THE ENCYCLOPEDIA OF
TRUE CRIME

THE ENCYCLOPEDIA OF TRUE CRIME

THE PICK OF HISTORY'S WORST CRIMINALS FROM FRAUDSTERS AND MOBSTERS TO THRILL KILLERS AND PSYCHOPATHS

CHARLOTTE GREIG with PAUL ROLAND, JO DURDEN SMITH, JOHN MARLOWE and KAREN FARRINGTON

CHARTWELL
BOOKS, INC.

This edition printed in 2008 by

CHARTWELL BOOKS, INC.
A Division of **BOOK SALES, INC.**
114 Northfield Avenue
Edison, New Jersey 08837

Copyright © 2008 Arcturus Publishing Limited
26/27 Bickels Yard, 151–153 Bermondsey Street,
London SE1 3HA

ISBN-13: 978-0-7858-2469-5
ISBN-10: 0-7858-2469-3

Printed in China

PICTURE CREDITS

Corbis: 22, 24, 29, 38, 50, 53, 54, 72, 80, 86, 96, 98, 100, 103,
104, 130, 133, 134, 157, 177, 178, 195, 212, 214, 221, 222, 224,
227, 229, 230, 231, 232, 233, 234, 238, 241, 243, 245, 249, 250,
252, 259, 263, 269, 273, 274, 275, 277, 281, 282, 286, 287, 290,
293, 295, 303
Topfoto: 8, 10, 12, 20, 31, 60, 62, 63, 64, 66, 67, 68, 69, 74, 76,
78, 83, 84, 87, 132, 145, 147, 149, 150, 154, 156, 158, 159, 160,
161, 163, 164, 165, 176, 185, 189, 190, 192, 200, 203, 208, 217,
253, 255, 256, 262, 265, 291
Getty: 13, 21, 26, 28, 32, 36, 37, 47, 49, 57, 58, 94, 102, 106,
109, 111, 1112, 113, 115, 116, 118, 121, 123, 125, 126, 128, 137,
153, 171, 175, 181, 186, 198, 284, 289
Rex Features: 15, 16, 18, 68, 122, 138, 142, 166, 167, 169, 173,
197, 201, 205, 206, 219, 228, 237, 242
PA Photos: 89, 90, 92, 292, 297
Mary Evans: 34, 45
Crime Library: 42, 43
Barrington Barber: 48
Kobal: 183
Picture Desk: 210, 266
Larry Halff: 260

We have made every effort to contact the copyright-holders of
the photographs and illustrations within this book. Any
oversights or omissions will be corrected in future editions.

Contents

POLICE LINE DO NOT CROSS

Introduction

Criminals come in all shapes and sizes and belong to every creed and colour. Despite being the product of their different lives and times, wrongdoers have much in common, leading secretive lives, living off their wits and keeping very different hours from the rest of us. Few are stuck in the old nine to five routine.

Perhaps that's the enduring appeal of crime: most of us spend our lives doing as we are told, but criminals are working against the laws which tie more timid citizens down. In the world of crime you are very much your own person, and in the rogues gallery which follows you will find out exactly what that means. It isn't always pretty.

The Killing Never Ends features some of the world's most gruesome serial killers. 'The Rostov Ripper', Andrei Chikatilo, haunted deserted bus and train stations of the old Soviet Union until he was brought to justice after 52 grisly murders. In Germany between the wars when food was scarce, Fritz Haarmann sold the flesh of his victims as pork on the black market. More recently, Jeffrey Dahmer became obsessed with the notion of creating zombies – half-humans – to be his playthings, to which end he liked to drill into his victims' heads, dripping acid in their brains. But compared to Ed Kemper these fellows were quite well adjusted…

In **Robbers – Masters of the Heist**, you can read about 19th-century criminal mastermind Jonathan Wild, who led the authorities a merry dance and gave us the term 'double-cross', along with a merry band of safe-crackers, conmen and armed robbers, who include the real Butch Cassidy and the Sundance Kid. **Forensic Detection: Following the Trail** gives you the inside track on how police discover clues at crimes scenes, revealing how criminals as diverse as Fred and Rosemary West, The Green River Killer, Clifford Irving and The Woodchip Killer ended up in court.

Gangs, Mobs and Outlaws: Running with the Pack covers mobsters from Al Capone and Machine Gun Kelly to the Kray Brothers and Ned Kelly, while **Fraudsters and Spies: White-Collar Crime** introduces you to the exploits of the likes of Frank Abagnale, 'The Skywayman', Victor Lustig, the man who sold the Eiffel Tower twice, and the true story behind the film *The Falcon and The Snowman*. **Drug Barons: Dealing with Death** takes you into the murky world of drug cartels and worldwide drug distribution, while **Assassinations: Proving a Point** examines deaths that shook the world – the assassinations of Martin Luther King, John Lennon, Leon Trotsky and Gianni Versace, among others.

Bringing this book to a conclusion are three sections about what happens to criminals when they are caught – **Behind Bars: The End of the Road, Prison Culture** and **Prison Riots**. Somehow a life of crime no longer seems to be quite so appealing.

POLICE LINE DO NOT CROSS

Elizabeth Bathory

When Countess Elizabeth Bathory, aged fifteen, married Count Nadasdy in around 1576, it was an alliance between two of the greatest dynasties in Hungary. For Nadasdy, the master of Castle Csejthe in the Carpathians, came from a line of warriors, and Elizabeth's family was even more distinguished: it had produced generals and governors, high princes and cardinals – her cousin was the country's prime minister. Long after they've been forgotten, though, she will still be remembered. For she was an alchemist, a bather in blood – and one of the models for Bram Stoker's *Dracula*.

VOLUPTUOUS

She was beautiful, voluptuous, savage – a fine match for her 21-year-old husband, the so-called 'Black Warrior'. But he was forever off campaigning, and she remained childless. More and more, then, she gave in to the constant cajolings of her old nurse, Ilona Joo, who was a black witch, a satanist. She began to surround herself with alchemists and sorcerers; and when she conceived – she eventually had four children – she may have been finally convinced of their efficacy. For after her husband's death, when she was about forty-one, she surrendered to the black arts completely.

There had long been rumours about the castle: of lesbian orgies, of the kidnappings of young peasant women, of flagellation, of torture. But one day after her husband's death, Elizabeth Bathory slapped the face of a servant girl and drew blood; and she noticed that, where it had dripped on her hand, the skin seemed to grow smoother and more supple. She was soon convinced that drinking the blood of young virgins and bathing in it would keep her young forever. Her entourage of witches and magicians – who were now calling for human sacrifice to make their magic work – agreed enthusiastically.

HUNG IN CHAINS

Elizabeth and her cronies then began scouring the countryside for children and young girls, who were either lured to the castle or kidnapped. There they were hung in chains in the dungeons, fattened and milked for their blood before being tortured to death. Their bones were used in alchemical experiments. The countess, it was said later, kept some of them alive to lick the blood from her body when she emerged from her baths. However, if they either failed to arouse her or showed the slightest signs of displeasure, she had them brutally killed.

Peasant girls, somehow, failed to stay the signs of ageing; and after five years, Elizabeth decided to set up an academy for young noblewomen. Now she bathed in blue blood, the blood of her own class. But this time, inevitably, news of her depravities reached the royal court, and her cousin, the prime minister, was forced to investigate. A surprise raid on the castle found the Countess in mid-orgy, bodies lying strewn, drained of blood, and dozens of girls and young women awaiting their turn in the dungeons.

Elizabeth's grisly entourage was taken into custody and then tortured to obtain confessions. At the subsequent trial for

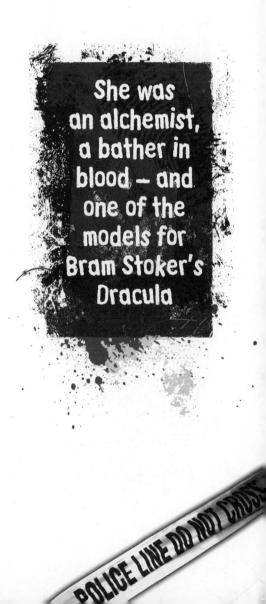

She was an alchemist, a bather in blood – and one of the models for Bram Stoker's Dracula

POLICE LINE DO NOT CROSS

the murder of the eighty victims who were actually found dead at the castle, her old nurse, Ilona Joo, and one of the Countess's procurers of young girls were sentenced to be burned at the stake after having their fingers pulled off; many of the rest were beheaded. The Countess, who as an aristocrat could not be arrested, was given a separate hearing in her absence at which she was accused of murdering more than 600 women and children. She was bricked up in a tiny room in her castle, with holes left only for ventilation and the passing of food. Still relatively young and curiously youthful, she was never seen alive again. She is presumed to have died – since the food was left uneaten – four years later, on 21 August 1614.

> The Countess, who as an aristocrat could not be arrested, was accused of murdering more than 600 women and children

Countess Elizabeth Bathory pursued a grisly beauty regime

Andrei Chikatilo

Andrei Chikatilo, the 'Rostov Ripper', killer of over fifty women, young men, girls and boys, came to the attention of the world following his arrest in 1990, just as the Soviet Union was starting to break up. Indeed, had he been caught earlier it is more than likely that his name would have remained obscure. Soviet Russia liked to pretend that such crimes as serial murder were purely a product of the decadent West; we still do not know the full extent of criminality during the years of the communist regime.

HANNIBAL LECTER

Chikatilo was born in Yablochnoye, a village deep in the heart of rural Ukraine, on 19 October 1936. The baby was found to have water on the brain, which gave him a misshapen head and, it was later revealed, a certain degree of brain damage. He was also unlucky enough to be born during the period of forced collectivization imposed by Stalin, a time of terrible famine and untold suffering. According to Chikatilo's mother, Andrei had an older brother named Stepan who was kidnapped and eaten by starving neighbours during this time. It is unclear if this was actually true – there is no record of a Stepan Chikatilo ever existing – but it was certainly a tale that succeeded in traumatizing the young Chikatilo. (Thomas Harris later borrowed this awful story to explain the pathology of his fictional serial killer Hannibal Lecter.) To make matters worse, the boy's early childhood was spent during the Second World War, when the region's misery grew even worse. His father was taken prisoner during the war, then sent to a Russian prison camp on his return.

On leaving school, Chikatilo joined the army. He also joined the Communist Party, which was essential for any ambitious young person who wanted to succeed in Soviet Russia. On leaving the army, he worked as a telephone engineer and studied in his spare time to gain a university degree, which eventually allowed him to became a schoolteacher near his home in Rostov-on-Don. At the same time he married a woman named Fayina, found for him by his sister. As it emerged later, Chikatilo had lifelong problems with impotence, but he did manage to father two children.

FALSE ALIBI

Chikatilo appeared to be living a regular life. By the time his darker urges began to express themselves, he was forty-two, much older than most serial killers. In 1979 he chose his first victim, a 9-year-old girl called Lenochka Zakotnova. He took her to a vacant house in the town of Shakhty, attempted to rape her, failed, and then, using a knife, stabbed her to death and dumped her body into the Grushovka River. She was found there on Christmas Eve. Luckily for Chikatilo – who was questioned as a suspect in the case but was given a false alibi by his wife – a known local rapist, Alexander Kravchenko, was beaten into confessing to the crime and put to death.

Nevertheless, evidence of Chikatilo's true nature was starting to leak out and he was fired from his teaching job for

The 'Rostov Ripper' had lifelong problems with impotence but did manage to father two children

POLICE LINE DO NOT CROSS

molesting boys in the school dormitory. His party membership stood him in good stead, however, and he was soon given a new job as a travelling procurement officer for a factory in Shakhty. The job involved a lot of moving around the area and thus plenty of opportunity to kill. His preferred method was to approach his victims at a train or bus station and lure them into nearby woodland to kill them.

He started in earnest in 1982 with the murder of seventeen-year-old Larisa Tkachenko, a girl known locally for exchanging sexual favours for food and drink. Chikatilo strangled her and piled dirt into her mouth to muffle her screams. He later claimed that his first killing had upset him, but that this second one thrilled him. In June 1982 he killed his next victim, 13-year-old Lyuba Biryuk, cutting out her eyes, an act that became his gruesome trademark.

INCREASING SAVAGERY

Over the next year he killed six more times, with two of the victims young men. What the killings had in common was their increasing savagery and the removal of body parts, particularly the genitals. It is believed that Chikatilo ate the parts he removed in a hideous echo of his brother's fate. However, he himself only confessed to 'nibbling on them'.

The murders attracted much police concern, but the Soviet media were not permitted to publicize the existence of a maniacal killer on the loose. In the single month of August 1984, eight victims were found. The only clue the police had was that, judging by the semen found on the bodies of some of the

Chikatilo was traumatized by the story of his brother's death

POLICE LINE DO NOT CROSS

Chikatilo had a bag that he kept stocked with the tools that helped him in his monstrous crimes

more recent victims, the killer's blood group was a very rare AB.

Soon afterwards, in late 1984, Chikatilo was arrested at a railway station where he was importuning young girls. He was found to have a knife and a length of rope in his bag but, because his blood group was A, not AB, he was released. This discrepancy in the blood groups has never been explained.

BUS STOPS AND STATIONS

Released by the police, Chikatilo simply carried on killing. Dozens more innocents lost their lives over the next five years. In 1988, he claimed eight lives and in his last year of freedom, in 1990, he killed nine more. By then, a new detective, Issa Kostoyev, had taken over the case. Kostoyev hit on a strategy of flooding the

train and bus stations with detectives, and eventually the plan paid off. Immediately after murdering his final victim, 20-year-old Svetlana Korostik, Chikatilo was spotted, perspiring heavily and apparently bloodstained, at a station. A detective took his name and, when it was realized that he had previously been a suspect, Chikatilov was arrested. After ten days in custody he finally confessed to fifty-two murders, more than the police had been aware of. He was charged and brought to trial in April 1992.

Locked inside a cage during the trial to protect him from attack by the victims' relatives, Chikatilo was a shaven-headed madman who ranted and raved in the courtroom. He was found guilty on 15 February 1994 and executed by a single bullet to the back of the head.

Chikatilo was a shaven-headed madman who ranted and raved in the courtroom

POLICE LINE DO NOT CROSS

Fritz Haarmann

Fritz Haarmann was one of the first serial killers to hit the headlines in modern times. He confessed to the murders of at least twenty-seven young men and boys in the town of Hanover, Germany, between 1918 and 1924. What made Haarmann uniquely terrifying was the mixture of frenzy and orderliness that characterized his crimes. He would kill his victims in a savage onslaught, often biting through their windpipes as he raped them. Then, with considerable care, he would remove their clothes and sell them, dismember the bodies, dispose of the bones, and finally cook the flesh and sell it on the black market as pork. If that seems hard to believe, one should remember that during the years after the First World War Germany was on the brink of starvation; food was food, and people at that time did not ask too many questions as to its provenance.

> He would kill his victims in a savage onslaught, biting through their windpipes as he raped them.

MOTHER'S FAVOURITE

Fritz (Friedrich) Haarmann was born on 25 October 1879 in Hanover, the sixth child of Olle and Johanna Haarmann. Olle was a drunk and a womanizer. Johanna was older than her husband, forty-one at the time Fritz was born, and in poor health. Fritz, the baby of the family, was his mother's favourite and he constantly sided with her against his father. As a child he preferred dolls to boys' toys. More worrying was a fondness for frightening people, particularly his sisters; he liked to play games that involved tying them up or scaring them by tapping on their windows at night.

Fritz's mother died when he was twelve and his feuding with his father intensified. After school, he became apprenticed to a locksmith. When that did not work out he was sent to military school. After six months there, he was sent home because he seemed to be suffering from epileptic fits. Back home in Hanover, he took to molesting children. Complaints were made, and Haarmann was examined by a doctor, who sent him to the insane asylum. This was a deeply traumatic experience for Haarmann. He eventually escaped and fled to Switzerland, before returning to Hanover in 1900. By this time, he appeared to be a reformed character. He married a woman named Erna Loewert and seemed ready to settle down. But, when Erna became pregnant, Fritz left her, joined the army and became involved in petty crime. He was soon arrested for burglary, pick-pocketing and small-scale cons. In 1914 Fritz was convicted of a warehouse burglary and sent to prison for his longest stint yet, enabling him to see out the First World War from his prison cell. On release in 1918 he found himself in a poverty-stricken society as Germany struggled to recover from the war.

POST-WAR CRIMES

Crime was flourishing as people desperately sought means of survival. This was the ideal environment for Haarmann. He immediately joined a smuggling ring and simultaneously became a police informer, managing to profit from both sides at once.

Police pictures of Fritz Haarmann at the time of his arrest: he used to pick up boys at the station, introducing himself as 'Detective Haarmann'

POLICE LINE DO NOT CROSS

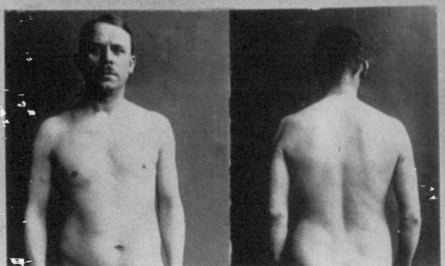

In the post-war years many homeless and displaced people milled around the city and resorted to prostitution, so it was easy for Haarmann to pick up boys and youths, particularly at the railway station. Often he introduced himself as 'Detective Haarmann' and used that pretext to get the boys to go with him. At one time, Haarmann had been satisfied with sexual abuse, but now he needed to kill his victims to satisfy his lust.

SEVERED HEAD

One of his first victims was named Friedel Rothe. Rothe's parents found out that their son had gone with 'Detective Haarmann', and the police went round to Haarmaan's apartment but failed to notice the boy's severed head, hidden behind the stove. Shortly afterwards, Haarmann received a nine-month prison sentence for indecency. On release he met a young homosexual called Hans Grans. They became lovers and moved in together. Next they became business partners, trading on the black market as Fritz continued to act as a police informer. Over the next couple of years their business began to include a gruesome new sideline: selling the clothes and cooked flesh of Haarmann's victims.

For the most part the pair's victims were not missed. Even when they were, the authorities seemed to make one elementary blunder after another in following up clues: the parents of one victim told the police they suspected Grans of having been the murderer, but Grans was in prison at the time; however, Haarmann was never investigated, even though he had visited the

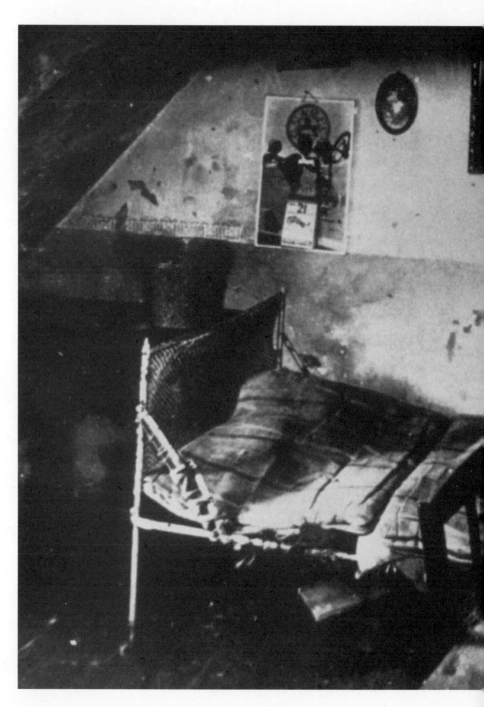

He liked to frequent the railway station and find likely prospects there

Haarmann's apartment: there wasn't much to search but police still managed to miss vital evidence that the man was a killer

POLICE LINE DO NOT CROSS

parents pretending to be a criminologist and laughed hysterically as they told him of their fears. Another time, a suspicious customer took some of Haarmann's meat to the authorities for examination; the police expert duly pronounced it to be pork. It seems that, as long as the murders were confined to a homosexual netherworld, people in general preferred to look the other way.

MACABRE JOKE?

All that changed in May 1924 when several human skulls were found by the River Leine. At first, the authorities tried to calm the public's fear, suggesting that this was some kind of macabre joke, the skulls having been left there by grave robbers. However, when, on 24 July, children found a sack stuffed full of human bones, there was no stopping the panic. In all the police found 500 bones belonging to at least twenty-seven bodies.

The police investigated all the local sex offenders, among them Fritz Haarmann, but still found no evidence to connect him to the apparent murders. In the end it was Haarmann's own arrogance that led to his downfall. For some reason – perhaps to stop himself from committing another murder – he took a 15-year-old boy to the police to report him for insolent behaviour. Once under arrest, the boy accused Haarmann of making sexual advances. Haarmann was arrested and his flat searched. The police found garments belonging to missing children, some of them bloodstained. Haarmann at first explained them away by saying that he was a dealer in used clothing and that he had no idea where the blood had

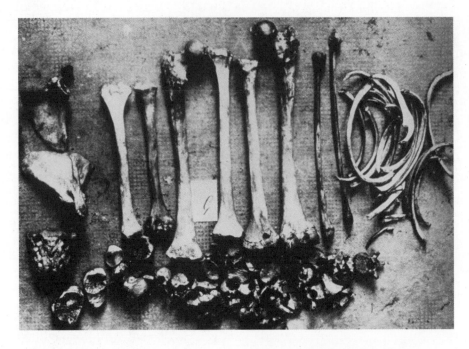

come from. However, after a week in custody, under questioning, Haarmann finally confessed to the murders. He took detectives to a number of sites around Hanover where he had buried further bodies, seeming to take pride in his crimes. His testimony only varied when it came to the role of Hans Grans, whom he alternately blamed and exculpated.

When the case came to court, Haarmann was tried and sentenced to death. The jury decided that Grans was no more than an accessory after the fact and sentenced him to twelve years in prison. Haarmann appeared to enjoy his trial, conducting his own defence, smoking cigars and complaining about the presence of women in the courtroom. It was his final act of bravado, however. On 25 April 1925 he – like so many of his victims – was put to death by beheading.

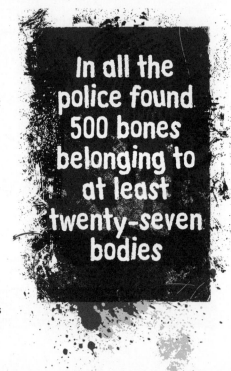

In all the police found 500 bones belonging to at least twenty-seven bodies

Jeffrey Dahmer

The case of Jeffrey Dahmer is among the most troubling of all serial killers – an apparently regular guy, Dahmer turned into a psychopathic murderer, necrophile and cannibal.

Jeffrey Dahmer was born on 21 May 1960, the son of Lionel, a chemist, and Joyce, a homemaker. Joyce was highly strung, while Lionel worked long hours; the pair argued a great deal but to all appearances this was still a normal family household. However, at an early age, Jeffrey developed a fascination with dead animals. Then, aged six, following a hernia operation and the birth of his younger brother David, he became withdrawn. He remained solitary and friendless throughout his childhood. In his teens, his fascination with dead creatures intensified. He would cycle around looking for road kill, which he would carefully dismember. He had also become a heavy drinker.

Jeffrey's parents did not appear to notice his troubles, as by this time they were locked in an acrimonious divorce. During the summer of 1978, just as Jeffrey was due to graduate, they both moved out of the house, leaving Jeffrey there alone. His response was to pick up a hitchhiker, Stephen Hicks, take him home and have sex with him. When Hicks tried to leave, Jeffrey hit him on the head with a bar bell, strangled him, dismembered his corpse and buried it nearby.

ALCOHOLIC

Jeffrey's father Lionel had by this time moved in with his second wife Shari, who pointed out to her new husband that his son was an alcoholic. Lionel responded by giving Jeffrey an ultimatum: to stop drinking or to join the army. Jeffrey refused to stop drinking, so his father saw to it that he enlisted in January 1979, aged eighteen. Dahmer appeared to enjoy army life, but he was soon discharged for habitual drunkenness. Soon after, he moved into an apartment in his grandmother's basement and his life continued its downward spiral.

In 1982, Dahmer was arrested for indecent exposure, and then again in 1986. Each time his father paid for lawyers, and for his second offence Dahmer was given a suspended sentence and counselling. The counselling clearly had little effect, however, as he went on to kill three times during the next year.

FIRST VICTIM

His first victim that year was Steven Tuomi, whom he met in a gay bar. He murdered Tuomi in a hotel, put the body in a suitcase, took it home, had sex with it and then dismembered it. Next, Dahmer murdered a 14-year-old Native American boy called James Doxtator, who hung around the Milwaukee gay scene. After Doxtator came a Mexican youth named Richard Guerrero. (Dahmer's career of savagery categorically disproved a previously held theory that serial killers only murder within their own race.)

At this point Dahmer's grandmother, who was bothered by his drunkenness and the terrible smells coming from his apartment, evicted him. Dahmer moved into his own flat in Milwaukee, Wisconsin, in September 1988. The next day, he lured a 13-year-old Laotian boy there,

He murdered Tuomi in a hotel, put the body in a suitcase and then had sex with it

POLICE LINE DO NOT CROSS

offering to pay him for a nude modelling session. He drugged the boy and fondled him but did not become violent. The boy's parents reported Dahmer to the police. He was sentenced to a year in prison for sexual assault. While waiting for sentence, however, he killed his next victim, Anthony Sears.

A MURDER A WEEK

Dahmer served ten months in prison before beginning his final killing spree. Between June 1990 and July 1991, he murdered another twelve men. In the end he was committing a murder almost every week, and his treatment of his victims was becoming ever more bizarre. He was obsessed with the notion of creating zombies – half-humans who would be his playthings. To this end he drilled holes in his victims' skulls while they were still alive and dripped acid into their heads. (Unsurprisingly, none of his victims survived.) In at least one case, he also tried cannibalism. He kept his victims' body parts in his refrigerator, and placed their skulls on an altar in his bedroom.

Most disturbing of all was the case of Konerak Sinthasomphone, the brother of the Laotian teenager he had previously molested. Dahmer drugged Konerak, but the boy managed to escape from the apartment. Two young black women found Konerak and called the police, but when they arrived on the scene, Dahmer persuaded the police that the drugged and bleeding Konerak was his boyfriend. Incredibly, the police returned the boy to Dahmer, who promptly took him home and murdered him.

In the next few weeks, a frenzied Dahmer went

Jeffrey Dahmer graduated from a fascination with dead animals to psychopathic murders

POLICE LINE DO NOT CROSS

In prison, Dahmer refused to be placed in solitary confinement. On 28 November 1994, a fellow inmate took an iron bar and smashed it down on Dahmer's skull. The blow killed him

on to kill his last four victims. On 22 July 1991, his final intended victim, an adult black man, Tracy Edwards, escaped from the apartment, a pair of handcuffs trailing from his wrist. He managed to flag down a police car and led the police back to the apartment, where they were horrified to find a human head in the refrigerator.

Dahmer's killing spree was finally over. As details of the story emerged in the press, the full picture of Dahmer's horrific crimes shocked an America that had become wearily accustomed to tales of murder and perversion. By 22 August 1991 Dahmer had been charged with fifteen counts of murder. His trial began on 30 January 1992. He pleaded guilty but insane. The jury found him sane and he was sentenced to fifteen consecutive life sentences but was killed in prison.

Ted Bundy

Ted Bundy was one of the most terrifying of all serial killers, not simply because he was a sadist and necrophile who confessed to the murders of more than thirty women, and may conceivably have murdered as many as a hundred. Worryingly, he could actually pass for a regular guy – the good-looking young lawyer who lives down the street. Bundy was not a skid-row slasher who operated a safe distance away from respectable folk. He was a killer who moved around the university campus, the mall, the park over the holiday weekend.

APPARENT NORMALITY

Perhaps the most deadly aspect of Bundy's modus operandi was that he played ruthlessly on his apparent normality. Typically, a victim – always a young woman with long dark hair in a centre parting – would be walking back to her student dorm, or out in the park. She would be approached by a personable, tousle-haired young man with his arm in a cast. He would explain that he needed help lifting something into his car. The woman would offer to help the nice young man and she would follow him to his car. She would then disappear forever, or would be found in the woods, her body raped and sodomized, her head staved in by a furious assault with a blunt instrument.

Ted Bundy was born Theodore Robert Cowell in November 1946 in Vermont. However, he enjoyed little of the privilege typically credited to his

While Ted Bundy confessed to murdering more than thirty women, the true figure may have been nearer a hundred

POLICE LINE DO NOT C

generation. His mother, Louise Cowell, had become pregnant by a serviceman who had disappeared before Ted was born. She and her baby lived with her strict parents in Philadelphia, and in an effort to avoid scandal the family pretended that Ted was actually his grandparents' child, and that his mother was in fact his sister. When Ted was four years old, his mother moved to Tacoma, Washington, and married a man called John Bundy; a year later, in 1951, Ted took his stepfather's name.

Bundy was a bright child who consistently achieved good grades in school. However, he was not an easy mixer. He was bullied when he was young and later, while becoming more apparently gregarious, he also acquired a reputation for petty theft and lying.

After high school he attended the University of Puget Sound in Washington. Around this time he met a young, pretty woman called Stephanie Brooks, who had long dark hair worn in a centre parting. Stephanie came from a moneyed Californian family, and she and Bundy went out together for a time. However, while Bundy became obsessed with her, she found him lacking in ambition and, when she left college, she broke off with him. Bundy was devastated.

MURDEROUS RAGE

Bundy left college and moped for a while. Then he turned his disappointment into motivation to succeed. He re-enrolled in college, studied psychology and became active in the Republican Party. Bundy also worked for a suicide hotline, and received a commendation from the Seattle Police Department for catching

a mugger. He found a new girlfriend, divorcee Meg Anders. He could scarcely have looked more like a model citizen.

TALK OF MARRIAGE

Underneath, however, a murderous rage was building. First, he got back in touch with Stephanie Brooks, meeting up with her in California while on a business trip in 1973. She was impressed by the new go-ahead Ted, and – unbeknown to Meg Anders – Stephanie and Ted began to talk of marriage.

In February 1974, Bundy broke off all contact with Brooks. Just as suddenly as she had dumped him, he did the same to her. What she did not know was that, just beforehand, Bundy had committed his first murder. The victim was a young woman called Lynda Healy whom he had abducted from her basement flat in Seattle. Over the next few months, five more young women would vanish in the surrounding area. Each one was last seen out walking, and each one had long dark hair with a centre parting.

It was clear that there was a serial killer on the loose, but at this stage the police had no bodies and no clues. Then came the events of 14 July. On that hot summer's day crowds had flocked to the shores of Lake Sammamish, but two young women – 23-year-old Janice Ott and 19-year-old Denise Naslund – had failed to make the journey back. Both had wandered off from their friends and vanished. When police investigated, several passers-by reported seeing Ott in conversation with a man whose arm was in a sling and who was heard to say his name was Ted. Then another witness came forward and said that this Ted had

When the police found the corpses there were fresh bite marks on them

POLICE LINE DO NOT CROSS

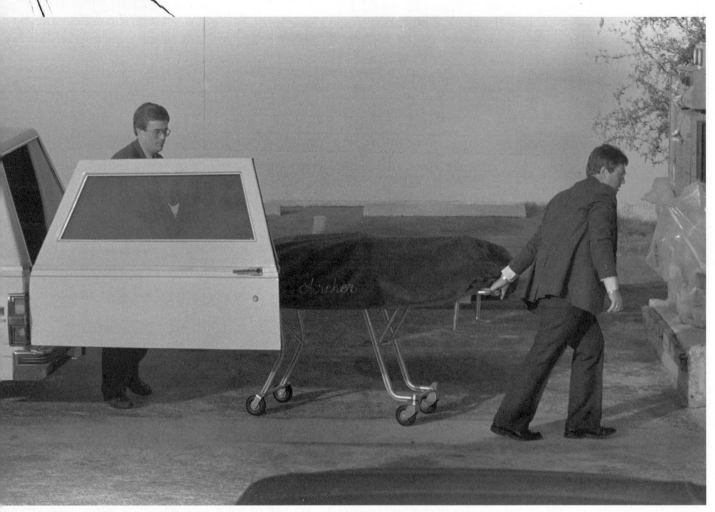

Ted Bundy's body is taken to the County Medical Examiner's office following his execution

asked her to help secure a sailboat to his car, a tan Volkswagen Beetle. She had gone with him as far as his car but, when he told her the boat was somewhere up the road and they would have to drive there to get it, she had become suspicious and declined.

The police put out a description of the man called Ted and various calls came in. One of these was an anonymous call from Meg Anders, saying she thought the man might be her boyfriend Ted Bundy, who was starting to alarm her with his interest in violent sex and bondage. The police checked him out, but the young law student seemed too innocuous to worry about, and the lead was dropped.

Over the next three months several bodies started to be discovered. Janice Ott and Denise Naslund were found buried in the woods, along with the skeleton of a third woman who could not be identified. Two more bodies were found the following month. Then Bundy seemed to get cold feet and moved his murderous operations out of the state.

POLICE LINE DO NOT CROSS

Bundy's next three victims were all abducted in Utah during the month of October. At this point, Bundy made his first mistake. On 8 November he attempted to abduct Carol DaRonch from a shopping mall in Salt Lake City. He pretended to be a police officer and lured her into his car, a VW Beetle, but she became suspicious and escaped after a struggle. Later that night, 17-year-old Debbie Kent was not so lucky: Bundy abducted and murdered her.

ARRESTED

In the New Year, Bundy moved his hunting ground again, this time to Colorado. He abducted four more women there in the first half of 1975. Just before the fourth body was discovered, however, he was finally arrested. A policeman had stopped Bundy in Salt Lake City and looked inside the car, finding handcuffs and a stocking mask. Carol DaRonch was called in and picked Bundy out of a line-up as the man who had tried to abduct her. Her evidence was enough to have him convicted and sentenced to jail for attempted kidnapping.

Meanwhile other evidence linked Bundy to the killings in Colorado, and in January 1977 he was taken to Aspen to be tried for the murder of Caryn Campbell. The game was clearly up for the serial killer. However respectable his exterior, it was all too plain that underneath the model citizen was an appalling sexual sadist and murderer.

This should have been the end of the story but, while he was waiting for trial, Bundy demonstrated new levels of resourcefulness. He escaped from custody during a court appearance and spent eight days hiding out in Aspen before being recaptured. Incredibly, he then managed to escape again, cutting a hole in the roof of his cell, crawling along and cutting another hole down into a janitor's room, then walking unchallenged out of prison. This escape would last longer, and have far worse consequences.

AT LARGE

Bundy fled to Tallahassee, Florida, where he rented a room under an assumed name, close to the university. Two weeks after his escape, on 15 January 1978, he murdered again, this time giving up all subtlety in his approach. He broke into a sorority house and brutally raped and murdered two young women, leaving a third badly injured.

The following month, he failed in his attempt to abduct a schoolgirl. Three days later, he succeeded in abducting and murdering his final victim, 12-year-old Kimberley Leach. After another three days, he was finally recaptured and this time he was convicted of first-degree murder: the evidence against him was the match of his teeth with the bite marks left on his victims. In July 1979 he was sentenced to death by electric chair.

Law student Ted Bundy launched several increasingly tenuous appeals and became a celebrity. While in prison, he confessed to more than thirty murders. Women proposed marriage to him; one even succeeded in exchanging marriage vows with Bundy when she appeared as a defence witness during an appeal court appearance. The courts were not impressed however, and finally, on 24 January 1989, Ted Bundy was put to death by electrocution.

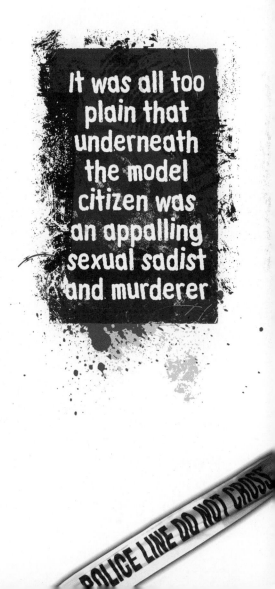

It was all too plain that underneath the model citizen was an appalling sexual sadist and murderer

POLICE LINE DO NOT CROSS

POLICE LINE DO NOT C

Albert DeSalvo

The case of the 'Boston Strangler' is one of the most enduringly mysterious in the annals of serial murder. What is known for sure is that between June 1962 and July 1964 eleven women were murdered in the Boston area – all were raped and strangled. Most people at the time assumed there was a single serial killer on the loose, and dubbed him the Boston Strangler. Others, including many on the police investigation, thought that there were two killers, because the first set of victims were all older women between the ages of fifty-five and seventy-five, while five of the last six to die were women in their late teens and early twenties. These latter murders were also significantly more violent than the others. For this reason, some concluded that there was a first murderer fixated on older women (perhaps motivated by a hatred of his mother), followed by a copycat killer using the same modus operandi but preying on younger women.

However, all this speculation was quelled when, in early 1965, a man named Albert DeSalvo, who had recently been arrested for a series of rapes, confessed to all eleven murders, as well as some other killings that had not previously been attributed to the Strangler.

PHYSICALLY ABUSED
Albert DeSalvo was born in Chelsea, Massachusetts, on 3 September 1931. He was one of six children born to Frank and

Albert DeSalvo confessed to being the Boston Strangler, but many people who knew him personally doubt that he could have committed the crimes

Charlotte DeSalvo. Frank DeSalvo was a violent man who dealt out regular physical abuse to his family, and was jailed twice before Charlotte eventually divorced him in 1944. Albert became a troubled teenager, repeatedly arrested for breaking and entering, assault and other minor offences.

In 1948, aged seventeen, Albert joined the army and was stationed in Germany. While living there he met and married a German woman, Irmgard Beck, who came with him when he was transferred back to the States, to Fort Dix in New Jersey. At Fort Dix, DeSalvo was accused of molesting a 9-year-old girl but the matter was dropped when the mother declined to press charges. However, the affair resulted in him being discharged from the army in 1956.

SEXUAL DEMANDS
At this point Albert and Irmgard, plus their baby daughter Judy, moved back to Massachusetts. Over the next few years DeSalvo worked a series of jobs, and was generally regarded as a likeable man by his fellow workers. Not all was well, though: he was arrested several times for burglary and there was considerable sexual discord between him and his wife. Irmgard became very unenthusiastic sexually after their daughter was born with a hereditary disease and she was terrified of having another handicapped child. Albert, meanwhile, demanded sex from his wife five or six times a day.

This manic sexual behaviour soon led DeSalvo into trouble. During the late 1950s reports began to come in from Massachusetts women about the 'Measuring Man': a man who claimed

DeSalvo was accused of molesting a 9-year-old child but the matter was dropped when the mother declined to press charges

POLICE LINE DO NOT CROSS

> He was known as the 'Green Man' rapist, since he often made his assaults while wearing green work clothes

DNA evidence taken from Mary Sullivan, one of the victims of the Boston Strangler, did not match the DNA of Albert DeSalvo, leading to theories that his confession to George Nassar may have been a plot

to be from a modelling agency and would persuade women to let him measure them. When DeSalvo was once more arrested for burglary, on 17 March 1960, he surprised police by confessing that he was the Measuring Man.

Due to the lack of violence involved in his crime, DeSalvo received a relatively lenient two-year sentence. With time off for good behaviour, he was released after eleven months. Far from teaching him a lesson, however, his time in prison

POLICE LINE DO NOT CROSS

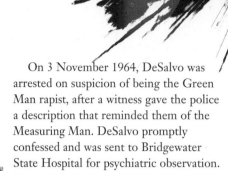

seemed to have turned him into a more aggressive predator. Over the next two years he raped hundreds of women (300 by police estimates, 2,000 by his own exaggerated account), often several on the same day. He was known as the 'Green Man' rapist, since he often made his assaults while wearing green work clothes. These rapes were carried out during the same time period as the Boston Strangler killings, but the police still made no connection between them at the time.

On 3 November 1964, DeSalvo was arrested on suspicion of being the Green Man rapist, after a witness gave the police a description that reminded them of the Measuring Man. DeSalvo promptly confessed and was sent to Bridgewater State Hospital for psychiatric observation. There he confessed first to a fellow inmate, George Nassar, then to the police, that he was also the Boston Strangler.

MAKING A DEAL

The police were delighted to have the Strangler presented to them on a plate in this way. However, various problems remained. In particular, none of the witnesses who had seen the Boston Strangler, including his one surviving victim, were able to pick DeSalvo out of a police line-up. In the end DeSalvo, represented by the infamous lawyer F. Lee Bailey, made a deal with the police: he received a life sentence for the Green Man rapes, but was never formally charged with the Strangler murders.

In November 1973, DeSalvo was stabbed to death by a fellow prisoner. However, his death failed to bring speculation to an end. Many people believed that DeSalvo only confessed to the killings as part of a deal with George Nassar, whereby Nassar would claim the reward for finding the Boston Strangler and give half the money to DeSalvo's family to provide for them while he was in jail. Today, however, the consensus from experts who spent a substantial amount of time with DeSalvo is that the man imprisoned as the Green Man rapist was indeed the legendary Boston Strangler.

Attorney F. Lee Bailey, here seen holding a photograph of DeSalvo in custody, became famous for taking on high-profile criminal cases such as that of the Boston Strangler

POLICE LINE DO NOT CROSS

John Wayne Gacy

Even by comparison with his fellow serial killers, John Wayne Gacy, 'the killer clown', has become something of an icon of pure evil. This is partly to do with the way he dressed up as a clown to entertain children at parties near his suburban Chicago home – what more sinister notion could there be than that beneath the clown's make-up lies a sex killer? And partly it is because of the sheer enormity of his crime: thirty-three young men raped and murdered, almost all of them buried beneath his suburban house.

John Wayne Gacy was born on 17 March 1942, St Patrick's Day, the second of three children born to Elaine Robinson Gacy and John Wayne Gacy Sr. He grew up in a middle-class district of northern Chicago, and was raised as a good Catholic boy. His childhood was largely uneventful.

Look a little closer, though, and there were signs of troubles. John Gacy Sr was a misanthropic man who frequently took out his anger on his son through physical beatings and verbal abuse. John Gacy Jr in turn became very close to his mother. Aged eleven, he sustained a nasty accident when he was struck on the head by a swing. It caused him to have regular blackouts during his teens. During his teenage years he also first complained of heart problems, though this seems likely to be just a symptom of a lifelong tendency to hypochondria – whenever he was under pressure he would claim to be on the brink of a heart attack.

Gacy did poorly in high school; he left without graduating and headed for Las Vegas in a bid to make his fortune. Instead, he ended up working in a mortuary, where he showed an unhealthy interest in the corpses. He then returned to Chicago and began attending business college. While there, he discovered his considerable ability as a salesman: he was able to talk people into anything.

MODEL CITIZEN

In 1964, Gacy married Marlyn Myers, a woman he had met through work and whose father had a string of Kentucky Fried Chicken franchises. Gacy decided to join the family business and became a restaurant manager. The couple had a child and Gacy became extremely active on the local charity and community group circuit around their new home in Waterloo, Iowa.

All this came to an end suddenly in May 1968, when Gacy was charged with raping a young employee named Mark Miller. Gacy was sentenced to ten years in prison for sodomy, and his wife promptly divorced him.

GOOD BEHAVIOUR

Gacy was released from prison after just eighteen months, thanks to his good behaviour while inside. His father had died while he was in prison, but now his mother – to whom he had always been close – stood by him and helped him to set up in business again. He bought a new house in the Chicago suburbs and established himself as a building contractor. In June 1972 he remarried, this time divorcee Carole Hoff. Carole and her two daughters moved into Gacy's

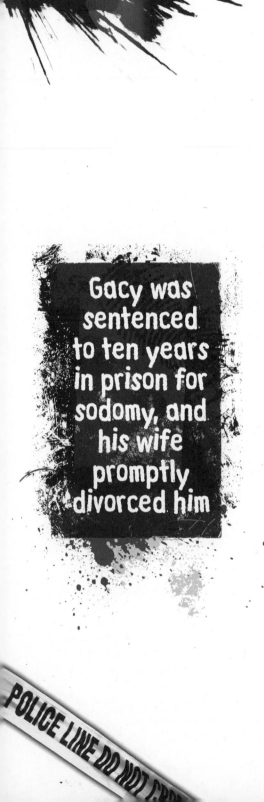

Gacy was sentenced to ten years in prison for sodomy, and his wife promptly divorced him

Gacy preferred men to women, and accordingly his marriage to Carole Hoff was soon on the rocks

house and the family soon became popular in their neighbourhood. Gacy would give parties with Western or Hawaiian themes and was active in local Democratic politics.

COURT CASE

Carole Hoff was aware of Gacy's past but under the impression that he had put it all behind him. This was far from true. In fact, just before they married, Gacy had been charged with sexually assaulting a minor, but the case had collapsed when his accuser failed to come to court. However, rumours soon began to circulate about Gacy's conduct with the teenage boys he liked to employ in his business. By 1975, his marriage was definitely deteriorating. Carole was profoundly disturbed to find homosexual pornography around the house. Gacy refused to apologize and even told her he preferred men to women. The couple divorced in 1976. It emerged that throughout their marriage Gacy had been picking up strangers in Chicago's gay bars and had carried out several murders, burying the bodies under the house. Neighbours had even complained about the terrible smell.

Now that his marriage was over, Gacy gave full vent to his lust for killing. He developed a modus operandi: victims, either picked up on the streets or chosen from his workforce, would be lured back to the house and given plenty of alcohol and marijuana. Gacy would then offer to show them a magic trick. The victim would be asked to put on

POLICE LINE DO NOT CROSS

a pair of handcuffs – which is when they would find out that this was no trick at all: the handcuffs were all too real and they were now in Gacy's power. Gacy would proceed to torture his victims before finally killing them by strangling them to death while raping them.

SICK CLOWN VISITS

Time and again, Gacy got, quite literally, away with murder. His neighbours suspected absolutely nothing, although they persistently complained about the terrible smells coming from his house. He carried on giving parties and started dressing up as 'Pogo the Clown' to visit sick children in hospitals. He became such a valued member of the local Democratic Party that he had his photograph taken shaking hands with the then First Lady, Roslyn Carter.

Finally, in 1978, his secret life began to catch up with him. In February of that year he abducted a young man called Jeffrey Rignall. Gacy chloroformed him, raped and tortured him and then – oddly – dumped him in a park rather than killing him. Rignall went to the police who showed little interest, but, acting alone, he managed to track down his abductor and filed an official complaint that was just starting to be investigated late that summer.

HOUSE SEARCH

Gacy had still not been charged with anything when, on 16 October, a 15-year-old boy called Robert Piest went missing. His parents discovered that he had been going to meet John Wayne Gacy about a job. When he was questioned, Gacy pleaded ignorance but the investigating officer decided to press ahead with a search of Gacy's house. They discovered an array of suspicious objects: handcuffs, pornography, drugs and so forth.

The police also noted the terrible smell. Gacy was confronted with this evidence and eventually confessed to having carried out a single murder. The police returned to the house and began to dig. Soon they realized that there was not one victim but dozens. In all, twenty-eight bodies were found around the house; the five most recent victims had been dumped in nearby rivers, as Gacy had run out of burial space under his house.

Charged with thirty-three counts of murder, Gacy entered a plea of insanity. However, the jury found it hard to believe that a man who dug graves for his victims in advance was the victim of uncontrollable violent impulses, so he was duly sentenced to death. While in prison he became a grotesque celebrity: credulous admirers were able to call a premium-rate number to hear his refutation of the charges against him. He gave frequent interviews and also showed admirers his paintings. Towards the end of his time on Death Row, Gacy began to claim that he had not killed after all, but had been the victim of a mysterious conspiracy. All to no avail, however. On 10 May 1994 he was put to death by lethal injection.

Protesters were able to express a little of how they felt about the killer as they threw John Wayne Gacy's belongings on to a bonfire

POLICE LINE DO NOT

Jack the Ripper

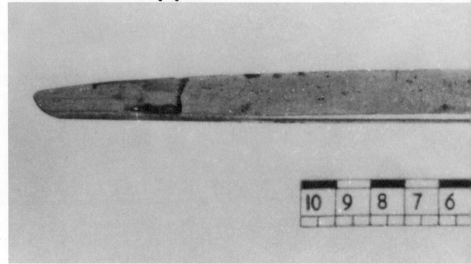

> It was possible the killer had medical training and was familiar with dissecting bodies in the post-mortem room

Jack the Ripper is the definitive serial killer. His brief and monstrous career established the serial killer in the public mind as the most terrifying of all the criminals. So why does this killer, whose crimes were committed over a century ago, still haunt us today? Partly, it is because of the sheer ferocity of his crimes: the disembowelling, the removal of body organs. Partly, it is the setting: Victorian Whitechapel is fixed in our minds as a seedy location for murder. Mostly, however, what has made the Ripper an immortal among murderers is the simple fact that he was never caught.

WHO WAS THE RIPPER?

The Ripper's crimes provide endless scope for speculation. Scarcely a year passes without another book being published that promises to name the real killer – a trend that reached its zenith when the crime novelist Patricia Cornwell spent a reputed $8 million of her own money in an effort to prove that the Victorian painter Walter Sickert was the murderer – at best a tenuous claim.

The killer we now know as Jack the Ripper announced himself to the world on 31 August 1888 with the murder of a prostitute named Mary 'Polly' Nichols. This was the third prostitute murder of the year in London's East End and did not initially attract too much attention, even though it was an unusually brutal killing: her throat and torso had been cut, and there were stab wounds to the genitals. At this stage, of course, there was nothing to suggest a serial killer at large.

It was little more than a week, however, before the murderer struck again. The victim was another prostitute, Annie Chapman, known as 'Dark Annie'. Like Polly Nichols, she had been killed by

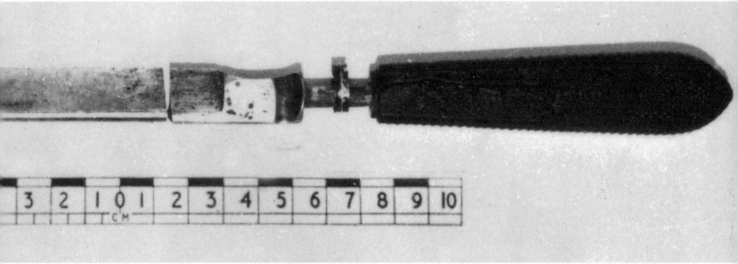

3 2 1 0 1 2 3 4 5 6 7 8 9 10
CM

a knife slash to the throat, but this time the killer had disembowelled her, pulled out her entrails and draped them over one shoulder, and then cut out her vagina and ovaries. What struck investigators, apart from the sheer horror of the scene, was the precision of the cuts. It seemed quite possible that the killer had medical training and was familiar with dissecting bodies in the post-mortem room.

TWICE IN ONE NIGHT

This gruesome crime already had the public in an uproar, but it was as nothing compared to the reaction that followed the murderer's next atrocity, committed on 30 September. This time, he killed not once but twice on the same night. The first victim was Elizabeth Stride, 'Long Liz', a seamstress and occasional prostitute. She had been killed by a knife wound to the throat, but there was no other visible

mutilation. One can only presume that the killer was interrupted in his work, and thus dissatisfied, because, before the night was over, he also killed prostitute Catherine Eddowes – and this time the attack had all his characteristic savagery. In addition, someone had written on the wall: 'The Juwes are not the men that will be blamed for nothing.' The police were not sure if the killer had written it, nor what it meant, so the investigating officer ordered it to be removed to avoid anti-Jewish hysteria developing.

LETTERS FROM HELL

Immediately before the double murder, the Central News Agency had received a letter that purported to be from the killer. There had already been many such letters, most of them obvious hoaxes, but when a second letter came from the same writer within hours of the double murder,

A knife found at the scene of one of the killings: its design sparked yet another theory, that the murderer was employed in the butchery trade

the agency passed them on to the police. The writer had signed himself 'Jack the Ripper', which caused a sensation in the press. Now, the murderer had a name.

Two weeks later another letter arrived, this one sent to George Lusk, head of the Whitechapel Vigilance Committee. It appeared to have a different author from the previous ones – this correspondent was clearly far less literate – but it was even more chilling. In place of a return address it simply said 'From Hell'. Enclosed in the letter was a piece of human kidney, which the writer claimed belonged to Eddowes. Eddowes had indeed had a kidney removed by her killer.

POLICE LINE DO NOT CROSS

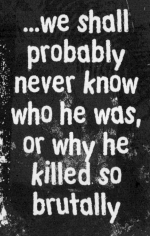

...we shall probably never know who he was, or why he killed so brutally

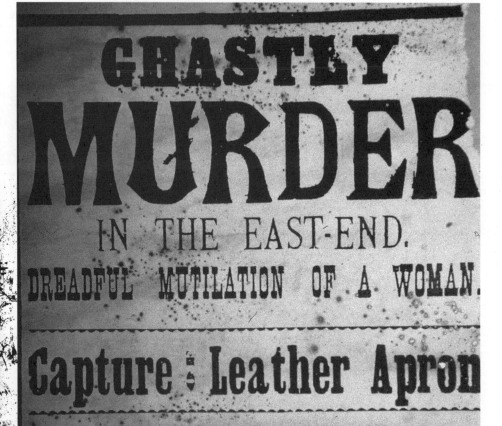

GHASTLY MURDER

IN THE EAST-END.

DREADFUL MUTILATION OF A WOMAN.

Capture : Leather Apron

Another murder of a character even more diabolical than that perpetrated in Buck's Row, on Friday week, was discovered in the same neighbourhood, on Saturday morning. At about six o'clock a woman was found lying in a back yard at the foot of a passage leading into a lodging house in a Old Brown's Lane, Spitalfields. The house is occupied by Mrs. Richardson, who lets it out to lodgers, and the door which admits to this passage, at the foot of which lies the yard where the body was found, is always open for the convenience of lodgers. A lodger named Davis was going down to work at the time mentioned and found the woman lying on her back close to the flight of steps leading into the yard. Her throat was cut in a fearful manner. The woman's body had been completely ripped open and the heart and other organs laying about the place, and portions of the entrails round the victim's neck. An excited crowd gathered in front of Mrs. Richardson's house and also round the mortuary in old Montague Street, whither the body was quickly conveyed. As the body lies in the rough coffin in which it has been placed in the mortuary the same coffin in which the unfortunate Mrs. Nicholls was first placed—it presents a fearful sight. The body is that of a woman about 45 years of age. The height is exactly five feet. The complexion is fair, with wavy dark brown hair; the eyes are blue, and two...

A newspaper shows the extent to which the killings took over the public imagination

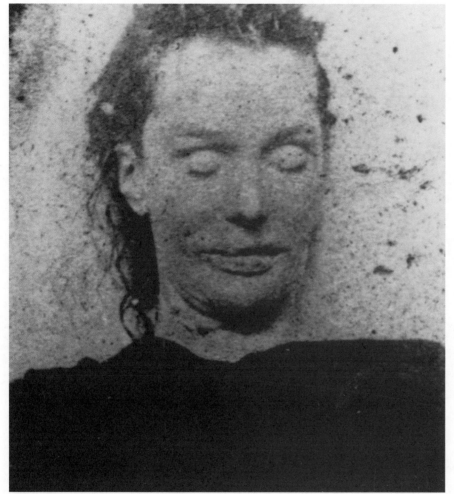

Elizabeth Stride, known as 'Long Liz'; she held the dubious claim to fame of being one of the two women who were killed by Jack the Ripper on the same night

However, the next killing never came. There was a knife murder of a prostitute two years later, and another one two years after that, but neither had any of the hallmarks of a gruesome Ripper killing. As mysteriously as he had appeared, the Ripper had vanished.

LIKELY SUSPECTS

Since that time, detectives – both amateur and professional – have speculated about who he (or even she in some far-fetched accounts) was. To date, suspects have included Queen Victoria's grandson Prince Eddy, in a rage against the prostitute who supposedly gave him syphilis; Sir William Gull, the Queen's surgeon, as part of a conspiracy to cover up the fact that Prince Eddy had conceived an illegitimate child with a Whitechapel girl (another theory sadly lacking in evidence); and Liverpool businessman James Maybrick, the supposed author of *The Ripper Diaries*, published in 1994 and generally deemed to be fake.

The truth is that we shall probably never know who he was, or why he killed so brutally. However, there is a likely explanation for the sudden end to his reign of terror, put forward at the time by Sir Melville Macnaghten, the Chief Commissioner of the Metropolitan Police. He speculated that 'the murderer's brain gave way altogether after his awful glut in Miller's Court, and that he immediately committed suicide, or, as a possible alternative, was found to be so hopelessly mad by his relations that they confined him to an asylum'.

UNIMAGINABLE CARNAGE

Three more weeks went by without murders, and then the Ripper struck again. Once again, the victim was a prostitute, Mary Kelly. In a change from his previous behaviour, she was killed indoors, in a room in Miller's Court. Mary Kelly's body was utterly destroyed; she was partially skinned, disembowelled, grotesquely arranged and numerous trophies were taken, including her uterus which, as she was pregnant at the time, had contained a foetus. It was a scene of unimaginable carnage and one that left Whitechapel – and the world – bracing itself for the Ripper's next atrocity.

POLICE LINE DO NOT CROSS

Edmund Kemper

Edmund Kemper, 'the co-ed killer', was a disturbed child who grew up very tall, very bright and very dangerous. He earned his nickname by killing six young women whom he picked up hitchhiking. There may well have been more victims, but Kemper very carefully avoided leaving any clues. However, he eventually lost all sense of caution when his killing rage turned on his own mother. This time, there was only one obvious suspect.

TROUBLED CHILDHOOD

Edmund Kemper was born in Burbank, California, on 18 December 1948, one of a cluster of serial killer baby boomers. Something else he had in common with his fellow serial killers was a troubled childhood. His father, known as E.E., was a Second World War hero and gun collector; his mother was named Clarnell. The couple split up when Ed was nine and his mother took him, along with his sister, to live in Helena, Montana. Ed reacted badly to the break-up and began to manifest some of the warning signs of serious disturbance. He killed the family cat by burying it alive in the back garden, then he dug it up, cut off its head and mounted it on a stick, keeping it in his bedroom as a trophy. He also took to mutilating his sister's dolls.

Once he confided in his sister that he had a crush on a female teacher. Joking, his sister asked him why he did not try to kiss her. Edmund answered, in all seriousness, that if he did that 'I would have to kill her first'. It was not just

Edmund's behaviour that was disturbing: his size was also a problem. Both his parents were very tall and, as he reached his teens, Edmund became far taller than his peers, although despite his size, he was also unusually afraid of being bullied.

Edmund's relationship with his mother deteriorated until she could take no more. Branding him a 'real weirdo' she sent him to live with his father. His father could not handle him either and in turn sent the boy, aged fifteen, to live with his paternal grandparents on their California farm. This arrangement worked tolerably well for a while, country living at least providing Edmund with plenty of opportunity to shoot animals and birds; but on 27 August 1964 Kemper moved from wild animals to innocent humans: he shot dead first his grandmother and then his grandfather.

Kemper was promptly arrested and, when he explained his actions by saying 'I just wondered how it would feel to shoot Grandma', he was judged to be mentally ill and placed in a secure hospital at Atascadero. Five years later, in 1969, Kemper, who was by now over 2 metres (6 feet 9 inches) tall and 136 kg (300 lbs) in weight, managed to persuade doctors that he was a reformed character, and he was paroled to his mother's care.

CUSTOMIZED CAR
This was, to put it mildly, a mistake. His mother, Clarnell, had now relocated to Santa Cruz, a college town in the San Francisco Bay area. For the next two years Kemper bided his time. He applied

Kemper graduated from shooting wild animals to killing his own grandparents – just to find out what it might feel like, or so he said

He killed the family cat by burying it alive in the back garden to join the police, but was turned down on the grounds that he was too tall. Undeterred, he became a regular drinker at a police bar called the Jury Room, where he befriended detectives. He also worked odd jobs and bought himself a car, similar to those used by the police as undercover vehicles. He started using the car to pick up young female hitchhikers, gradually learning to put them at ease. Next he customized the car, making it impossible to open the passenger door from the inside. In retrospect it is obvious that he was just waiting for his moment.

GRISLY PHOTOGRAPHS

The moment finally arrived on 7 May 1972, when he picked up two 18-year-old students, Mary Ann Pesce and Anita Luchessa, who were hitching to Stanford University. He drove them down a dirt road, stabbed them both to death, and then took them back to his apartment. There he sexually assaulted the bodies and photographed them. Then he cut off their heads, put the bodies in plastic bags, buried them on a nearby mountainside and threw the heads into a ravine.

It was four months before he killed again. This time the victim was 15-year-old Aiko Koo. He strangled her, raped her corpse, and then took her body home to dissect. He had her head in the boot of his car the next day when he went for a meeting with court psychiatrists – who were pleased with his progress and declared him officially 'safe'.

They could, of course, hardly have been more wrong. Another four months went by and Kemper murdered another student, Cindy Schell. By this

time he had acquired a gun that he used to shoot Schell dead after forcing her into the boot of his car. Now following a pattern, he raped, beheaded and dissected her before disposing of the corpse. He buried her head in his mother's garden.

Less then a month passed before Kemper struck again. This time, it was two more hitchhikers, Rosalind Thorpe and Alice Lin. They hardly had time to get into the car before he shot them both dead. He put both bodies in the boot and left them there while he went to dine with his mother, then returned to the car to decapitate the women, taking Lin's headless corpse inside to rape.

Kemper's madness was now a long way out of control. At this point he apparently contemplated trying to murder everyone on his block. Instead, though, he decided to stay closer to home. Over the Easter weekend, 1973, he murdered his mother with a hammer, decapitated and raped her, and tried to force her larynx down the waste disposal unit. In a muddled attempt to cover up his crime, he then invited one of his mother's friends over, Sally Hallett. He murdered Hallett, and then, on Easter Sunday, he got in his car and started driving west.

DEATH BY TORTURE

By the time he reached Colorado he realized the game was up. At this stage, he telephoned his friends on the Santa Cruz police force and told them what he had done, where and when.

Kemper's confession left no room for legal manoeuvring, except on grounds of insanity, but the jury decided that he was sane and found him guilty on eight counts of murder. Asked what the appropriate

punishment would be, Kemper reportedly said 'death by torture'. He was sentenced to life in prison, a sentence he is still serving.

Fuelling the court's belief that here was a sociopath not a psychopath, Kemper understands and enjoys his notoriety. He has given regular interviews (including one shared with John Wayne Gacy). Asking himself the rhetorical question, 'What do you think when you see a pretty girl walking down the street?', Kemper provided this for an answer: 'One side of me says I'd like to talk to her, date her. The other half of me says "I wonder how her head would look on a stick." '

In the light of such remarks, it is unsurprising that Kemper's parole requests have been turned down.

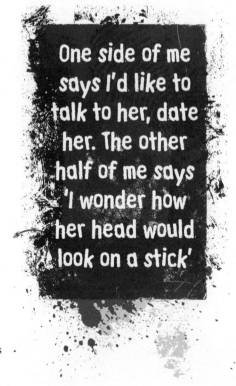

One side of me says I'd like to talk to her, date her. The other half of me says 'I wonder how her head would look on a stick'

POLICE LINE DO NOT CROSS

Bela Kiss

Very little is known about the early life of Bela Kiss, one of the most horrifying serial killers of all time. His story only comes fully into focus when he began his career of murder, as a young man apparently searching for a wife.

A handsome man with blue eyes and fair hair, Kiss was very attractive to women, not only because of his good looks, but also because he was educated, intelligent and well-mannered. However, when his crimes came to light, it emerged that Kiss was a lady killer in a more literal sense. He murdered over twenty women and pickled their bodies in alcohol, inside large metal drums that he hid in his home and around the countryside nearby. Perhaps most horrifying of all, he actually managed to get away with it.

BARRELS

In 1912, Bela Kiss was living in the village of Czinkota, just outside Budapest in Hungary. He shared a house with his housekeeper, an elderly woman named Mrs Jakubec. Although well-liked in the village, Kiss was not on intimate terms with any of his neighbours. A single man, he had a series of relationships with several attractive young women who often came to the house, but who were never introduced to the housekeeper or to any of his neighbours. Kiss also collected metal drums, telling the local police that they were for storing gasoline, which was likely to be in short supply in the future because of the impending war.

In 1914, Kiss was called up into the army. While he was away, soldiers went to his house to look for the extra supplies of gasoline he was said to keep there. They found the drums and opened them. Instead of gasoline, inside each drum they found the dead body of a woman who had been strangled and whose body had then been preserved in alcohol. A further search through Kiss' papers revealed dozens of letters from the women, who had visited the house after replying to his newspaper advertisements for a wife.

Kiss lured well-to-do, attractive women by correspondence, promising to marry them and often divesting them of their savings in the process. He then invited them to his home. Once there, he would strangle them, pickle their bodies in alcohol and seal them in the metal drums. The bodies also had puncture marks on their necks and they were drained of blood. Bela Kiss was not just a murderer, but a vampire too.

Why he chose to preserve the bodies in this way nobody knows to this day. It was obviously a risky thing to do. Firstly, the drums were big and hard to hide; secondly, the bodies inside were so perfectly preserved that in some cases even the labels on their clothing could be read. Surely Kiss must have known that if ever the drums were opened, his crimes could easily be traced.

CHANGING IDENTITY

Several local women who had gone missing were discovered in the drums, along with many others whose absence had not been noticed. Kiss had repeated his crimes again and again, with a series of innocent, unsuspecting victims, using a false name, 'Herr Hoffmann'. Until the discovery of the bodies, the connection

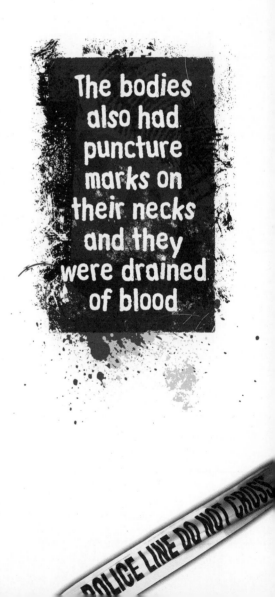
The bodies also had puncture marks on their necks and they were drained of blood

POLICE LINE DO NOT CROSS

A picture taken inside the outhouse where some of the bodies were found

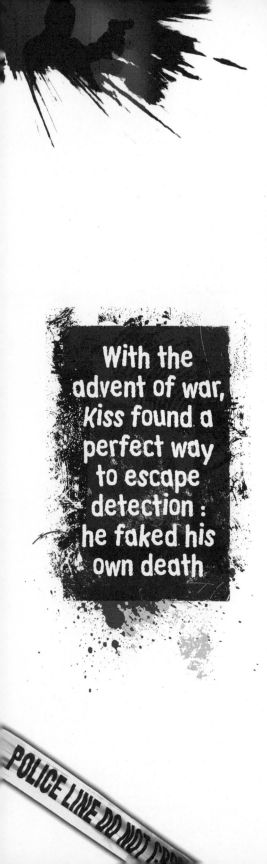

With the advent of war, Kiss found a perfect way to escape detection : he faked his own death

between Bela Kiss and 'Herr Hoffman', who was wanted for questioning in regard to the disappearance of two widows, had never been made.

FAKING DEATH

With the advent of war, Kiss found a perfect way to escape detection: he faked his own death. He assumed the identity of an army comrade who had been killed in combat, switching his papers with those of the dead man. However, his plan was foiled when, in the spring of 1919, he was spotted in Budapest by someone who knew him. Police investigated, and found out about the fraud, but were still unable to catch up with the killer. Later, a soldier called Hoffman boasted to his comrades of his prowess as a strangler; but once again, when police tried to find Bela Kiss, the trail quickly went cold.

Many years later, Kiss was apparently spotted in New York by a homicide detective called Henry Oswald, who was renowned for his ability to remember faces. By this time, Kiss would have been in his late sixties. Oswald pursued Kiss but lost him among the crowds of Times Square. A few years later, Kiss was again seen in New York, this time working as the janitor of an apartment block; but unbelievably he again escaped police and was never apprehended.

Nobody knows how or when Bela Kiss died. The true number of his victims is also unknown. Did he cease killing women when he went on the run, or did he continue his hideous crimes undetected? How many women who went missing at that time in Hungary could have been lured to their death by Bela Kiss? These are questions to which we will never know the answers.

POLICE LINE DO NOT CROSS

Pedro López

Pedro López, known as the 'Monster of the Andes', has a claim to being the most prolific serial killer of modern times. If his own unverified estimate of three hundred victims is to be taken seriously, then only Harold Shipman can rival him for the sheer number of lives he brought to an untimely end.

Tired of being a victim, Lopez became a monster – one of the most prolific serial killers of all time

STREET LIFE

Pedro López was born in the town of Tolmia, Colombia, in 1949, the seventh of thirteen children born to a prostitute mother. At any time this would have been a hard start in life, but in 1949 Colombia was going through what became known as 'La Violencia', a time of brutal lawlessness and civil war. Pedro's mother was a tyrannical figure, but he realized from a young age that home life was preferable to being out on the streets. When Pedro was eight years old, however, that is exactly where he found himself. His mother discovered him making sexual advances to a younger sister and threw him out.

The first person to take him in posed as a Good Samaritan, but turned out to be a paedophile who raped Pedro repeatedly, before casting him back out on to the streets. Utterly traumatized, the boy became a feral, nocturnal being, hiding inside buildings and emerging at night to scavenge for food.

He endured this existence for a year, finally ending up in the town of Bogotá, where an American couple saw him begging on the streets, felt sorry for him and took him in. They gave him room and board and sent him to a local school for

orphans. This good fortune did not last, however. Aged twelve, Pedro ran away from school after breaking into the school office and stealing money. Later he would claimed that this theft was in response to a teacher at the school making sexual advances to him.

PRISON RAPE

Whatever the reason, Pedro López was soon back on the streets again. La Violencia was over and times were a little easier. López was able to survive by a combination of begging and petty theft, building up, in his mid-teens, to a specialization in car theft. Aged eighteen, he was finally arrested and sentenced to seven years in prison. After only two days behind bars he was gang-raped by four of his fellow inmates. López, however, had grown tired of being a victim; he made a knife from various prison utensils, and in the following weeks succeeded in killing three of his attackers. The prison authorities, little interested in the wellbeing of the inmates, added on a mere two years to his sentence.

> After a day of confession, the priest asked to be released – he could not stand to listen to any more

POLICE LINE DO NOT CROSS

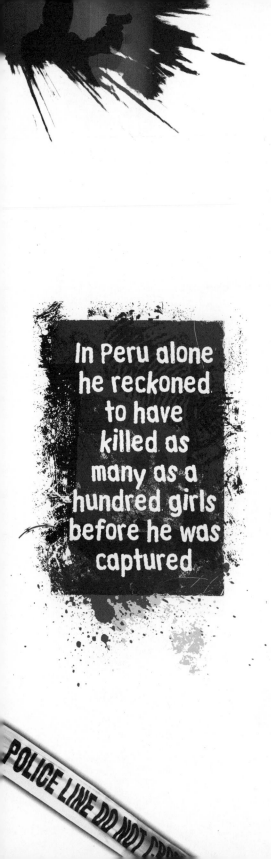

In Peru alone he reckoned to have killed as many as a hundred girls before he was captured

By the time of his release in 1978, López was a very angry and dangerous individual, with a grudge against society in general and women in particular – he blamed his mother for everything that had gone wrong in his life. On release, he started to take revenge and embarked on a two-year killing rampage. His targets were invariably young girls, mostly from Indian tribes, as he knew the authorities would be particularly uninterested in their fate. Nor did he confine himself to Colombia; his murderous spree saw him following the Andes south to Peru and Ecuador. In Peru alone he reckoned to have killed as many as a hundred girls before he was captured by Ayachuco Indians while attempting to abduct a 9-year-old girl. They were about to bury him alive when an American missionary intervened and persuaded them to hand López over to the authorities. The authorities simply deported him over the border to Ecuador and let him go.

CAUGHT

For the next year or so, Pedro López moved back and forth between Ecuador and Colombia, killing with apparent impunity. The authorities did notice an increase in missing girls but put this down to slave traders. Then, in April 1980, there was a flash flood in the Ecuadorian town of Ambato and the bodies of four missing children were washed up. A few days later, still in Ambato, a woman named Carvina Poveda spotted López in the act of trying to abduct her 12-year-old daughter. She called for help. López was overpowered and handed in to the police.

López started to confide in the prison priest. After a day of grisly confession, the priest had to ask to be released as he could

not stand to listen any more. The priest told the interrogators what he had learned; they put the new evidence to López and he began to confess.

DAYLIGHT MURDER

López told them that he had murdered a hundred girls in Colombia, at least 110 in Ecuador, and many more than that in Peru. He expressed a particular enthusiasm for Ecuadorian girls, who he said were much more innocent and trusting than Colombians, and stated a preference for murdering by daylight so he could see the life leave his victims' eyes as he strangled them.

At first the police were not sure whether all this was anything more than the ravings of a madman. Preferring to be branded a monster rather than a liar, López promised he would take the officers to his burial sites. He was placed in leg irons, then allowed to lead the police to a site outside Ambato, where they found the remains of fifty-three girls. The police had now seen more than enough to convince them that Pedro López was indeed the monster he claimed to be.

Further detailed confessions by the serial killer allowed the prosecutors to charge López with having committed 110 murders in Ecuador. He was duly sentenced to life imprisonment. In the unlikely event that he is ever released, he would be required to stand trial in Colombia, where he would certainly face the death penalty.

Today, López does not appear to be in any way remorseful; rather, he seems proud of his crimes: 'I am the man of the century', he boasted in a recent interview given from his prison cell.

POLICE LINE DO NOT CROSS

Vlad III Draculea

Vlad III Draculea was known in his day as Vlad the Impaler. The origins of this epithet most probably lie with the Turks, who came to call him Kaziglu Bey – 'the Prince Impaler'. It is a reference to his preferred method of execution. Most often a sharpened stake was inserted in a victim's anus and forced through the body until it came out of the mouth. Stakes might be pushed through other orifices. Infants were said to be impaled on a stake driven through their mothers' breasts.

He was born late in the year 1431, probably in the Transylvanian fortress city of Sighisoara. His father was Vlad II Dracul; his Romanian surname can be translated as 'Dragon'. Thus, Vlad III was Draculea, 'Son of the Dragon'. Five years after his birth, Vlad III became Prince of Wallachia, in present-day Romania.

TURKISH HOSTAGE

When Vlad was ten, his father sent him and his younger brother Radu the Handsome as hostages to the Ottoman Sultan Murad II. Vlad spent much of the next six years locked in an underground dungeon in Turkey where he was whipped and beaten. Radu, on the other hand, became a favourite of the sultan's son. He lived a life of comfort and became a convert to Islam.

Vlad's return to Wallachia was made possible only through the murder of his older brother, Mircea, who was buried alive after having first been blinded by red-hot iron stakes, and the subsequent

Even during the Middle Ages, the torture methods of Vlad III stood out as particularly brutal and sadistic

POLICE LINE DO NOT CROSS

Vlad the Impaler had unusual notions of hospitality: when he executed prisoners in his castle, his preferred method was to insert a sharpened stake in the anus and force it through the body until it came out of the mouth

assassination of his father. Murad II then installed Vlad III as a puppet prince. Mere months later, Vlad was pushed out of Wallachia by troops loyal to the kingdom of Hungary. He fled to Moldavia, where he was put under the protection of his uncle. After his uncle, too, was assassinated, Vlad switched his allegiance from the Ottoman empire to the kingdom of Hungary. In 1456, he led a successful campaign sweeping the Turks out of Wallachia, and was again installed as prince. The next six years were spent in an effort to consolidate his power. This Vlad achieved through a variety of means, not the least of which were torture and murder.

CLAPPED IN IRONS

In 1462, Vlad lost Wallachia when troops of the Ottoman empire again invaded. His wife, whose name is left unrecorded, committed suicide to avoid capture. Vlad's brother Radu became the new prince. Under an agreement struck between the Hungarian king and Sultan Mehmed II, Vlad was imprisoned in Hungary. It is doubtful that his confinement lasted four years; in 1466, he married into the Hungarian royal family and was officially released from custody eight years later.

In 1475, he attempted to take back Wallachia. Radu was now dead, but he had a new foe, Basarb the Elder, with whom to contend. It was an easy victory, but afterwards the troops that had helped to restore Vlad returned to Transylvania. He was left with the citizenry which he had once terrorized. When the Turks returned with reinforcements, Vlad was at their mercy.

Vlad III died in December 1476. Most accounts place him on the battlefield at the moment of death, facing defeat, surrounded by his men. One story has it that he was accidentally killed by one of his own as the battle's end drew near.

The story of Vlad the Impaler inspired Bram Stoker's novel Dracula

He was said to delight in cutting off various body parts – the nose, the ears, the genitals and the tongue – as punishment

After his death, Vlad's corpse was decapitated, preserved in honey and sent to Istanbul where the head was displayed, appropriately, atop a stake. According to records, his body was buried at the monastery at Snagof, on an island close to Bucharest. However, recent excavations there have uncovered only some bones of horses. Dating from the Neolithic era, they do not at all correspond with what one would expect of a Wallachian prince.

CLAPPED IN IRONS

It is an indication of the particularly brutal and sadistic nature of Vlad that his torture methods stand out in the Middle Ages. The earliest written record in which his atrocities are detailed is a German pamphlet issued in the Holy Roman Empire. Printed in 1488, twelve years after his death, it paints the late prince as a sadistic monster, forever terrorizing his people. Romanian oral tradition, however, appears divided. Some tales portray him as harsh but fair; a ruler who expected his people to be honest and moral. Only those who deviated from this path were dealt with in a brutal manner. Other oral accounts depict a cruel man who delighted in torture and punishment. This Vlad was a prince who employed a variety of methods in torturing his victims, including skinning, boiling, scalping, decapitation, blinding, strangling, hanging, burning and frying. He was said to delight in cutting off various body parts – the nose, the ears, the genitals and the tongue – as punishment.

Oral tradition has it that these techniques were not used exclusively against the Turks, but also on his own people. In the years 1457, 1459 and 1460, he tortured and murdered tradesmen and merchants who dared rebel against his laws. It is said that in August 1459, Vlad had impaled 30,000 merchants and administrators in the city of Brasov.

The Ottoman invasion of 1462 was caused, in part, by the reception he had given an emissary of the sultan. Vlad had told the emissary to remove his turban. After the order was ignored, the prince had the turban nailed to the man's head.

POLICE LINE DO NOT CROSS

Carl Panzram

Carl Panzram was a true misanthrope – a man who positively loathed his fellow human beings. His thirty-nine years on earth saw him drift from an abusive childhood to a nomadic adulthood spent in and out of a hellish prison system. In between, he took his revenge by killing at least twenty-one victims, and robbing and raping many more. When he was put to death in 1930, his last action was to spit in the hangman's face and say: 'Hurry it up, you Hoosier bastard, I could hang a dozen men while you're fooling around.'

Panzram was born on a farm in Warren, Minnesota, on 28 June 1891, one of seven children in a dirt-poor German immigrant family. Theirs was a desperately hard life that became even harder when Carl was seven years old: his father walked out one day and never came back. His mother and brothers struggled to keep the farm going, working from dawn till dusk in the fields. During this time, his brothers used to beat him unmercifully for no reason at all. At the age of eleven Carl gave them a good reason: he broke into a neighbour's house and stole whatever he could find, including a handgun. His brothers beat him unconscious when they found out.

BRUTAL CORRECTIONAL INSTITUTION

Panzram was arrested for the crime and sent to the Minnesota State Training School in 1903, aged twelve. This was a brutal institution in which he was regularly beaten and raped by the staff. Here he acquired a taste for forced gay sex and an abiding hatred of authority. In 1905 he expressed this hatred by burning part of the school down. He was not identified as the culprit, however, and was able to persuade a parole panel that year that he was a reformed character. The opposite was closer to the truth: the Carl Panzram who emerged from the school was in reality a deformed character.

TEENAGE HOBO

Panzram returned home for a while, went to school briefly, then left after an altercation with a teacher. He worked on his mother's farm until, at fourteen, he jumped on a freight train and headed westwards. For the next few years he lived the life of a teenage hobo. He committed crimes and was the victim of them; he was sent to reform schools and broke out of them. When he was sixteen, in 1907, he joined the army but refused to accept the discipline and was then caught trying to desert with a bundle of stolen clothing. He was dishonourably discharged and sent to the fearsome Leavenworth Prison, where he spent two hard years, breaking rocks and becoming a very strong and very dangerous man.

On his release, he returned to his roaming. He was arrested at various times and under various names for vagrancy, burglary, arson and robbery. The one crime he was not arrested for, but took particular pleasure in carrying out, was homosexual rape. Once he even raped a policeman who was trying to arrest him. His crimes escalated in savagery and so did his prison sentences; he served time in both Montana and Oregon.

In 1918, Panzram escaped from Oregon State Prison, where he had been serving a

During one of his frequent stints in jail, Panzram was sent to Sing Sing, but proved so unruly he was moved – only to go on to murder a fellow inmate

sentence under the name Jefferson Baldwin. He decided to leave the North-east, where he had become very well known to the police. He changed his name to John O'Leary and headed for the east coast, where he would make the final transition from robber and rapist to cold-blooded killer.

POLICE LINE DO NOT CROSS

BAIT

Panzram began by carrying out a string of burglaries that made him enough money to buy a yacht. He would lure sailors on to the yacht, get them drunk, rape them, kill them and then dump their bodies in the sea. This went on until his boat crashed and sank, by which time he reckoned he had killed ten men. Broke once more, Panzram stowed away on a ship and ended up in Angola, Africa. He signed on with an oil company who were drilling off the coast of the Congo. While he was there, he raped and killed a 12-year-old boy. Then he went on a crocodile hunting expedition that ended when he killed the six local guides he had hired, raped their corpses and fed them to the crocodiles.

CAPTURED

Panzram fled back to the States, as witnesses had seen him engage the guides. He went on to rape and murder an 11-year-old boy, George McMahon, in Salem, Massachusetts. Over the next months, he carried out two more murders and numerous robberies. Finally, he was captured while in the act of burgling a railway station. He received his toughest sentence yet: he began it in Sing Sing, but proved so unruly that he was sent on to Dannemora, an infamous jail where he was beaten and tortured by the guards. His legs were broken and left untreated, leaving him semi-crippled and in constant pain for the rest of his life.

Panzram seemed to positively welcome his sentence of death by hanging, going so far as to curse campaigners who tried to get the decision overturned

Immediately after his release in July 1928, Panzram carried out a string of burglaries and at least one murder before being rearrested. By now he was tired of life. On arrest he gave his real name for the first time and, while in prison in Washington DC, confessed to several murders of young boys.

A TALE TO TELL

Encouraged by a prison guard with whom he struck up an unlikely friendship, he went on to write a 20,000-word account of his terrible life and crimes. This remains a remarkable document, a horrifying but unusually even-handed account of a serial killer's inner life. Following the confessions, and amid a flurry of media interest, Panzram was tried for the most recent of his murders: the strangling of Alexander Uszacke. He was found guilty and sentenced to serve twenty-five years at the federal prison in Leavenworth, Kansas.

Following the sentence, Panzram warned the world that he would kill the first man who crossed him when he was inside. He was as good as his word. He was given work in the laundry and there murdered his supervisor, Robert Warnke, by staving in his head with an iron bar.

This time, Panzram was sentenced to hang. He positively welcomed the court's verdict and claimed that now his only ambition was to die. When anti-death penalty campaigners tried to have his sentence commuted, he ungraciously wrote to them to say: 'I wish you all had one neck and I had my hands on it.' Shortly afterwards, on 3 September 1930, he was duly hanged.

On a hunting expedition, he killed six local guides, raped them and fed them to the crocodiles

Aileen Wuornos

Aileen Wuornos has become one of the most famous of all serial killers, not because she killed a huge number of victims, nor because she killed them in an exceptionally brutal way, but because of the simple fact that she was a woman. Before her arrest, the received wisdom was that there was no such thing as a female serial killer.

This was not the case. There had in fact been many female serial killers before Wuornos, but they had mostly committed domestic murders, such as poisoning husbands or killing elderly invalids. In addition, there were a few female serial killers who had acted as accomplices to men. Wuornos, however, did not fit either pattern; she conformed more closely to the image of the reckless male gunslinger, robbing and killing victims in cold blood. It was no wonder that she sold the movie rights to her story within two days of being arrested.

SEVERE BURNS

Of course, Hollywood would never have come calling if Wuornos had remained a petty thief instead of a murderer. Hers was the kind of life that the movies prefer to ignore. She was born Aileen Pittman in Rochester, Michigan, on 29 February 1956. Her teenage parents had split up before she was born. Her father, Leo, later became a convicted child molester. Her mother, Diane, proved unable to cope alone and, in 1960, Aileen and her brother Keith were legally adopted by Diane's parents, Lauri and Britta Wuornos. This failed to improve

matters. Aged six, Aileen suffered severe burns to her face when she and her brother had been setting fires. Aged fifteen, she gave birth to a child, who was adopted. Her grandmother died that same year, apparently of liver failure, though Diane suspected her father, Lauri, of murder.

SCHOOL DROP-OUT

Aileen dropped out of school early, left home and hit the streets. It was not long before she started to work as a prostitute. She had regular run-ins with the law, mostly for drink-related offences. A brief marriage was annulled after her elderly husband took out a restraining order. She then served one year in prison following a farcical attempt at armed robbery conducted while wearing a bikini. In 1986, she met lesbian Tyria Moore, who became the love of her life. Aileen and Tyria set up home together, living off Aileen's prostitution. Aileen became a notoriously belligerent individual, often in fights and always carrying a gun in her purse. In her efforts to keep Tyria happy, she supplemented her income with theft, mainly from her clients. Some time in November 1989, Aileen Wuornos went one giant step further – into murder.

Her first victim was Richard Mallory, a 51-year-old electrician whose main interests were commercial sex and drinking. Wuornos would later claim that she killed Mallory to defend herself against rape. While she went on to make this claim in regard to all her murders, in this case there may have been some truth

Aileen Wuornos surprised the experts who had assumed that all serial killers were male – here was a woman who could be just as brutal as any man

She sold the movie rights to her story within two days of being arrested

POLICE LINE DO NOT

POLICE LINE DO NOT CROSS

to it, as it later emerged that Mallory had a conviction for rape.

Mallory's body was found in the woods near Daytona Beach, Florida, on 13 December, shot with a .22. In June 1990, another body was found in the woods, again shot with a .22 and this time naked. The corpse was identified a week later as David Spears. By then another victim had been found, Charles Carskaddon; again he had been shot with a .22 and, like Spears, had last been seen travelling down the main Florida freeway, I-75. The next victim was Peter Siems, who had last been seen on 7 June. His car was found a month later, dumped by two women whose descriptions matched those of Wuornos and Moore. Victims five, six and seven followed in August, September and November of 1990. All of them were shot with a .22. The police were reluctant to admit that a serial killer was at large but they finally released the sketches of the women who had dumped Peter Siems' car.

BIKER BAR

Soon reports came in that the two women might be Aileen Wuornos and Tyria Moore. The police arrested Wuornos in a biker bar in Florida on 9 January 1991. They found Moore at her sister's house in Philadelphia. In order to save her own skin, Moore helped the police to extract a confession from Wuornos. The ploy worked. Rather than see Moore charged with murder, Wuornos confessed to six of the murders; however, she did not confess to the killing of Peter Siems, whose body has not been found to this day.

MEDIA CIRCUS

At that point, the media furore began. Film-makers and journalists vied for the rights to tell Wuornos' story. Some portrayed her as a monster, others presented her as a victim. The truth of the matter seems to be that Wuornos was a woman brutalized by a miserable life, but that the murders she committed were motivated by rage rather than, as she argued, by the need to defend herself.

Certainly that was the verdict of the jury that sentenced her to death on 27 January 1992. Wuornos spent the next ten years on death row while campaigners attempted to have the death penalty rescinded. However, in the end, Wuornos herself demanded that the death penalty be carried out. She was executed by lethal injection on 9 October 2002.

> Before her arrest, the received wisdom was that there was no such thing as a female serial killer

Hollywood's version of Wuornos' story, Monster, earned Charlize Theron an Oscar for her portrayal of the serial killer

POLICE LINE DO NOT CROSS

George Hennard

George Hennard considered Steely Dan's 'Don't Take Me Alive' to be his theme song. The lyrics of this very bleak piece of music, inspired by the constant eruptions of violence in 1970s Los Angeles, concern a cornered murderer who is surrounded by police. Whether he knew it or not – and it is likely that he did – Hennard would one day be in a very similar position.

A WAY OF LIFE

George Hennard was born on 15 October 1956, the son of an army surgeon and his wife. He had a difficult relationship with his mother, and would depict her in drawings with a serpent's body. After graduating from high school in 1974, he joined the United States Navy, and later the Merchant Marine. In 1989, after 15 years of service, Hennard was dismissed for possessing a small amount of marijuana. The end of his duty left him extremely depressed. He told a judge, 'It means a way of life. It means my livelihood. It means all I've got. It's all I know.' Although he underwent drug treatment, he became reclusive.

He lived alone in a large, two-storey colonial-style house in Belton, Texas, the seat of Bell County. Belonging to his mother, this once grand home had fallen into disrepair, a state that had led to several confrontations with local officials. A good-looking man, Hennard appeared to have a great deal of problems with women. Those who knew him best often

> Hennard had a difficult relationship with his mother, and would depict her in drawings with a serpent's body

described him as a misogynist. He was given to shouting obscene remarks at women as they passed his home, and appeared threatening to his neighbours.

LOADED WEAPON

In the winter of 1991, on a trip to Nevada, Hennard bought a 9mm Glock-17 semi-automatic pistol and a 9mm Ruger. In May, he was carrying one of the guns when he was arrested by a park ranger in Lake Mead, Nevada, for driving while intoxicated and carrying a loaded weapon.

The next month, Hennard expressed his bitterness towards women in a five-page letter to Jill Fritz and Jana Jernigan, two sisters who lived down the street. Made public within twenty-four hours of the shooting that was to come, it is a rambling, venomous document. Hennard begins by mistakenly referring to the young women as 'Stacee' and 'Robin'. It reads, in part, 'Do you think the three of us can get together some day? Please give me the satisfaction of someday laughing in the face of all those mostly white treacherous female vipers from those two towns who tried to destroy me and my family.' At another point, Hennard expresses his appreciation of the sisters: 'It is very ironic about Belton, Texas. I found the best and worst in women there. You and your sister are the one side. Then the abundance of evil women that make up the worst on the other side.' Hennard included photographs of himself and concluded by asking that the two women not disclose the contents of the letter to anyone other than their immediate family.

Although Hennard saw Jernigan and her sister to be on the opposite side of 'the abundance of evil women', she was

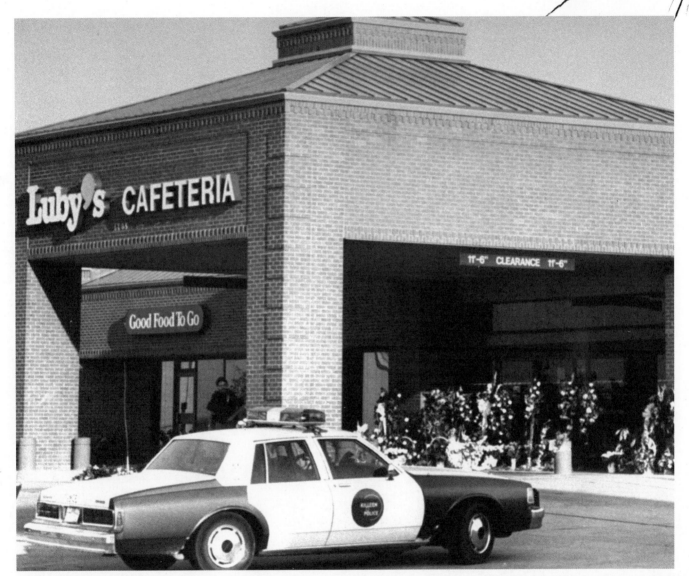

A police car stands guard outside Luby's Cafeteria. The delivery bay around the side is packed with wreaths and baskets of flowers placed there by mourners for those killed in the massacre by psychopathic gunman George Hennard

not spared his threatening phone calls, nor was the sisters' mother. Both went to the police with their concerns that he would one day explode into violence.

Though disconcerting, none of these communications would have been particularly newsworthy, had it not been for a ten-minute incident which took

place on 16 October 1991, the day after Hennard's thirty-fifth birthday. That day, he left his

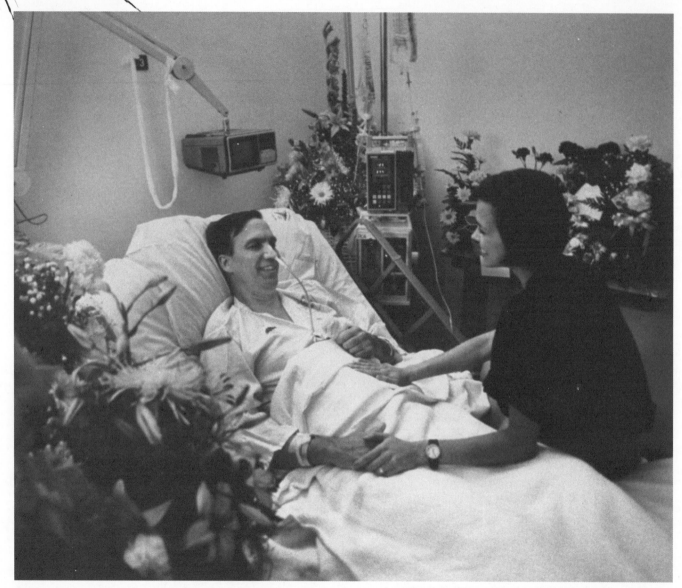

Gunshot victim Steve Ernst chats with his daughter Amy as he lies in hospital convalescing from wounds to the stomach. He was one of the lucky ones: twenty-three people died in the worst mass shooting in the history of Texas

Belton home and drove 25 km (15 miles) to Killeen, the largest city in Bell County. At about 12.40 pm, he drove his blue Ford Ranger pick-up into the parking lot of Luby's Cafeteria, a chain restaurant on the interstate highway. Hennard gunned the engine and rammed the truck through the restaurant's plate

POLICE LINE DO NOT CRO

glass window, striking an elderly male diner. The assumption was that there had been a terrible accident, and several members of the lunchtime crowd rushed to help. He then emerged from the cab with his Glock and Ruger.

'This is what Bell County has done to me!' he yelled, and began to shoot.

The first person to die was the man he had struck with his pick-up; Hennard shot him in the head. He was methodical in his killing, making certain that each was dead or mortally wounded before moving on to the next victim.

At one point he paused and spoke to a woman with a 4-year-old girl, saying 'Get the baby and get out of here, lady, right now.' He then returned to firing, shooting the woman's mother. Witnesses later said that he appeared to focus on shooting women.

There were some patrons who managed to escape. One man hurled himself through one of the restaurant's plate glass windows, creating an opening through which others followed. Those who could not escape sought to hide themselves behind overturned tables.

Police arrived at the bloody scene ten minutes into the slaughter. They exchanged fire and hit the gunman four times. Hennard sought refuge in one of the restaurant washrooms, where he committed suicide by shooting himself in the head, ending the nightmare.

PLAYING DEAD

It was then the worst mass shooting in the history of the United States: fourteen women and nine men lay dead; one other victim was mortally wounded. Another twenty people had been injured, some having cut wounds from trying to escape through the broken window.

The first paramedics to enter later reported discovering people playing dead, despite the fact that the shooting had ceased minutes earlier. One Luby's employee had to be treated for hypothermia after spending over two hours hiding in the restaurant freezer, unaware that the gunman was dead. Another hid for nearly twenty-four hours in a commercial dishwasher before being discovered.

After the shooting, Luby's Cafeteria stayed closed for about five months. Understandably, it never regained the popularity it had once enjoyed. In 2000, the restaurant shut its doors for good.

CONCEALED WEAPONS

Two days after the shooting, a proposed ban on semi-automatic assault weapons that had been before the United States Congress failed. However, the Texas shootings did have a lasting legacy; one that was markedly different from that of the Montreal Massacre, which had taken place less than two years earlier. As students at the École Polytechnique pushed for tighter gun control laws north of the border, a survivor of the Killeen shooting was crossing the United States campaigning in support of concealed handgun laws. Suzanna Hupp had been eating at Luby's Cafeteria when Hennard began his shooting spree. Although she managed to escape, both her parents, who had been at the table with her, were killed without mercy.

She had left her handgun in her truck as Texas state law then forbade the carrying of a concealed weapon. Hupp argued that she would have had an opportunity to stop the killing if she'd been permitted to carry the handgun in her handbag. Today she is credited with having helped to bring about the state's current concealed weapons law.

In 1998, she became the first woman to be awarded a lifetime membership of the National Rifle Association.

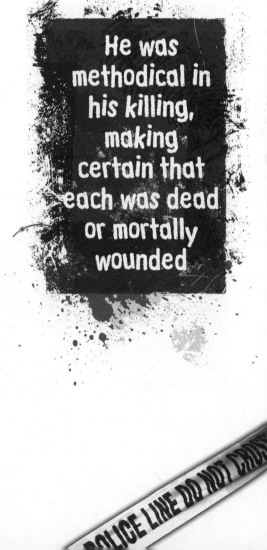

He was methodical in his killing, making certain that each was dead or mortally wounded

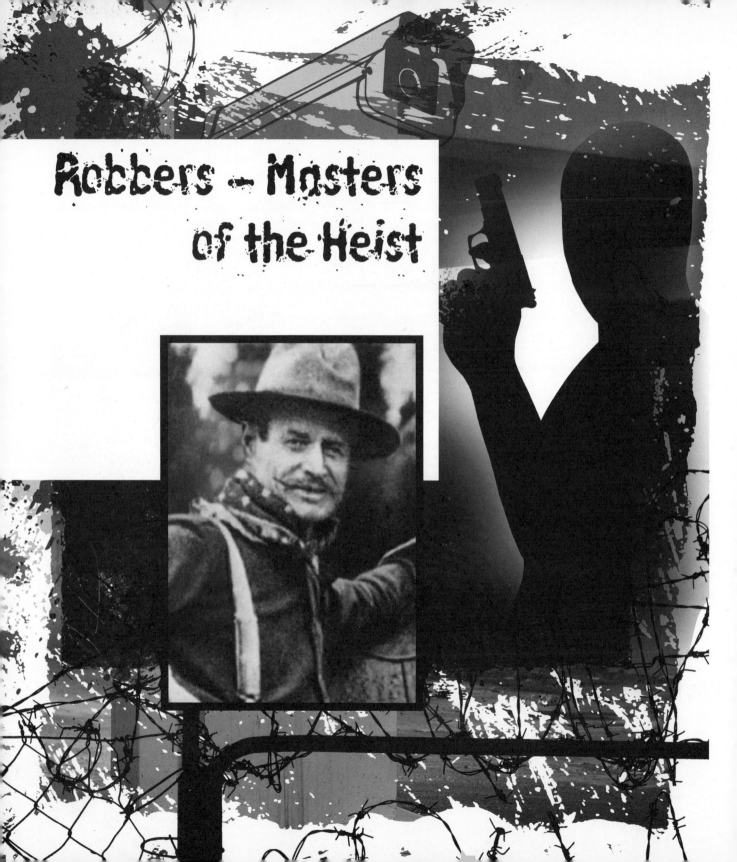

Robbers – Masters of the Heist

D.B. Cooper

The name D.B. Cooper refers to an aeroplane hijacker who hit the headlines in 1971, first extorting money and then parachuting out of the plane. He was never found, and thus the incident remains a mystery, prompting a great deal of speculation as to who the hijacker was and what became of him.

The hijacker made his appearance on 24 November 1971, on the eve of Thanksgiving. He bought his one-way ticket under the name of Dan Cooper and boarded his plane, a Northwest Orient Airlines Boeing 727, flying from Portland, Oregon, to Seattle, Washington. He was a well-dressed, middle-aged man, and did not attract attention in any way.

'NO FUNNY STUFF'

At that period, aeroplane hijackings were relatively common. However, most of them were political in nature, designed to attract attention to an anti-establishment cause. Cooper was unusual in this area in that he was, apparently, a conventional man who appears to have pulled off his stunt for one reason only: money.

Cooper sat at the back of the plane, and passed a note to the air hostess, Flo Schaffner. In the note, he wrote that he had brought a bomb on board, and wanted two hundred thousand dollars in unmarked bills, four parachutes and 'no funny stuff'. Ms Schaffner was used to male passengers passing her notes asking for a date, so she simply put the note in her pocket. It was only when the plane was taking off that she read it. She immediately told the flight crew about

the note, and they radioed the airport for help. Meanwhile, Ms Schaffner went to talk to Cooper, to see if he really did have a bomb. When he opened his briefcase, she saw some red sticks and some wires, which managed to convince her that he was telling the truth.

Before the plane landed, the FBI sent a message to say that the parachutes and money would be available for the hijacker at the airport. In accordance with the hijacker's demands, the bills would be unmarked – but unbeknown to him, they had all been copied on a Xerox machine, so that the serial numbers could be traced later by the police.

ESCAPE BY PARACHUTE

Once the plane landed, Cooper let all the passengers off. He then waited for the money and parachutes to be delivered to the plane. It is likely that he asked for four parachutes because he was afraid that if only one was delivered, it would be deliberately faulty. By asking for four, he was confusing the authorities, who may have thought the other parachutes were intended for members of the flight crew, and would therefore ensure that all of them were working properly.

Cooper asked the pilot to fly to Mexico at a low height, with the landing gear and plane flaps down. The pilot told the hijacker that, because the plane was flying low, it would be necessary to stop for refuelling in Reno, Nevada, on the way. Cooper agreed to touch down in Reno. On the flight there, he asked the crew to remain in the cockpit and told the stewardess to close the curtain in the first-class section behind them. The last the crew saw of him was when he was trying

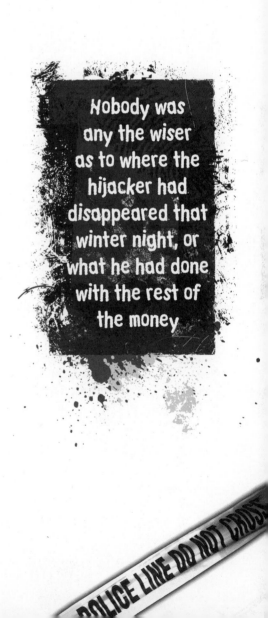

Nobody was any the wiser as to where the hijacker had disappeared that winter night, or what he had done with the rest of the money

POLICE LINE DO NOT CROSS

to tie something around his waist, most probably the bag containing the unnumbered bills that he had received.

A while later, the pilot noticed that the warning light, which showed that a door was open on the plane, had come on. He shouted out to ask if there was anything they could do for the hijacker, who responded 'No!' Cooper then disappeared, apparently by jumping off the back staircase of the plane, which he had forced open.

VANISHING INTO THE BLUE

Despite the fact that the plane was being followed by air force planes and an FBI helicopter, the hijacker was not actually seen jumping out. When the plane landed in Reno, it was searched, but all that remained of the mysterious hijacker were two parachutes, some cigarette ends, a tie and a tie clip. Cooper himself had completely vanished.

No one knows to this day whether he survived his parachute jump out of the plane. The plane was flying at almost 320 km (200 miles) an hour through a temperature of -7 °C (19.4 °F), with a wind-chill factor of -70 °C (-94 °F). However, the hijacker may well have survived this, because he would not have remained in these temperatures for more than fifteen seconds before landing. Even so, he was certainly not dressed for parachuting through winter conditions, wearing only a suit and an overcoat. When he landed in the snowy forest below without adequate clothing or provisions, he might well have frozen to death overnight.

Although a huge search of the area was made,

Did he survive to spend his ill-gotten gains? Neither the photofit made up from airport staff's descriptions of the mysterious D.B. Cooper nor the photocopied banknotes helped to find the hijacker

and two bodies were eventually found (both missing persons, neither of them connected to the case), there was no trace of the hijacker. Many years later, in 1980, some of the twenty-dollar bills that Cooper had taken turned up. They were found on the shore of a river near Vancouver, Washington, by a boy and his family on a picnic. The total amount was more than $ 5,000, and the serial numbers on the bills matched the ones copied by the FBI almost a decade before. The police took in a man named Daniel B. Cooper for questioning, but released him since he appeared to have no connection with the case. (After this episode, the hijacking case became known as that of 'D.B. Cooper', even though the hijacker had only ever given his name as Dan.)

In the end, the finding of the bills did little to solve the mystery. Nobody was any the wiser as to where the hijacker had disappeared to, or what he had done with the rest of the money. To this day, the case of D.B. Cooper remains a riddle.

POLICE LINE DO NOT CROSS

Jonathan Wild.

During the late 18th century, Jonathan Wild organized crime on a grand scale in London: his illegal operations were complex, but essentially, he ran gangs of robbers and thieves who stole goods, and then returned them to their rightful owners for a reward. His business made him a handsome profit, and he became a well-known public figure, dressing in fine clothes and carrying a silver-topped cane. However, eventually the law caught up with him, and overnight he became a villain, despised by the public and the press who had once lionized him.

A GANG OF THIEVES AND WHORES

Born in Wolverhampton in 1683, Wild came from a poor family. As a small boy, he was apprenticed to a buckle-maker and afterwards worked as a servant. As a young man, he ran up debts and spent time in a debtor's prison, where he met a prostitute named Mary Milliner. When the pair were released, he lived with her and became part of her gang of thieves and whores. During this time, Wild became a pimp and also bought and sold stolen goods. He developed an ingenious scam whereby thieves would let him know what property they had stolen, and victims of theft would also come to him to get their goods back. He took care never to have the stolen goods in his possession, and took a cut from both thieves and victims for his services. He posed as a do-gooder, recovering stolen items from thieves and returning them to their rightful owners, even working with

Jonathan Wild – a criminal disguised as a gentleman. Society took against him when he was found out and the crowd called for the hangman to make haste at his execution

the police to help the victims of theft; but in reality, it was he who was organizing the thefts in the first place.

AN EXPANDING BUSINESS

It was not long before Wild built up substantial wealth. His business rapidly expanded, and he began to employ jewellers to melt down gold and reset precious stones. In addition, he hired out tools to burglars, and exported stolen goods to Holland in his own ship. Wild became a well-known, successful public figure, calling himself 'Thief-Taker General of

POLICE LINE DO NOT CROSS

A 'ticket' inviting fellow bad characters to Wild's execution. Having been fêted by a society that was unaware of his crimes, his fall from grace was a long one

Great Britain and Ireland', and posing as a hero, a man who spent his time catching criminals on behalf of the public.

DOUBLE-CROSSING 'THIEF-TAKER'

As crime in London escalated, Wild became more famous. Yet he was secretly running a large gang of thieves, keeping records of their names and their thefts in a ledger. He kept control of his gang by threatening to turn them in to the police; when one of them annoyed him, he would cross out their name in the ledger and send them to the gallows, gaining a reward of forty pounds each time he did so. It is from Wild's practice of betraying his employees and crossing out their names in the ledger that we get the expression 'to double cross'.

By now, Wild had an office at the Old Bailey, London's famous criminal court, where victims would call and miraculously find their stolen goods waiting for them, apparently recovered by Wild's 'thief-takers'. Wild was by now being consulted by the government on how to deter crime in the city. He recommended an increase in the reward for capturing thieves, from £40 to £140, thereby raising his own pay while continuing to maintain his pose as a national crime-fighting hero.

HANGED ON THE GALLOWS

Eventually, however, his luck ran out. The authorities became aware of what Wild was up to, and in 1718 passed a law that informally became known as the 'Wild Act'. The law made it a crime to accept a reward without prosecuting the thief. At first, Wild was able to get around this by asking his clients to leave money for him at a safe house, but in the end he slipped up and was caught taking a reward fee. He was convicted of the crime and sentenced to be hanged.

The public was furious when it found out that, instead of being a respected public servant, Wild had actually been organizing crime in London on a grand scale. Crowds gathered in the streets to pelt him with rotten fruit as he and his jailers made their way to the gallows and, while he was waiting to meet his death, yelled at the executioner to make haste. A story that went down in legend has it that before Wild died, he made one last typical and flamboyant gesture: he picked the executioner's pocket.

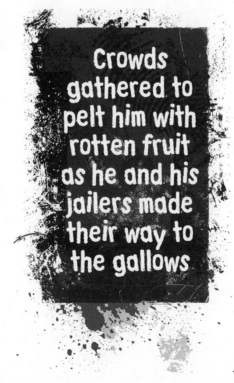

Crowds gathered to pelt him with rotten fruit as he and his jailers made their way to the gallows

Brinks Mat Robbers

The Brinks Mat Robbery, which took place on 26 November 1983, is one of the most famous in criminal history. The sheer size of the haul – several tons of gold, worth about twenty-six million pounds sterling – made it the biggest robbery ever to take place in Britain. What makes the robbery even more extraordinary is that, to this day, a great deal of the gold has never been recovered. Some of it was melted down and mixed with copper to make it untraceable and some found its way, through the criminal underworld, into private foreign bank accounts in the West Indies and Switzerland. Not only that, but it is also thought that many people connected to the robbery continue to live a life of luxury. For all these reasons, the Brinks Mat Robbery remains a mystery, one that the police and the authorities will probably never entirely solve.

John Palmer was acquitted of charges of handling the stolen Brinks Mat gold. It has been said that all gold jewellery sold in the UK since the robbery is partly composed of Brinks Mat bars

A STASH OF GOLD BULLION

To get away with such an enormous quantity of gold seems an incredible feat, yet the Brinks Mat Robbers had never planned the heist on such a large scale. Originally, the plan was to steal three million pounds sterling in cash. However, when they broke into the Brinks Mat warehouse at Heathrow Airport they found a little more than they were expecting: 6,800 bars of pure gold, packed into seventy-six boxes, all waiting to be taken to the Far East.

The gang consisted of six well-organized South London armed robbers. Through a family connection with a security guard who worked at the warehouse, they had insider knowledge of the interior of the building. They knew of a safe that was stashed with large amounts of cash. On the night of the robbery, the six men broke into the warehouse, terrorizing the security guards by pouring petrol over them and threatening to set them alight unless they revealed the combination numbers of the safe. (The security guard known to the robbers had phoned in sick that evening, an action that later aroused a great deal of suspicion.)

SAFE COMBINATION

Under pressure, the security guards told the intruders the combination for the safe. However, the gangsters were in for a surprise. When they opened the safe, instead of finding wads of cash, they found it full of gold bullion. Undaunted, the thieves decided to steal the whole lot. What should have been a smash'n'grab raid ended up taking about two hours, as the robbers found themselves having to organize a bigger getaway vehicle to cope with the heavy stash of gold upon which they had stumbled. Amazingly, given the time it took to complete the robbery, the gang got clean away that night.

POLICE LINE DO NOT CROSS

However, such a large amount of gold bullion was not easy to hide. Before long, the police were on the case of two well-known South London armed robbers, Brian Robinson, known as 'The Colonel', and Mickey McAvoy. Both men had been living in ordinary working-class houses in London before the robbery, but had suddenly moved to a mansion in nearby Kent. They had apparently paid for the property in cash. It was also believed that they had acquired two Rottweiler dogs named 'Brinks' and 'Mat'.

'THE FOX'

Robinson and McAvoy may have been experienced armed robbers, but neither was a particularly astute criminal. As it later emerged, in order to dispose of the gold, the pair had called in an underworld character with a little more finesse than they themselves possessed. This person was known as 'The Fox'. The Fox, in conjunction with a jeweller called Solly Nahome, had arranged for the gold to be melted down into smaller goods. In this way, Robinson and McAvoy hoped to escape detection.

However, in planning the robbery, they had made some elementary mistakes. Police were now on the trail of Anthony Black, the security guard who had given the gang inside information about the safe. It did not take long to find out that Black was Brian Robinson's brother-in-law. Under pressure from the police, Black soon gave evidence against the gang, which resulted in a prison sentence of twenty-five years each for Robinson and McAvoy. Black himself received a six-year sentence, of which he served three years, for providing the robbers with a

Squeaky clean? Gordon Parry was tried as a money-launderer for the Brinks Mat Robbers – one of the drawbacks of the unexpected windfall of gold was how to process it without attracting attention

key to the main door and for divulging the details of the warehouse's layout.

TRACKING DOWN THE CULPRITS

The main culprits in the robbery were now in prison, but it soon became clear that the gold itself would be hard to recover. Much of it was now circulating in different forms, as jewellery or mixed with copper so that it was impossible to trace. A man named Kenneth Noye, who had experience in the gold-smelting trade, had been brought in to help mask the gold's origins in this way.

Noye may have been a clever operator in the gold-smelting

Brian Perry was also accused of involvement with the Brinks Mat case. He subsequently became the victim of a gangland killing

When they broke into the Brinks Mat warehouse at Heathrow Airport they found a little more than they were expecting: 6,800 bars of pure gold

trade, but – like McAvoy and Robinson – as a criminal, he was not exactly subtle in his actions. His first mistake was to open a bank account in Bristol, withdrawing enormous amounts of money from one single branch, so much that the branch had to request extra funds from the Bank of England. Attention was soon drawn to Noye, and he was placed under police surveillance. When Noye discovered DC John Fordham in his garden working undercover, he stabbed the detective to death. Brought to trial in 1985 for the murder, Noye managed to convince the jury that he was innocent, and had acted in self-defence. The following year, however, Noye was in court once more, this time because several gold bars had been found at his house. This time, he received a huge fine and a fourteen-year prison sentence.

ROAD RAGE

In 1996, Noye hit the headlines once more. His vicious temper had again got him into trouble. In an incident of road rage, he had killed motorist Stephen Cameron in front of Cameron's fiancée. After a long hunt, Noye was finally captured, and received a life sentence for the senseless murder.

Over a long period, Noye's stash of gold was eventually found, but to this day much of the Brinks Mat bullion has yet to be recovered. Some believe that it never will be. It is even said that all gold jewellery sold in the UK since the robbery is partly composed of Brinks Mat bars. Whatever the case, the combination of skill, cunning and remarkable stupidity on the part of the robbers and their associates make this one of the most fascinating heists in criminal history.

Gold handler and double murderer Kenneth Noye, now in prison for life, and DC John Fordham

POLICE LINE DO NOT CROSS

Another suspect, John Fleming, aka 'Goldfinger', did his best to avoid answering police questions about his alleged involvement with the robbery by moving to Costa Rica, but he was brought back to face the music

To this day a large amount of the Brinks Mat bullion has yet to be recovered

POLICE LINE DO NOT CROSS

Anthony 'Fats' Pino

Anthony 'Fats' Pino was the mastermind behind the Great Brinks Robbery. Carried out in Boston on 17 January 1950, this was a minutely planned, audacious bank robbery that was later dubbed the crime of the century. The gang, led by Pino, got away with nearly three million dollars, which was an extraordinary sum for the time. For years, too, it appeared that they had got away with it: there were virtually no clues left at the scene, and the team avoided all the usual pitfalls of being seen spending their newly acquired wealth. Instead, all eight of the men involved agreed that they would not touch the loot for six years, by which time all memory of the crime would have receded. This was a classic crime of the sort normally only seen in the movies, a heist carried out by seasoned professionals with meticulous planning and rigorous discipline, a scam that worked like clockwork – and at its heart were the organizational talents of Anthony 'Fats' Pino.

> Pino was the mastermind behind the Great Brinks Robbery, later dubbed the crime of the century

THE CRIMINAL LIFE

Anthony Pino was born in Italy in 1907, but was brought to the United States by his parents while still a young child. Growing up in Boston, he soon gravitated to the criminal life, quickly specializing in burglary. In 1928 he was convicted of sexual abuse of a minor, and in 1941 he was sentenced to prison for breaking and entering with intent to commit a felony and for having burglary tools in his possession. At that point, the Immigration and Naturalization Service initiated proceedings to deport him, having discovered that he had never become a naturalized citizen.

In the late summer of 1944, Pino was released from the state prison and taken into custody by immigration authorities. He fought against this and, because part of the justification for deporting him was his criminal record, he appealed for a pardon in the matter of the burglary conviction. His appeal was successful and, in September 1949, the authorities agreed to drop the deportation proceedings.

They may, of course, have looked at matters differently had they known that Pino was in the midst of planning the largest bank robbery ever carried out in the United States at that time.

PLANNING THE PERFECT SCAM

Pino had begun a year before by identifying his target, the new Brinks building in Boston. He then assembled the core members of the team – Joseph 'Specs' O'Keefe, Joseph 'Big Joe' McGinnis and Stanley 'Gus' Gusciora. The gang staked out the building, learning in minute detail the routines of its workforce. Pino discovered that, in the evenings, Brinks employees on the second floor would count the money collected from customers that day. It was a huge amount. The only question was how to get to the second floor: there were alarms and at least five locked doors to go through.

Pino came up with a simple but effective plan that just needed immense patience. Over a period of months, the team would frequent the building and identify the locked doors they needed to get through. Each time one of the doors was left open and unattended during daylight hours, one of the gang would remove the central chamber of the lock, take it to a compliant locksmith who would cut a key to fit it, then return the cylinder to the door before anyone realized it was missing. Eventually, the team had keys to all five doors.

Next, they had to wait for the perfect time to strike: when they knew that the take would be high; that there were only a few employees on the premises; and that the surrounding area was quiet. So disciplined was the team in this regard that six times they called off the operation at the very last moment. Finally, on the evening of 17 January 1950, they struck.

HALLOWEEN MASKS
They donned clothing outwardly similar to the Brinks uniform, with navy suits and chauffeur's caps. In addition, they wore rubber Halloween masks, gloves and rubber-soled shoes. At 6.55 pm, while Pino and driver Banfield waited in the car, seven men entered the building.

With their copied keys, the robbers gained access to the second floor, binding and gagging five Brinks employees who were storing and counting money. They carefully loaded up all the money and valuables available. At one point, they were interrupted by the sound of the door buzzer. Horrified, the gang looked out of the window to see a Brinks employee at the door. However, before they could get downstairs and attempt to subdue him, the employee left again, apparently unconcerned. The gang went back to loading up the loot. Within half an hour, they were ready to go.

As soon as the robbers had left, an employee called the police. Minutes later, the police arrived, and were soon joined by FBI agents. There were virtually no clues on the scene: each robber's face had been completely concealed behind a mask and the only physical evidence was the rope and adhesive tape used to bind and gag the staff, and a chauffeur's cap left by one of the robbers at the crime scene.

The FBI learned that, as well as money, four revolvers had been taken by the gang. The descriptions and serial numbers of these weapons were carefully noted in case they might provide a link to the men responsible for the crime. All the police and the FBI had to go on at this stage was the certainty that the crime had been carried out by professionals, men who would in all likelihood already be known bank robbers. Men like career criminal Anthony Pino.

Strangely enough, all these suspects turned out to have clear alibis for the evening in question. The investigators roamed ever wider. Even old-time criminal outfits like the 'Purple Gang' of the 1930s, and a bootlegging gang that had specialized in hijacking whiskey in the Boston area during Prohibition, became the subjects of inquiries.

THE CRIME OF THE CENTURY
Public interest was immense. The Brinks case was called the crime of the century by the newspapers. The company offered a $100,000 reward for information leading to the arrest and conviction of the persons responsible. Soon the police were deluged with tip-offs from hopeful bounty hunters but were no closer to finding the actual criminals, or at least no nearer to proving

their culpability – for many already had their suspicions as to which local robbers were capable of such an audacious sting.

RUMOURS IN JAIL
Suspicions grew stronger when one of the revolvers used in the robbery was found by children on a sand bar at the edge of the Mystic River in Somerville. Then the remains of the truck the gang had used were found in Stoughton, Massachusetts. Two of the gang members in the Brinks case, Specs O'Keefe and Gus Gusciora, lived in Stoughton. Local officers went to search their homes, but no evidence linking them with the truck or the robbery was found.

In June 1950, however, both men were arrested in connection with some entirely separate burglaries. They were both sentenced to prison and, while they were inside, rumours started to circulate that O'Keefe had been asking certain other criminals on the outside for money to help with his defence. The police tried hard to drive a wedge between O'Keefe and his fellow robbers but failed. However, once O'Keefe was released in 1955, a rift did indeed develop. O'Keefe accused the others of cheating him out of his money and Pino responded by hiring a hit man to kill him. The hit man in question, Elmer 'Trigger' Burke, shot O'Keefe several times with a machine gun but failed to kill him. In hospital, O'Keefe finally agreed to testify against his fellow gang members.

On 12 January 1956, the FBI arrested Anthony Pino along with several other members of the gang. Gusciora died before he

could stand trial. The trial began on 12 August 1956. Eight of the gang received maximum life sentences; O'Keefe was sentenced to only four years in prison, and he was duly released in 1960. Most of the money from the Great Brinks Robbery, however, was never recovered by the police.

Most of the money from the robbery, however, was never recovered by the police

'Fats' Pino nearly planned and pulled off the perfect heist, but was arrested when a fellow gang member agreed to testify against him

POLICE LINE DO NOT CROSS

The Great Train Robbers

The Great Train Robbery of 1963 counts as one of the most famous crimes in British history. A gang of fifteen London criminals hijacked a train and stole over two million pounds sterling in used banknotes; the same amount today would be equivalent to about forty million pounds. However, it was not only the huge amount of money stolen that

Fifteen criminals hijacked a train and stole today's equivalent of about £40 million

The Great Train Robbers reunited in 1978, fifteen years on from their heist. The notorious Ronnie Biggs had settled in Brazil, and was at this time making a film with the Sex Pistols

*Ronnie Biggs with his long-time
girlfriend and eventual wife, Raimunda
Nascimento de Castro, in 1974*

ensured their notoriety: the heist was also seen by many sections of the popular British press as a highly romantic, flamboyant act on the part of the London underworld. In particular, gang member Ronnie Biggs came to be regarded as a swashbuckling figure who had flouted all the rules and got away with it. One central feature of the robbery that appealed to the public was that no guns were used – although, in actual fact, the robbery was a violent crime, since the train driver was hit over the head with iron bars and was permanently injured. This unpleasant reality was, in some quarters, conveniently forgotten, and in time the train robbers became working-class heroes who were regarded with a great deal of affection and admiration by the British public.

PLANNING THE HEIST

The gang was led by a man named Bruce Reynolds, who planned the operation from the beginning. He was an antiques dealer who drove an Aston Martin, and liked to flash his money around. The front man for the gang was John Wheater, a solicitor with an upper-class background who rented the farmhouse where the gang hid after the heist.

Next was Buster Edwards, an ex-boxer turned conman, who was later immortalized by Phil Collins in the film *Buster*. Other gang members included Charlie Wilson, a bookmaker, and two very big men known as Gordon Goody and Jimmy Hussey, who became the brawn of the operation. Last, but not least, was the youngest member of the gang, Ronnie Biggs, who as yet had little experience of criminal life.

The operation was meticulously planned, using information about the times large amounts of cash were carried on postal trains going in and out of London. The robbers selected a quiet site outside Cheddington, in Buckinghamshire, so that they could flag down the train and bag the money without attracting too much attention. The site was also chosen because it was located near a military base, where large supply vehicles often travelled around. In this way, the robbers hoped that their movements would not arouse suspicion.

ATTACKED WITH IRON BARS

On 8 August 1963, a few minutes after three o'clock in the morning, the raid began. Wearing railway workers' overalls, the gang rigged up some temporary signals on the line, using batteries for power. Seeing the red 'stop' light ahead, the driver brought the train to a halt. When it stopped, a fireman, David Whitby, got out to find out what the trouble was. Whitby was pulled off the track by Buster Edwards and, once he realized that a robbery was in progress, did not try to resist. However, when the driver, Jack Mills, got off, other members of the gang attacked him with iron bars, causing him to bleed from the head. Mills collapsed on the side of the track.

Mistakes also started being made because the train robbers began to panic. The gang included a retired train driver, brought in by Ronnie Biggs to move the train into position so that the mailbags could be easily dropped off. However, the elderly train driver did not understand the workings of modern trains, and was unable to move the stopped train. The

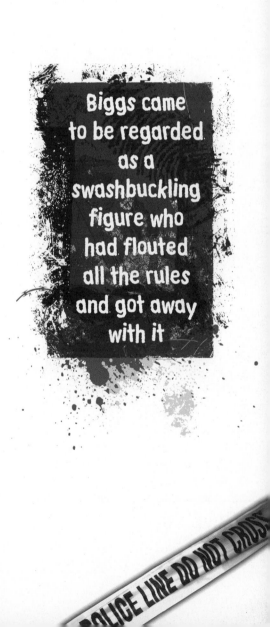

Biggs came to be regarded as a swashbuckling figure who had flouted all the rules and got away with it

POLICE LINE DO NOT CROSS

injured Mills, still bleeding, was forced to take over and drive the train into position. The gang then formed a human chain to unload over a hundred sacks of money, and made their getaway.

ROUNDING UP THE GANG

The gang hid out at a nearby farmhouse, Leatherslade Farm. Here, they drank cups of tea and played the boardgame Monopoly, allegedly using the real banknotes from their haul as money. This proved to be their downfall. By the time the police reached the farmhouse, the gang had scattered, but they had left incriminating fingerprints on the Monopoly board and elsewhere, and so police were able to identify the men, many of whom were known criminals.

Eventually, thirteen of the fifteen gang members were apprehended and brought to justice. Bruce Reynolds spent five years on the run before the police finally caught up with him. He was then tried and received a prison sentence, of which he served ten years. Buster Edwards fled to Mexico but later gave himself up. Charlie Wilson made a daring escape from prison while serving his sentence, and lived quietly outside Montreal, Canada, for a time until police traced him via a telephone call his wife made to her parents in England.

THE LATER YEARS

Biggs also made a dramatic escape from jail, after serving over the first year of his sentence. He underwent plastic surgery, travelled around the world and then settled in Rio de Janeiro, Brazil.

In his later years, Biggs became notorious as

Ronnie Biggs in his later years in Brazil. Despite living the good life there, when his health began to fail he returned to England and arrest

the one Great Train Robber to avoid capture – even though his initial role in the robbery had been a small one. However, in his later years he became ill, having suffered several strokes, and grew tired of living abroad. He announced his intention of coming back to Britain, even if he risked being imprisoned in his bad state of health. When he returned, he was duly apprehended and today

continues to serve out his sentence in prison hospital in Britain.

In the end, most of the Great Train Robbers were eventually brought to justice. However, the money that had been stolen in the robbery was never recovered. Thus, the Monopoly players of the gang may have collected their money, but they did not pass 'Go' – instead, they went straight to jail.

POLICE LINE DO NOT

Willie Sutton

Willie Sutton was the nearest thing real life has produced to the kind of bank robber one sees only in the movies. Most bank robbers are brutal, unimaginative types. Willie Sutton, by contrast, was charming and funny, a snappy dresser and a ladies' man. He used cunning and nerve rather than brute force to pull off his scams. In a thirty-year career during the first half of the 20th century, he robbed over a hundred banks and netted an estimated two million dollars, an enormous sum for the times.

Willie Sutton was born into an Irish family in Brooklyn, New York, on 30 June 1901, the fourth of five children. He stayed in school until the eighth grade, then left home and got a job. At various times he worked as a clerk, a driller and a gardener, never staying in any one job for more than eighteen months. This was because by then he had already found his true vocation in life – as a thief. Willie started stealing when he was nine or ten years old, graduating to breaking and entering in his late teens, when he robbed his girlfriend's father's business so that the pair of them could elope.

THE BIRTH OF THE ACTOR

Sutton received a brief prison sentence for this but refused to be discouraged. A veteran safe-cracker called Doc Tate introduced him to the dangerous world of professional crime, robbing banks and jewellers. Before long, Sutton was also an expert safe-cracker.

Being able to crack a safe was useful, but it did not solve the question of how to gain access to the safe in the first place. Initially, Sutton went along with the traditional approach of storming a bank while waving a gun. Then one day, while staking out a bank, he watched uniformed guards get out of an armoured truck and make their way into the bank to collect the day's takings. It was then that Sutton had a brainwave. He realized that if you are wearing the right uniform, no one really looks at your face too hard or asks many questions. He resolved that in the future, rather than storm into a bank, he would disguise himself as a security guard – or mailman or whatever – and gain access that way. As he later recalled, 'That afternoon, "Willie the Actor" was born.'

It was a stunningly effective ploy. One day he would rob a Philadelphia bank in the guise of a mailman; another day it would be a Broadway jewellery store and he would be impersonating a postal telegraph messenger. Other favourite disguises included a policeman and a maintenance man. Along with the disguises, Sutton cultivated a gentlemanly approach. He was polite to his victims. He carried a gun, but prided himself on never having to use it. One victim said that the experience of being caught up in one of his robberies was like being at the movies, except that the usher had a gun.

THE GREAT ESCAPES

Sutton spent his ill-gotten gains on fast living and expensive clothes. He married for the first time in 1929, but his wife divorced him after he was finally caught and sentenced to thirty years in jail. He was sent to the much feared Sing Sing Prison. However, the same ingenuity that had made him such a successful bank

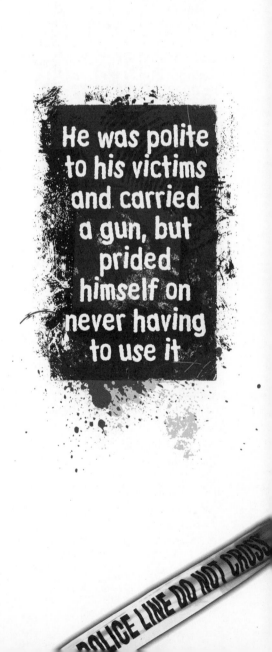

He was polite to his victims and carried a gun, but prided himself on never having to use it

POLICE LINE DO NOT CROSS

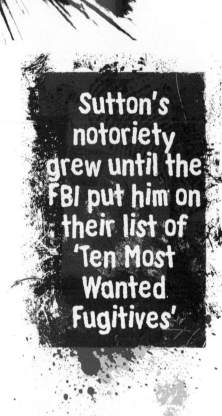

Sutton's notoriety grew until the FBI put him on their list of 'Ten Most Wanted Fugitives'

robber also helped him to become a highly skilled prison escapee. His first escape was on 11 December 1932, when he scaled the prison wall using a pair of 2.7 m (9 ft) ladders joined together.

Outside, Sutton went straight back to robbing banks. One particularly audacious raid was on the Corn Exchange Bank and Trust Company in Philadelphia, Pennsylvania, on 15 January 1934. A month later, the police caught up with him again. This time he was sentenced to serve twenty-five to fifty years in Eastern

Sutton took another route altogether when robbing banks, preferring to gain access to a bank by, quite literally, sheer bare face rather than masked and brandishing a gun

POLICE LINE DO NOT C

Due to his love of high-quality tailoring, his photo was circulated to New York tailors

State Penitentiary, Philadelphia. There, he continued to make escape attempts. Four attempts were foiled. Finally, on 3 April 1945, Sutton was one of twelve convicts who escaped through a tunnel. However, he was recaptured the same day by Philadelphia police officers.

For his part in the escape attempt, Sutton's sentence was increased to life imprisonment and he was transferred to the Philadelphia County Prison, in Homesburg, Pennsylvania. Not for long. On 10 February 1947, after dark, Sutton and other prisoners dressed as prison guards carried two ladders across the yard to the outside wall. As the prison's searchlight traversed the yard, it lighted on Sutton and his companions. Sutton called out 'It's okay,' and the searchlight operator let him carry on. This time, he got clean away.

MEDIA FURORE

After three more years of bank robberies, Sutton's notoriety had grown to the point that the FBI put him on their list of 'Ten Most Wanted Fugitives'. Cleverly, the FBI noted Sutton's love of high-quality tailoring and his photo was circulated not only to police departments but also to New York tailors. This tactic paid off when Arnold Schuster, a 24-year-old tailor's son, recognized Sutton on the New York subway on 18 February 1952. Schuster told the police, who later arrested Sutton.

Sutton's arrest provoked a media furore. He had gained a reputation as something of a Robin Hood figure (though while he robbed the rich, he certainly never gave to the poor), and was famous for answering the question 'Why

do you rob banks?' with the immortal line: 'Because that's where the money is.' The furore was to have an unfortunate consequence for Schuster. Two weeks later, he was murdered by mob assassins determined to let the public know that turning in wanted criminals was a dangerous pastime.

Sutton was sent to Attica Prison to serve his outstanding life sentence plus a further 150 years. Now in his fifties, Sutton was unable to escape from Attica and remained there until 1969, when he managed to persuade the authorities that he was seriously ill. On Christmas Eve, he was released from Attica State Prison. The following year, he cheekily made a television commercial to promote a new photo credit card for a bank. He then retired to Florida where he wrote an autobiography full of entertaining tales and the disappointing revelation that the 'that's where the money is' line was actually made up by a journalist. He died in Florida on 2 November 1980, at the age of seventy-nine.

Butch Cassidy and the Sundance Kid

Butch Cassidy and the Sundance Kid were among the last of a dying breed of outlaws and migrant cowboys in the Wild West at the turn of the 20th century. Along with their flamboyant gang, the Wild Bunch, they stole horses, robbed banks and trains, and generally lived outside the law. Eventually, as the authorities closed in on them, they decamped to South America, going straight but then continuing their life of crime and excitement until they met their end. After their deaths, they became legendary folk heroes, and were immortalized in the 1969 film *Butch Cassidy and the Sundance Kid.*

Butch Cassidy was born Robert Leroy Parker in 1866. He grew up on a ranch near Circleville, Utah, where his parents were Mormons. As a boy, he once stole a horse, under the influence of an old cattle rustler called Mike Cassidy – from whom he later derived his last name. Life on the strictly run family ranch proved too dull for young Robert and, before long, he left home to become a migrant cowboy, working around the country. For a short period, he also worked as a butcher, which is where it is thought he got his nickname 'Butch' from.

FEARLESS ADVENTURERS

Cassidy soon tired of trying to make an honest living, and began to steal cattle. He was caught and imprisoned in a

Butch Cassidy – a migrant cowboy and as stylish an outlaw as they came

Wyoming jail for two years. When he came out, he started to live the life of an outlaw in earnest. He was well suited to it: a quick-witted man with a great deal of charm, he was also a fearless

POLICE LINE DO NOT CR

adventurer who could always come up with an audacious plan to get himself out of a tight corner. Such was his charisma that he soon gathered a gang of notorious desperadoes around him, who became known as the Wild Bunch.

PARTNERS IN CRIME

His future partner in crime, Harry Alonzo Longabaugh, was born in Philadelphia, Pennsylvania, the youngest of five children. His parents were poor but had a strong religious faith. As a young man, Harry left home and travelled around the country seeking employment. In 1887, broke and out of work, he stole a horse in Sundance, Wyoming. He was caught and served an eighteen-month sentence in the Sundance town jail. The name of the town gave him his nickname from that time on: the Sundance Kid.

Soon after the pair met up, Sundance became Cassidy's right-hand man. They developed a strong partnership that lasted through thick and thin, until their deaths many years later. Ben 'The Tall Texan' Kirkpatrick was another gang member, known as a lady killer; others included Bill Tod Carver, 'Deaf Charlie' Hanks, Tom 'Peep' O'Day and 'Wat the Watcher' Punteney. Perhaps the most infamous of all was Harvey Logan, alias Kid Curry, who joined the Wild Bunch after committing a string of robberies with his own gang. Curry was described by William Pinkerton, head of the famous Pinkerton detective agency, as

The Wild Bunch (left to right): (standing) Bill Carver, Harvey 'Kid Curry' Logan; (sitting) Harry 'Sundance Kid' Longabaugh, Ben 'Tall Texan' Kirkpatrick and Butch Cassidy

'the most vicious outlaw in America', and was known to be a cold-blooded killer. Pinkerton wrote: 'He has not one single redeeming feature. He is the only criminal I know of who does not have one single good point.' However, popular reports attest that Curry was actually a quiet, polite fellow who had many friends, and who impressed women with his gentlemanly ways. It seems that he reserved his greatest viciousness for representatives of the law, especially those from Pinkerton's agency.

THE WILD BUNCH

Several women also rode with the outlaw band. The best known was Etta Place, who married the Sundance Kid and stayed with the gang throughout their adventures. Little is known about her, but it has been suggested that her real name was Ann Bassett, a girl from a ranch in Brown's Park, who at one time had been involved in cattle rustling. Some believe that, as well as being Sundance's wife, she was also Cassidy's girlfriend, but the relationship between the three remains unclear.

The Wild Bunch went on to commit the longest series of successful robberies in the history of the Wild West. Their first bank robbery was in Montpelier, Idaho, in 1896. Moving on to Wyoming, they robbed an Overland Flyer train, and, after a shoot-out, got away with $30,000. Their next train heist, also in Wyoming, netted them only about fifty dollars, but after that they robbed $30,000 from a bank in Winnemucca, Nevada. The Wild Bunch's last job was in 1901, when they robbed a Northern Pacific train in Montana and stole $40,000.

The Wild Bunch went on to commit the longest series of successful robberies in the history of the Wild West

POLICE LINE DO NOT CROSS

ESCAPE TO
SOUTH AMERICA

By now, the railroads had hired the Pinkerton Agency to catch the gang, and time was fast running out for them. With Pinkerton's men hot on their heels, they split up. Cassidy and the Sundance Kid, along with Etta Place, headed down to South America. The Tall Texan was caught and imprisoned, and later met his end while robbing a train. Carver and Deaf Charlie were also killed. Kid Curry was imprisoned in Knoxville, Tennessee, until he made a daring escape. Some believe he was later shot during a train robbery, but there is also some evidence that he lived to a ripe old age on a ranch in Patagonia, with a Spanish wife who bore him eight children.

Butch Cassidy, the Sundance Kid and Etta Place bought a ranch in Argentina and lived peacefully for several years before they ran out of money and the men turned to their old ways once more. The pair are thought to have met their end after holding up a payroll transport in the mountains of Bolivia, when they were pursued by troops and apparently killed in a shoot-out. However, there is some disagreement as to what really happened. Some believe that the bandits were not in fact Cassidy and Sundance, but another pair of outlaws. Others maintain that either Cassidy or Sundance, or both of them, committed suicide after being wounded in the shoot-out.

Whatever the truth, the legendary pair went down in American history – and in international movie history – as the last of the great outlaws of the Wild West. For many, their deaths spelt the

The Sundance Kid and his wife, Etta Place. She was rumoured to have been Butch Cassidy's lover too, but the exact relationships between the three remain unclear to this day

end of an era: a time when, at the end of the 19th century, the tough, freedom-loving spirit of the pioneers of the Wild West fought long and hard against the greedy profiteering and dreary bureaucracy of the state authorities.

POLICE LINE DO NOT CROSS

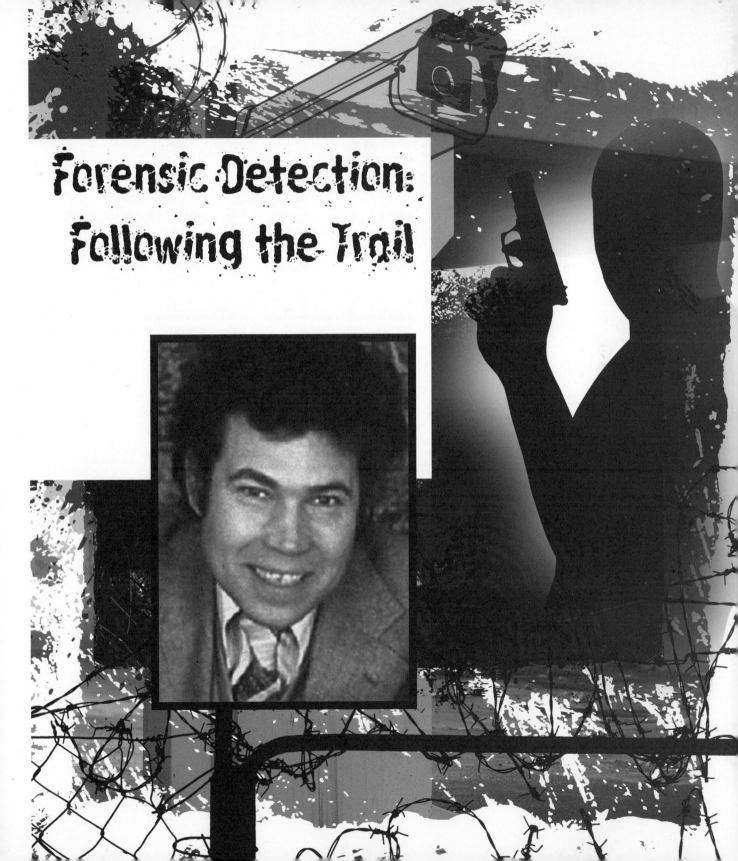

Forensic Detection: Following the Trail

Fred and Rosemary West

...when Rena came looking for Charmaine, Fred murdered her too, burying her body in the countryside

Fred and Rosemary West are among the most chilling serial killers of all time. During the 1970s, they murdered a string of female victims, including their own daughter. The Wests would probably have got away with their crimes, had it not been for the fact that, in 1992, a young girl they had raped finally went to the police, and the whole story began – literally – to be unearthed.

VIOLENCE AND SEXUAL ABUSE

Fred and Rosemary West were both from deprived rural backgrounds, where violence and sexual abuse were not uncommon. Born in the village of Much Marcle in 1941, Fred was one of six children, and later claimed that incest was rife in the family. He was backward at school, and left at the age of fifteen scarcely able to read or write. At the age of seventeen he suffered a serious motorcycle accident that possibly caused damage to his brain: it was after this that his behaviour became increasingly out of control. He was eventually arrested for having sex with an under-age girl, and narrowly avoided prison. His parents, finally tiring of his behaviour, threw him out of the family home.

Rosemary Letts was born in 1953 in Devon. From a young age, she was sexually abused by her schizophrenic father. Her mother, meanwhile, suffered from severe depression. As a teenager, Rosemary was overweight and sexually precocious. When she met Fred, who was twelve years older than she, she idolized him, and soon became pregnant by him, even though she was not yet sixteen years old at that time.

THE MURDERS BEGIN

Fred had already been married, to prostitute Rena Costello, who had a mixed-race child called Charmaine from a previous relationship. Fred and Rena's own child, Anna Marie, was born shortly before the pair split up. Fred then took up with a friend of Rena's named Anna McFall, who was pregnant with Fred's child when, as later emerged, he murdered her, dismembering her body and burying it near the trailer where they had lived. He was now free to concentrate on his burgeoning relationship with his new girlfriend, Rosemary.

During this time, Fred was in and out of prison on minor charges such as non-payment of fines, while Rosemary was left in charge of the children – Charmaine, Anna Marie, and the couple's own new daughter, Heather, who was born in 1970. Rosemary had a ferocious temper and was insanely cruel, especially to Charmaine. She abused the children while Fred was away, finally murdering Charmaine. Later, Fred buried the child's body under the house. When Rena came looking for Charmaine, Fred murdered her too, burying her body in the countryside.

In 1972, the couple moved to a house in Cromwell Street, Gloucester, where Rosemary worked as a prostitute and continued to bear children, some of

The picture of a loving couple: not even their closest neighbours had any idea about what was going on behind the façade of a normal, busy family

Clearing work gets under way in the garden at Midland Road, Gloucester, an address where Fred West lived before he married Rose

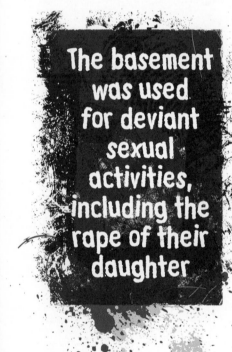

The basement was used for deviant sexual activities, including the rape of their daughter

which were Fred's, and some of which had been fathered by her clients. The basement of the house was used for deviant sexual activities, including the rape of their daughter, Anna Marie, and a girl they employed to care for the children, Caroline Owens. When Owens went to the police, Fred West was tried for the rape, but – unbelievably – he was let off with a fine. Tragically, the next girl they hired to care for the children,

Lynda Gough, was not so lucky: she did not escape with her life, and was murdered and buried under the cellar. The couple went on to abduct, torture and murder more young women, in a killing spree that was as brutal as it was depraved: Carol Anne Cooper, Lucy Partington, Alison Chambers, Therese Siegenthaler, Shirley Hubbard, Juanita Mott and Shirley Robinson all met their deaths in the most horrifying ways. The

Wests even killed their own daughter, Heather, after she told friends about her bizarre home life. Like many of the other victims, she was buried in the garden.

THE CASE GOES COLD

Then, suddenly, the killings stopped. There have been many theories about why this came about: perhaps the Wests found other ways of satisfying their violent sexual impulses; or perhaps there were actually many other victims who were never missed by anyone, and whose deaths were never reported. The Wests were careful to choose their victims from the bottom of the social pile; often girls who had lost touch with their families, or who were working as prostitutes, whose relatives and friends would not come looking for them. (Lucy Partington, a middle-class university student and a relative of the writer Martin Amis, was the exception.)

It looked as though the Wests had got away with their crimes, and that their victims would be forgotten. But in 1992, the couple's horrifying deeds came to light when a young girl they had raped went to the police to report her ordeal. This time, the victim's story was believed and investigated.

BURIED UNDER THE PATIO

On 6 August 1992, police arrived at the house in Cromwell Street. They searched the house for pornography and found more than enough evidence to arrest the couple for rape and sodomy of a minor. One of West's perversions was to film his wife on video, engaging in sex with different partners, both men and women. The older West children, Stephen and Anna Marie, both made statements supporting the allegation of rape, but the case later collapsed when they withdrew these, under pressure from the family.

Meanwhile, the younger children had been taken away from their parents and placed in social care. Their carers began to notice that they often joked about their sister Heather being buried under the patio. This was reported to the police, who returned to the house in

The Wests even killed their own daughter, Heather, after she told friends about her bizarre home life

Cromwell Street in February 1994 and began to dig up the garden. To their horror, they not only found Heather's remains, but a total of nine other bodies in the garden. Later, other bodies under the cellar were dug up.

Fred West initially confessed to the murder of his daughter Heather, but then retracted the confession. It seemed that he and Rosemary then made a pact, in which he would take the blame for the murder, emphasizing that his wife was not involved in any way. Accordingly, he re-confessed, stressing that Rosemary was not to blame, but by this time there was

POLICE LINE DO NOT CROSS

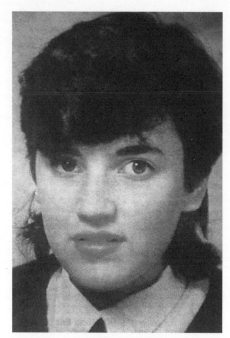

*The troubled face of Heather West, who
disappeared in 1987. Her remains were
subsequently found, buried under the patio
at 25 Cromwell Street*

> It seems
> incredible that
> two people who
> had committed
> so many hideous
> murders could
> have gone
> unpunished
> for so long

evidence to show that she too was
responsible for the murder not only of
Heather, but also of many other victims
who had now been found.

HANGED IN HIS CELL

Fred West was charged with twelve
murders in all, but before he could
come to trial, he hanged himself in his
prison cell, on New Year's Day in 1995.
Meanwhile, Rosemary maintained that
she was innocent, but in October that
same year, she was convicted of ten of the
murders, and received a life sentence.

What would have happened if that
young girl had not gone to the police
to report her rape in 1992? Is it possible
that Fred and Rosemary West would

have continued to evade the law until
the end of their natural lives, their crimes
never discovered? What if the authorities
had dismissed the girl's story, as they had
dismissed that of Caroline Owens, the
Wests' nanny, years before? It seems
incredible that two people who had
committed so many hideous murders
could have gone unpunished for so long –
but that is what happened.

Perhaps it was a change in the social
climate that helped to bring them to
justice. Perhaps the permissive climate
of the 1970s, in which the rules about
sexual morality were beginning to be
relaxed, impacted in a negative way on
the underclass to which both Fred and
Rosemary West belonged, so that the
bizarre sexual behaviour that took place
in their household went largely unnoticed
and unremarked on by friends and
neighbours, who might, in other times,
have found it unacceptable.

However one explains it, the fact
remains that it was only through the
bravery of one young girl that the
appalling brutality of this pair of vicious
killers came to light, years after the
murders happened, so that they finally
received the punishment they deserved.

Gary Ridgway

The trial of Gary Leon Ridgway, the Green River Killer, was one of the most sensational ever to take place in America. In the end, it was DNA technology that enabled the police to nail this brutal killer, who is now serving a total of forty-eight life sentences.

TEENAGE PROSTITUTES
On 15 July 1982 a group of children discovered the body of 16-year-old Wendy Lee Coffield in the Green River, King County, on the outer edges of Seattle's city limits. She had drifted up against a piling near the Meeker Street Bridge, naked save for her tennis shoes, strangled by her own blue jeans. On 15 August that same year, a slaughterhouse worker came across the body of Deborah Bonner, and only two days later, a man rafting the same stretch of river saw in the shallows what turned out to be 17-year-old Cynthia Hinds. Next to her was another body, that of 31-year-old Marcia Chapman. All had been strangled. When police searched the area they found the body of another girl, Opal Mills, sixteen, on the nearby bank, dead by no more than twenty-four hours. The King County Sheriff's Department were hot on the heels of a serial killer, but it was as close as they would get for some time.

The victims of the Green River Killer belonged to a very specific demographic group. All of them were women. All of them were believed to be prostitutes. And only a handful of them were older than twenty-one; almost half were eighteen or younger. Unfortunately, there was no shortage of these very vulnerable young women in the Seattle area. Street prostitution in and around the city during the years of the Green River Killer was rife, and changes in state legislation had meant that young runaways could no longer be forcibly detained. As a result, there was an abundance of isolated, inexperienced and defenceless teenage girls who were prepared to climb into a car with a strange man as a way of making a living. Once the act of running away had been decriminalized, police no longer even kept records on missing teenagers. Had they continued to do so, the monstrous scale of these murders might have been apparent much earlier.

THE KILLING GROUND
The area in which the prostitutes plied their trade straddled the city limits: when the King County Sheriff's Department were cracking down these women went north into the city, and when the Seattle Police Department did the same, the women returned. The two forces never combined their efforts, and this problem in dealing with street prostitution made Seattle a rich killing ground for a serial killer.

Furthermore, vice officers for King County did not work at weekends, when trade was busiest, and some even freelanced as security in local strip clubs, ensuring prostitutes were kept out of the lounges and thus forcing them out on to the streets, where they were most at risk. Similarly, in the city itself, police conducted a series of raids on brothels, although none of the girls that worked in them had ever fallen prey to

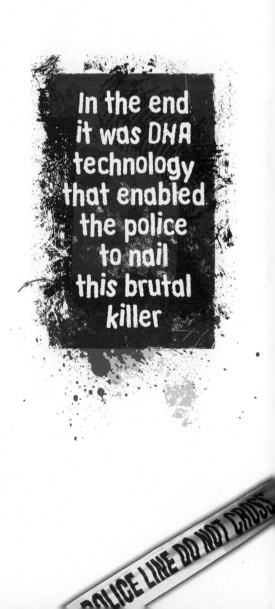

In the end it was DNA technology that enabled the police to nail this brutal killer

the killer. When arrests were made in the red light district it was invariably the prostitute who was arrested, rather than her customer. No effort was being made to keep a systematic record of the 'johns', not even of the licence plates on their cars. Inadvertently, the Green River Killer was being given a free hand.

On 16 August 1982, King County assembled its Green River Task Force. It was headed by Police Major Richard Kraske, and comprised twenty-five officers, the biggest task force since the Ted Bundy murders seven years earlier – although, as it transpired, these officers were far less experienced. The day after Kraske's appointment, the task force staked out the river, and an overhead news helicopter broadcast their position to anyone with a television.

PSYCHOLOGICAL PROFILE

The first suspect emerged that year in September: a cab driver and ex-con named Melvin Wayne Foster, who had approached police to inform on other cabbies he considered suspicious. A psychological profile of the Green River Killer had already been created by FBI agent John Douglas, and police considered Foster to fit perfectly. He was put under twenty-four-hour surveillance. After searches of his house, he was given a lie detector test, which he failed. Foster attributed his failure to a nervous condition and despite constant police observation of him, young women continued to disappear.

Forensic fingertip search: investigators search for the remains of one of Gary Leon Ridgway's victims at an unnamed location

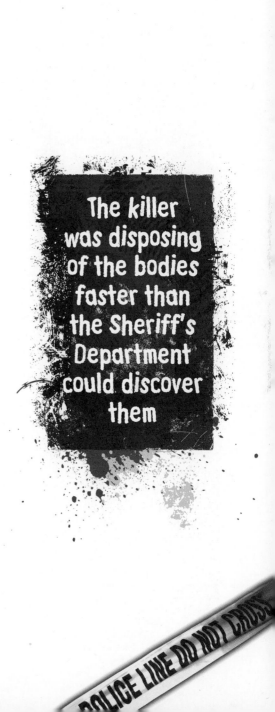

The killer was disposing of the bodies faster than the Sheriff's Department could discover them

POLICE LINE DO NOT CROSS

> ...he began visiting prostitutes for sex, and developed an intense hatred for these mostly young, inexperienced women

Eventually, the task force had to admit that they had suspected, arrested and investigated the wrong man.

Meanwhile, the death toll had risen to sixteen. The killer was disposing of the bodies faster than the Sheriff's Department could discover them.

The first task force was disbanded when Sheriff Bernard Winckoski left his position in January 1983, to be replaced three months later by Sheriff Vern Thomas. Sheriff Thomas began

Jose Malvar Jr, brother of Marie Malvar, on the witness stand at Gary Ridgway's trial. Malva Jr, his father and Marie's boyfriend searched the streets for the green pickup van that Marie was last seen getting into

POLICE LINE DO NOT CR

campaigning immediately for a new, larger task force. It took the rest of the year to organize, and to overcome his colleagues' concerns about the strain that it would put on police resources. But by January 1984, a task force of forty officers was ready to look again at the Green River Killer, and every one of them must have felt the pressure: the killer was operating seemingly unhindered in a small area that was routinely patrolled by plain clothes as well as uniformed officers. Furthermore, while Sheriff Thomas had been planning and politicking, these murders had continued unabated.

CLOSING IN ON THE KILLER

In a change of tactics, Thomas' task force began to arrest the prostitutes' clients instead of the prostitutes. Prior to this, arrests of women prostitutes were three times greater than the number of men arrested for trying to buy sex. Soon, the ratio was almost reversed, and the killings seemed to tail off. Progress was being made at last.

The killer had been scared away, or so it appeared. Police began to speculate that the culprit had moved, or was operating elsewhere. But although much good work had been done, the killer remained free, and morale in the task force began to plummet. Leads were few and far between and there were no physical descriptions of the killer, for the simple reason that no victim had ever been able to escape.

When the sixth victim, Marie Malvar, had got into a green pickup van with a dark-haired man on 30 April 1983, her boyfriend was there to see it. He followed in his own car, noticing that the two seemed to be arguing, and then lost them at a traffic light near Des Moines. He reported her missing four days later. He returned to the area with her brother and father, and searched the streets, looking for the pickup, which they found in a driveway. The Des Moines police sent a detective, but she was not inside the house. It was three months before Des Moines police informed King County Homicide of the incident. And it was three *years* before King County factored it into their investigations (another victim, Kimi Kai Pitsor, had also been seen getting into a similar vehicle, but the two events were never connected).

A STRANGE LONER

Gary Ridgway was not, in fact, unknown to police. He was a strange man whom people described as friendly but a bit odd. He had been raised in Seattle. His mother was a domineering woman, and he wet the bed as a child, but there was nothing in his childhood to suggest the burning rage that led him, as an adult, to become a serial killer. As a young man, he joined the Pentecostal church, and often went to collect for the church from door to door. However, at the same period, he began visiting prostitutes for sex, and developed an intense hatred for these mostly young, inexperienced women. In 1980, he was accused of choking a prostitute, but police let him go. In 1982 he was interviewed in a car with prostitute Kelli McGinness (an 18-year-old who disappeared the following year), and the same year pleaded guilty to soliciting a decoy female police officer.

Gary Ridgway was a strange man whom people described as friendly but a bit odd

Ridgway's mother was domineering, but nothing in his childhood suggested he would become a serial killer

Ridgway confessed to killing forty-eight women over fifteen years. He was sentenced to life imprisonment – commuted from the death sentence in return for helping police find the bodies

POLICE LINE DO NOT CROSS

In 1984, he approached Thomas' Green River Task Force to offer information, and was given a lie detector test, which he passed. Later that year, when police ascertained that he had had contact with at least three of the victims, Ridgway finally became chief suspect.

However, a house search provided no clues. In 1986, he passed another polygraph test ('I was too relaxed,' he later said). The following year, bodily samples were taken. Yet, despite the fact that he had been in the area, and had had contact with the women who were killed, Ridgway was not arrested.

THE VITAL CLUE

After this period, the killings tailed off dramatically, and by 1991 the Green River Task Force was staffed by a single officer. But there were many who had not forgotten the victims of the Green River Killer, and who were determined to seek justice for their murders. In 2001 King County gained a new sheriff, Dave Reichert, who formed a new team to solve the case, largely consisting of forensics and DNA experts. All viable evidence the county had collected was sent to the laboratory for investigation.

It was this initiative that was finally to yield results. The experts started with three of the earliest victims, who had been killed in 1982 and 1983 – Mills, Chapman and Carol Christensen. Semen taken from their bodies was tested using new DNA technology and the match with Gary Ridgway's sample was positive. The Green River Killer had been found at last.

Ridgway was fifty-two years old when he was arrested on 30 November 2001 on four counts of murder. At first the killer maintained his innocence, but as DNA testing continued on further remains, the evidence against Ridgway become incontrovertible. Two years later, he pleaded guilty to forty-eight counts of murder, mostly committed in 1982 and 1983, but one in 1990, and one as late as 1998.

JUSTICE AT LAST

In July 2003 Ridgway was moved from the county jail to an undisclosed location amid reports that he was prepared to co-operate if he could escape the death penalty. The plea bargain was defended by the prosecution as 'an avenue to the truth' for the victims and their families, a way to bring them 'closure'. While not all the families were happy with this turn of events, forty-one victims were eventually named in court who might never otherwise have been mentioned, and as a result, some of the bodies were located and could be given a proper burial by their families.

It is generally thought that Gary Ridgway killed many more than forty-eight women. Chillingly, he himself has admitted that he cannot remember all of the women he put to death. However, through a combination of police work and forensic technology, the case was finally solved, and he was made to pay for at least some of his hideous crimes. Today, with forty-eight life sentences to serve, there is absolutely no doubt that Ridgway will remain in jail for the rest of his life. After years of being hunted down, the Green River Killer is finally behind bars – for good.

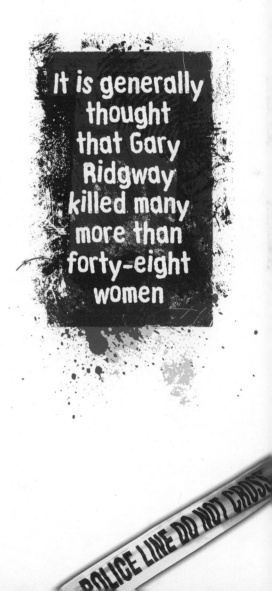

It is generally thought that Gary Ridgway killed many more than forty-eight women

POLICE LINE DO NOT CROSS

Byron de la Beckwith

Medgar Evers was born in Decatur, Mississippi on 2 July 1925. As a young man he served in the United States army during the Second World War, and went on to enrol in business studies at Alcorn State University in Lorman, Mississippi. He was a keen student, involved with many activities, including playing team sports, singing in the college choir, taking part in the debating society and editing the college newspaper. In fact, he was so successful that he was listed in the 'Who's Who' of American colleges. But not everyone rejoiced in his success.

At college, Evers met his future wife, Myrlie Beasley, and the pair married in December 1951. After he had received his degree, the newly-weds moved to Mound Bayou, Mississippi. Evers was a bright, ambitious young man, who was determined to combat the racism of the Mississippi establishment so that he could follow his career path and raise his family in peace in the place where he had grown up.

POLITICAL ACTIVISM

His first job after leaving college was as an insurance salesman, travelling round the South. On his travels, he saw for himself the abject poverty in which many black families lived, and was determined to do something about it.

> On his travels, he saw for himself the abject poverty in which many black families lived

Grief and defiance: mourners march and sing through Jackson, Mississippi, in a funeral procession for the slain civil rights leader Medgar Evers

POLICE LINE DO NOT CR

He was badly beaten several times, but he refused to be intimidated and carried on with his political activism

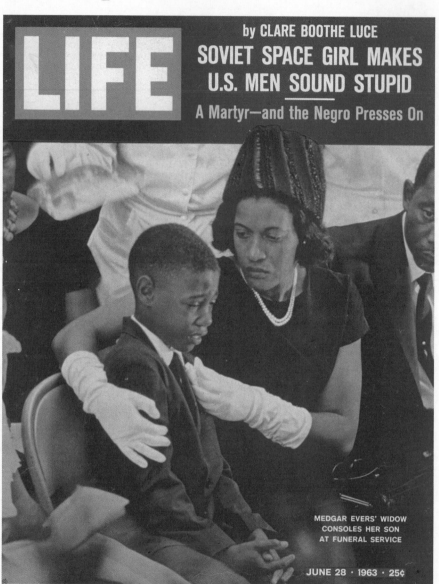

by CLARE BOOTHE LUCE

SOVIET SPACE GIRL MAKES U.S. MEN SOUND STUPID

A Martyr—and the Negro Presses On

MEDGAR EVERS' WIDOW CONSOLES HER SON AT FUNERAL SERVICE

JUNE 28 · 1963 · 25¢

The face of African America's despair: Medgar Evers' son and widow attend his funeral in June 1968

He became more active in politics, joining the National Association for the Advancement of Colored People (NAACP) and helping to organize boycotts of gasoline stations that were refusing to allow black people to use the restroom facilities. He also helped to set up local chapters of the NAACP around

Medgar Evers (left), as the President of the Mississippi NAACP, was with James H Meredith – the first African-American to go to the University of Mississippi – when Meredith announced he would be returning to the college, despite protest riots

the Mississippi delta. In recognition of his efforts, in 1952, Evers was appointed the first full-time field secretary of the NAACP in Mississippi. His job was to collect and disseminate information about civil rights violations. He also organized non-violent protests against segregation, for which he was imprisoned. He was badly beaten several times, but he refused to be intimidated.

FRESH FINGERPRINTS

In 1954, Evers applied to the University of Mississippi to study law. At that time the university was segregated, but Evers cited the ruling of the Supreme Court in the case of Brown v. Board of Education which ruled that segregation was unconstitutional. When his application was rejected, Evers campaigned for the desegregation of the university.

In 1962, the campaign finally bore fruit when it enrolled its first black student, James Meredith. This triumph came at a cost, however: it sparked riots that left two people dead. In some quarters, Evers was blamed for inciting the violence, although he had always stated that 'violence is not the way' and had supported civil disobedience as a way of bringing about real change.

On 12 June 1963, Evers pulled into his driveway after a meeting and was brutally shot as he stepped out of his car, right outside his home. When the police were called, a gun was found in the bushes nearby, covered in fresh fingerprints. After analysis, there was no doubt who they belonged to: Byron de la Beckwith, a well-known figure in the local white segregationist movement. De la Beckwith had been heard to say that he wanted to kill Evers. After the murder, de la Beckwith was arrested and charged, but despite the evidence, he was never convicted.

On two separate occasions, all-

POLICE LINE DO NOT CROSS

white juries failed to agree that de la Beckwith was guilty as charged. However, many years later, in 1989, new evidence came to light that the jury in both trials had been pressurized not to convict. There was also evidence of statements that de la Beckwith had made, implying that he had committed the murder.

BODY EXHUMED

In 1994, a new trial commenced, during which Evers' body had to be exhumed. It was found to be in a good enough state of preservation to corroborate the information. Byron de la Beckwith was finally convicted of the murder of Medgar Evers on 5 February 1994. He appealed against the verdict, but his appeal was rejected, and he went on to serve his sentence, dying in prison in 2001.

This was no ordinary cold case, however, in which new evidence alone resulted in a conviction. The years after Evers' death had seen a fundamental change in attitudes in the United States, as people began to realize the injustices of racism, prompted by the campaigns of the civil rights movement and the passing of a civil rights bill that at last enshrined the principles of equal rights in law. Over the years, it had become clear that segregation, and the violence involved in implementing it, was no longer excusable or acceptable.

COURAGE AND VISION

As part of this process, the reputation of Medgar Evers grew. Immediately after his death, he was mourned nationally, and buried with honours at Arlington

The cold face of a killer: Byron de la Beckwith (right) is shown conferring with his attorney at Jackson police station after his arrest for the murder of civil rights leader Medgar Evers

Cemetery. Nina Simone composed a song as a tribute to him ('Mississippi Goddamn'), as did Bob Dylan ('Only a Pawn in their Game'), which helped to establish him as a legendary figure. He became known as one of the earliest civil rights pioneers, whose courage and vision had been instrumental in kicking off the civil rights movement in the United

States. Thus, pressure to convict his murderer, and to overturn the biased decisions of the past trials, also grew. In a sense, the final Medgar Evers trial, taking place decades after his death, was not just a trial of his murderer, but of the racist attitudes that had allowed his murder to take place, and let it go unpunished for so many years.

Dennis Rabbitt

It was years before police even realized what was happening, but then rape is perhaps the most under-reported of crimes. According to a 1996 survey, only 39 per cent of such crimes are ever relayed to law enforcement officials. Even so, there are some women in St Louis, Missouri, who would claim bitterly that the police would rather the figure was even lower.

Nevertheless, the following modus operandi of the rapist concerned began to emerge: between 1988 and 1997, an individual was breaking into women's homes at night, after they had gone to bed, usually through an unlocked door or open window. He wore a ski-mask and gloves to protect his identity. After the rape, he would usually force the victim to bathe, presumably to destroy any forensic evidence of his crime.

The rapes took place in the better neighbourhoods of St Louis, towards the south of the city, areas that had always been relatively safe and crime-free, and for this anomaly the unknown criminal was dubbed the Southside Rapist. When DNA evidence finally brought his reign of terror to an end, the head of the city police department was compelled to open a new, dedicated crime lab, so no other criminal should escape this newer, longer arm of the law.

THE MAN BEHIND THE MASK

Dennis Nathaniel Rabbitt was born in St Louis in 1957, to a middle-class family. His father was blind, and he was brought up mostly by his stepfather and his mother. During his adolescence, Rabbitt claims his mother drilled a hole in the bathroom door so she could watch him masturbate. Later in his teenage years he returned home one day to find his mother unconscious near the living room, and his stepfather upstairs in their bedroom, dead, with a gun in his hand and blood on the walls.

Rabbitt later said he knew something was wrong with him from an early age. By seventeen, his criminal record had begun, and he had become a known burglar. This did not stop him from leading the semblance of a normal life, however, and Rabbitt eventually married, and became the father of two. During this time he ran a bar and restaurant in downtown St Louis, and those that knew him described him as a typical married father. He was to describe the break-up of his marriage as one of the worst events in his life, although it was he who filed for divorce, in 1987. Observers who watched the case unfold were quick to point out that the first rape of which he was suspected occurred the following year.

THE NIGHTMARE BEGINS

As the police found out, while his modus operandi remained fairly consistent, there was no link between the victims of the Southside Rapist, other than that they were women, and they were vulnerable. He had no preference for a physical or racial type. The age varied hugely too, starting in the mid-teens and ending in the early eighties. There were no other causative factors that linked them, none of the women knew each other, their daily movements were all

His mother drilled a hole in the bathroom door so she could watch him masturbate

POLICE LINE DO NOT CROSS

POLICE LINE DO NOT CROSS

different, and they worked and shopped in different areas. Yet each one would awake some time in the night with a masked man sitting on their chest or legs, holding a knife at their throat, or pointing a gun at their head. Other than the rape itself he inflicted no harm on them, which would categorize him as a power-assurance rapist, also described by police as a 'gentleman rapist'.

Rabbitt fits the profile reasonably well, being a man of average intelligence, who was rarely physically aggressive, who worried about his social status and may also have been insecure about his masculinity, and who had failed at maintaining a romantic relationship. He also fantasized that the rape was consensual sex, desired and enjoyed by his female victim. It was anything but; even Jennifer Jewer, a woman of strong Baptist faith, who famously forgave him in court, eventually slid into a paralysing depression that cost her her job.

'TO SERVE AND PROTECT'?

For over a decade, the St Louis Metropolitan Police were at a loss, while the rapes continued. 'He terrorized the city,' Police Chief Joe Mokwa confessed. 'We didn't know who he was or where he was going to strike next. We had no solid eyewitnesses to identify him.' In an attempt to narrow down the rapist's area of operations, they contacted James LeBeau, an administration of justice professor at Southern Illinois University,

Under heavy police protection, including a bullet-proof vest and riot helmet, Dennis Rabbitt is transferred across state. So prolific was the range of his attacks, authorities in St Louis had to decide which municipality would prosecute him first

in 1996. LeBeau was a pioneer of crime mapping – taking the locations of crimes and putting them on a map, thereby placing spatial information in a geographical format. But while crime mapping went on to prove itself useful for the purposes of trend-spotting and expending resources, it brought St Louis police no closer to the fleet-footed Southside Rapist.

Despite the Metropolitan Police's best efforts, however, many remain critical of their handling of the case, and their handling of rape cases in general. Statistically, St Louis officially had fewer rapes than most American cities, even while the Southside Rapist was at his busiest. As the *St Louis Post-Dispatch* has reported, this was largely because for decades huge numbers of rapes were never even filed on system, but simply kept as 'memos' for a period of months before being shredded. As late as 2005 the department had to increase its annual rape figure by 53 per cent. Physical evidence from rape kits was frequently destroyed too, often without ever having been analysed. In such a culture, critics argue, it is no wonder Dennis Rabbitt got away with so much for so long. There are also allegations that before Rabbitt was identified as the Southside Rapist he was found by police drunkenly passed out in public only a few houses away from where a rape had occurred the night before.

MANHUNT

Frustrated, the police returned to their crime mapping. Could this new technique be honed and refined to produce a better result? The case had been cold

'We didn't know who he was or where he was going to strike next'

for three years when the police extended their search outside the Southside area and began to look further afield, at rapes in less affluent parts of the city, even in other counties. With these extra cases taken into account, the profile of the perpetrator became clearer, and the list of suspects drastically shorter.

FAILED RAPES

Dennis Rabbitt, who had by now been arrested twice for attempted burglaries (failed rapes, he later confessed), was on the list. Crime mapping had worked after all: the officers had just needed to take in all of St Louis.

Under the guise of a peeping-tom investigation, the police obtained a saliva sample from Rabbitt and analysed his DNA. It was a perfect match for the Southside Rapist, but when the tests were finished they found Rabbitt had left his new job in waste disposal and fled the city, almost immediately after giving the sample.

The manhunt lasted for months. After an appearance on America's Most Wanted, a woman tipped off his whereabouts for a reward of $25,000. The FBI caught up with Rabbitt in a motel in Albuquerque, New Mexico, with a 15-year-old girl in tow. He initially claimed to be Nathan Babbitt, but this modest alias could not hide his tattoos, which matched the description on record.

BEHIND BARS

Dennis Rabbitt was tried not once but several times, in different counties, until he had been tried for each of the twenty rapes his DNA linked him to, and was

found guilty on each count. He was sentenced to five life sentences in Missouri and an additional sixty years in Illinois.

There are numerous but inconsistent reports that he has confessed to many more rapes than the twenty he was convicted of, from a total of twenty nine up to a hundred. 'It's only logical that there are many more rapes than we know about,' St Louis Detective Mark Kennedy once said. 'Even if he averaged only four a year, that's more than one hundred rapes.'

In April 2005 Dennis Rabbitt was stabbed, repeatedly but not fatally, in the exercise grounds of the South Central Correctional Center, and as a result he was moved elsewhere. Outside prison walls, St Louis police were so impressed by the efficacy of DNA evidence that they opened a new crime lab on Clarke Avenue that now oversees 100,000 cases a year. Meanwhile, in and around the Gateway City, a number of traumatized but relieved women are trying to get on with their lives.

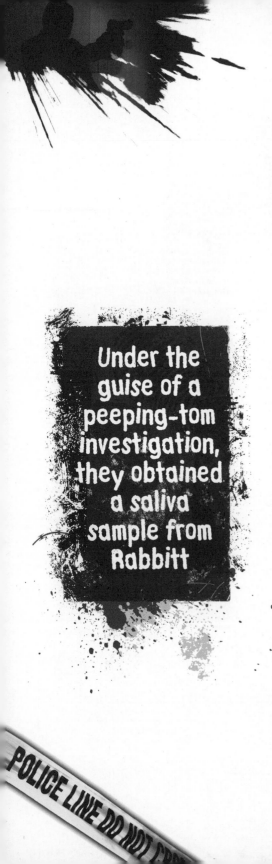

Under the guise of a peeping-tom investigation, they obtained a saliva sample from Rabbitt

POLICE LINE DO NOT CROSS

Lewis Felts

On the night of 26 September 2002, a fierce storm was raging through Front Royal, Virginia, making driving hazardous in this bleak rural part of Massachusetts. One driver returning home late slowed as he came to the flooded, aptly named Low Water Bridge and caught sight of something curious in his headlights. It was a vehicle with a man slumped at the wheel and another gravely wounded in the passenger seat. Both had been shot at close range. The passenger, 20-year-old Joe Kowaleski, was rushed to hospital where he remained in a coma for days, unable to give detectives the vital clues they needed if they were to catch the killer. His friend, Ty Lathon, was pronounced dead at the scene.

DRIVEN TO MURDER

When Kowaleski recovered he couldn't remember anything other than a glimpse of a red jeep approaching at high speed followed by a blinding flash. More bad luck came with the realization that the rain had washed away all clues. All the physical evidence that remained were two empty 12-gauge shotgun shell casings and a set of skidmarks from a vehicle that had evidently pulled up alongside just long enough to allow a gunman to empty both barrels into the victims. However, it was impossible to take prints from the tyre tracks because they were on gravel. Both the weather and the environment were

> ... just long enough to allow a gunman to empty both barrels into the victims

Sometimes weather and environment conspire to protect the killer

POLICE LINE DO NOT CROSS

conspiring to keep the killer's identity a secret, but the motive at least was clear. There was an assortment of drug paraphernalia in the victim's vehicle and three cellphones, two of which belonged to the victims, the other owned by Lathon's ex-girlfriend Julie Grubbs.

Grubbs didn't own a red jeep, but her new boyfriend did. His name was Lewis Felts and he was a known drug dealer. Investigators staked out his home and arrested him when he appeared with a box of cleaning products looking intent on eliminating the remaining clues. They confiscated the vehicle and searched the apartment, where they found a significant quantity of drugs and $1,200 in cash, together with a fourth cellphone.

CELLPHONE EVIDENCE
Felts and Grubbs denied being at the scene, claiming to have stayed that night in Grubbs' apartment, 96 km (60 miles) from the crime scene. But subsequent enquiries revealed that Grubbs had used the fourth phone to call Ty Lathon twenty-two times on the night of the murder and that her calls had been logged as being relayed from several towers along Route 50 as she had driven south. The final call was traced to Front Royal.

Although the cellphone records destroyed the couple's alibi they did

not prove they had committed the murder, only that they had been in the vicinity. They could have been lying to avoid incriminating themselves in drug dealing.

GEOLOGICAL FORENSICS
The detectives then called in a forensic geologist to examine dried mud found in the jeep's wheel wells. He sieved it to separate the coarser soil from the finer material and then subjected both to microscopic analysis. What he found sealed the guilt of the killer couple. In the samples of dried mud were fragments of sparkling blue azurite and emerald green malachite, copper-based minerals which had been washed downstream from a working quarry to Low Water Bridge. This discovery placed the jeep at the scene and all that remained was to place the weapon in Felts' hands. A friend of Felts came forward to tell how he had sold Felts a shotgun three weeks before the shooting. Better still, he had kept a couple of shells. These were shown to match those discarded at the scene. At the end of his trial Felts was found guilty of capital murder and attempted murder and sentenced to twenty-five years in prison.

What had at first appeared to be a drugs hit turned out to be an old-fashioned crime of passion. Lewis Felts had killed Ty Lathon over a girl.

The weather and the environment were conspiring to keep the killer's identity a secret

The Woodchip Killer

Forensic science is not simply a matter of running trace evidence through high-tech apparatus and printing out the criminal's ID after the database has produced a match. Even the most sophisticated equipment can only analyse the evidence. It takes a tenacious, imaginative and highly motivated CSI to gather all the elements, interpret the evidence and make a case. The following account is a good example of the lengths that any good forensic scientist must now go to and the attention to detail he or she needs to secure a conviction.

MISSING PERSON

Just before Christmas 1986, the police received a call from Keith Mayo, a private investigator, who said he was concerned that his client, flight attendant Helle Crafts, had gone missing from her home in Connecticut. When questioned, her husband Richard claimed that she had stormed out after an argument and that he had no idea of her whereabouts. Neither had her colleagues, but without a body there was nothing much the police officers could do except conduct a routine missing persons enquiry. Until, that is, a snowplough driver remembered seeing a man fitting Richard Crafts' description operating a wood-chipping machine by a river at 3.30 am in the midst of a blizzard.

The inference was clear: Richard Crafts had dismembered his wife's body and shredded it into compost. If he had tipped the contents into the river, the

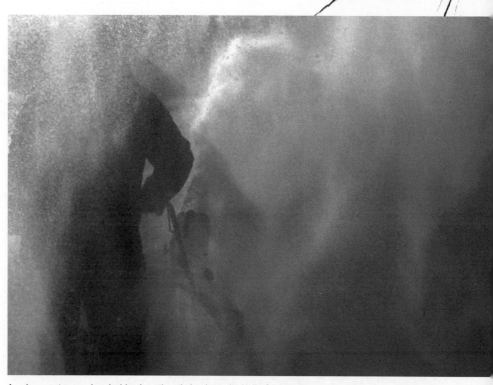

An observant snowplough driver's actions helped convict Helle Craft's killer

current would have distributed the shredded remains across the state and no amount of circumstantial evidence would be enough to convict him.

Fortunately the coroner in charge of the case, Henry C. Lee, possessed local knowledge and told the police precisely which spot on the river to search as body parts had been washed up there in earlier cases. Sure enough, the officers pulled a chainsaw from the water and were able to match it to the chipper and the truck that Crafts had rented. But even this lucky find proved only that Craft had – oddly – discarded a rented saw in a river. It did not prove conclusively that he had mulched his wife's remains.

A GRUESOME TASK

So for nearly a month investigators scoured the first location where Craft had been seen using the shredder during the snow storm and were able to bring back a small mountain of wood chippings and what appeared to be human tissue to Lee's laboratory. There the team sifted through the debris, putting plant material to one side and human hair, tooth fragments and tissue in another.

Each hair had to be analysed to see if it was animal or human and, if it was human, which race and gender it belonged to. Hair that had been pulled had to be separated from

POLICE LINE DO NOT CROSS

Flight attendant Helle Crafts who went missing in 1986, allegedly after an argument with her husband Richard

POLICE LINE DO NOT CROSS

Private investigator Keith Mayo was hired by Helle Crafts before she disappeared when she discovered that her husband had had a series of extra-marital affairs

that both chippings showed the distinctive cut marks made by the wood chipper that Crafts had hired.

If Richard Crafts had entertained hopes of evading arrest and prosecution for murder, he had underestimated the dedication and dogged persistence of the forensic investigators on his case, who had spent almost three years putting their case together. When he came to trial in 1989, Richard Crafts' defence was systematically demolished by Dr Lee and his team of expert witnesses. Crafts was found guilty and sentenced to fifty years in prison.

hair that had been shed naturally and then those that had been torn out had to be matched to a specific part of the body. Hair that had been cut had to be further examined to see if it had been cut cleanly by scissors or raggedly by a shredder. After separating body fragments from the wood chippings, Lee and his team were left with small findings: a fingernail, a dental crown, a bone fragment and pieces of plastic bag in which the body parts had been transported to the site.

BODY FRAGMENTS

Tooth fragments proved sufficient to positively identify the rest of the remains as belonging to the missing woman and when Dr Lee identified a bone fragment as part of the skull it proved conclusively that Mrs Crafts was dead. Moreover, the tissue on the chainsaw matched tissue found at the site; hair taken from Mrs Crafts' hairbrush was matched with hair recovered from the chippings and, if that wasn't enough, a sliver of nail polish was found to be identical with a sample taken from a bottle at the Crafts' house.

But the final flourish in Henry Lee's exemplary investigation was his decision to consult R. Bruce Hoadley, a forensic tree expert. By examining the chippings found at the river and those taken from the hire truck, Hoadley was able to state that they were from the same tree and

When Dr Lee identified a bone fragment it proved conclusively Mrs Crafts was dead

Clifford Irving

In 1971 rumours began circulating in the American media that eccentric billionaire industrialist Howard Hughes (the subject of Martin Scorsese's Academy Award-winning movie *The Aviator*) had finally broken his 30-year silence to tell the story of his life to a comparatively unknown writer, Clifford Irving. Among Hughes' surviving friends surprise was mixed with incredulity and even suspicion that the story may have been a hoax, since Hughes was a resolute recluse who had guarded his privacy as fiercely as he had protected himself from the germs he feared would infect him if he allowed contact with the outside world.

GHOST WRITER

For decades Hughes had remained in self-imposed exile on his palatial island paradise in the Bahamas, where he reputedly refused to have his hair cut or to trim his fingernails so that he now had the appearance of an ancient Chinese mandarin with waist-length hair and nails 20 cm (8 in) long.

Irving's publishers, McGraw-Hill, had reservations of their own, but these were allayed when Irving produced a sheaf of letters allegedly written by Hughes which were subsequently declared genuine by handwriting experts. No book had yet been published on Hughes' life to which the man himself had contributed and this would be an amazing publishing coup.

Duly satisfied, McGraw-Hill agreed to an advance of $765,000, which was an unprecedented amount at the time, but the company was convinced that they had

secured an international bestseller. They handed Irving a cheque made out to H.R. Hughes which the author promised to forward to the reclusive billionaire and they awaited delivery of the manuscript. Irving did not disappoint them. In due course he delivered a weighty 1,200-page biography which was eagerly read by Hughes' former associates, who declared themselves satisfied that the memoirs were genuine. They had the authentic 'voice' of Hughes – at least they did so on paper.

VOICE OF A RECLUSE

Just as the presses were about to roll, associates of the billionaire announced that Hughes would be holding a tele-conference at a Los Angeles hotel at which he would denounce Irving's biography as a work of 'fantastic fiction' and field questions from journalists.

During the two-hour session Hughes fielded a battery of probing enquiries which covered everything from technical details of the aeroplanes he had designed to trivial facts concerning the good luck charms given to him by female admirers. All were answered correctly. Then Hughes made a statement in which he denied collaborating with Irving or ever having met him. Furthermore, he wished it to be known that not a single cent of the $765,000 advance had been deposited in any of his many bank accounts. It was a convincing performance, but there was still the question of whether the deep voice on the end of the phone line was a clever, well-informed impostor. There was only one way to find out.

American industrialist, aviator, film producer and famous recluse Howard Hughes

The story may have been a hoax since Hughes was a resolute recluse who had guarded his privacy

Tapes of the conference were handed over to voiceprint analyst Lawrence Kersta, who compared the pitch, tone and intonation with an early recording of Hughes. Kersta's contention was that the underlying character of a person's voice remains constant even if the tone becomes frailer with age. After days of intense study Kersta declared himself to be convinced that the tele-conference voice was that of Hughes. But with a fortune at stake and the reputation of the publisher riding on the outcome it was decided that Kersta's verdict could not be considered conclusive, especially as he had a financial interest in the technology he had been using.

PHONETIC PROFILING

The final word was then given to Kersta's most vocal critic, Dr Peter Ladefoged, professor of phonetics at UCLA, who had no vested interest in the outcome himself. Ladefoged subjected the tapes to detailed spectrographic analysis to compare the peaks and troughs of key consonants, vowels and phrases. He too announced that he was satisfied that the voice was that of Hughes.

The intense speculation surrounding the deal prompted Irving's Swiss bank to investigate the matter. They released a statement to the press confirming that a cheque for $765,000 had been deposited in the account of H.R. Hughes and then transferred to another in the name of Helga R. Hughes, Irving's wife.

Caught in a lie, Irving finally admitted his guilt and was sentenced to thirty months in prison. He was released after serving just eighteen months and continued his career as a writer.

US writer Clifford Irving, author of the fake Howard Hughes biography

Stanley Cornet

During 1993 the 'sunshine state' of Florida was making headlines for all the wrong reasons. It had become a stalking ground for opportunist thieves who considered tourists easy prey. Holiday-makers were easy to spot as rental car companies marked each vehicle with a company sticker, and the criminals relied on the fact that out-of-state visitors would not want to return to testify, especially if court proceedings could be deliberately delayed on technicalities.

DAYLIGHT ATTACKS

Over the course of that summer local muggers had become increasingly bold and vicious, attacking visitors in broad daylight, relying on shock tactics to traumatize their victims and render them less than reliable witnesses. But one gang chose the wrong victim. Despite the adverse publicity German TV producer Helga West had no fears about taking a vacation in Miami with her elderly mother. She had recently wrapped up a special report on the Florida crime wave in which she offered safety advice to would-be travellers, so she was confident she could take care of herself.

At first, the holiday was all that Helga had hoped it would be. However, on the morning of their return flight she took a wrong turning en route to the airport and mother and daughter soon found themselves in an unfamiliar neighbourhood. While Helga tried to get her bearings, a car drove up, blocking her exit, and two

Helga West, whose vacation in Miami with her elderly mother was cut short by a violent robbery

On the morning of their return flight Helga took a wrong turning en route to the airport...

black males leapt out. One shattered the driver's window with a single kick while his partner screamed threats at Helga's elderly mother in the passenger seat. Helga fought back bravely, forcing the pair to abandon the robbery and flee empty-handed, but not before they had inflicted severe injuries on their distraught victims. Helga sustained two cracked vertebrae, a serious head wound and a spiteful bite mark in her arm so deep that it had almost severed a muscle. Doctors later confirmed that had the attack continued it is almost certain she would have been left severely disabled.

A CLEVER DETECTIVE

Fortunately Helga recovered from her injuries and her case was assigned to Miami detective Laura Le Febvre, who had many years' experience investigating sexual assaults. Detective Le Febvre knew the forensic value of a fresh bite mark and had the foresight to arrange for it to be photographed under ultra-violet light, which gives a three-dimensional image, making it easier to match to a dental impression taken from a suspect.

It was just as well that Le Febvre insisted on having the photograph taken as there were precious few other clues. The perpetrator who had left the bite mark lost his baseball cap in the struggle but it didn't help detectives because the hair samples inside didn't have a root and so there was no DNA to run through CODIS.

Just as the police began to despair of finding the perpetrators, Detective Le Febvre happened to visit the Miami-

Miami Beach: scene of many crimes in the 1990s

Dade Police department on an unrelated matter and overheard a conversation which put her on the trail of a prime suspect, factory worker Stanley Cornet. An officer was discussing the arrest of a suspect who had bitten him in an attempt to escape arrest.

To make absolutely sure of a positive ID, Detective Le Febvre put Cornet's photo among one hundred others, instead of the usual ten. When Helga picked his picture out without hesitation Le Febvre organized a warrant for Cornet's dental impression.

FORENSIC ODONTOLOGY

Knowing the game was up, Cornet protested violently and had to be restrained. Clenching his mouth tightly, he stubbornly refused to cooperate.

It was then that forensic odontologist Dr Richard Souviron had an idea: he brought in a lethal-looking device that looked as if it might have played a part in the Spanish Inquisition and placed it on the table before the belligerent suspect, the intimation being that he was ready to use it if Cornet continued to refuse to cooperate. In fact, the contraption was used to prise open the mouths of cadavers during an autopsy, and Dr Souviron had no intention of using it on the suspect. The ruse worked, and Dr Souviron managed to secure an impression of Cornet's teeth which were a perfect match to the bite mark on Helga West's arm.

Stanley Cornet was sentenced to life in prison, while Helga West set up an internet victim support organization, www.witnessjustice.org, to offer advice to victims of violent crime.

Knowing the game was up, Cornet protested violently and had to be restrained

POLICE LINE DO NOT CROSS

Lee Harvey Oswald.

Even those who have no patience with convoluted conspiracy theories must surely question the official government version of the assassination of John F. Kennedy as presented by the Warren Commission, which concluded that a lone marksman was responsible for shooting the president and was then himself conveniently killed before he could be questioned in open court. Quite apart from the numerous inconsistencies, accusations of evidence-tampering and mysterious deaths of key witnesses, the forensic evidence alone challenges the idea that a single sniper killed President Kennedy in Dallas on that fateful November afternoon in 1963.

HOME MOVIES
If the Kennedy assassination was indeed orchestrated by disaffected elements within the administration and the armed forces, as has been alleged, then it must be said that those responsible covered their tracks extremely well, but they could not have foreseen that the fatal moment would be captured on film by amateur home movie buff Abraham Zapruder.

Despite several attempts to suppress the controversial footage, those images could not be airbrushed out of history like the numerous witnesses who swore to hearing shots and seeing puffs of gunsmoke coming from a location other than the Dallas Book Depository where the lone gunman, Lee Harvey Oswald, is generally supposed to have fired three uncannily accurate shots in very rapid succession from a faulty bolt-action rifle, a feat even trained snipers failed to copy in subsequent tests.

THE MAGIC BULLET
The Zapruder footage establishes a timeframe of 5.6 seconds from the first shot, when Kennedy is clearly seen to flinch, as he instinctively reacts to the bullet whizzing past his ear, to the last in the frame which quite clearly shows the front right side of the president's head being smashed by a bullet.

The bullet obviously could not have come from the direction of the Book Depository which the motorcade had just passed. And this is when the myth of the 'magic bullet' was born. One of the most famous scenes in Oliver Stone's film *JFK* is the monologue on the subject of the magic bullet.

If there were only three shots, as the Commission contends, then the first was the one that made Kennedy instinctively react and Senator Connally turn round in the front passenger seat to see what had startled the president.

This first bullet appears to have ricocheted and a fragment of it, or piece of shrapnel, then struck a bystander, James Teague, who was standing by the underpass in front of the motorcade. If the third bullet caused the fatal head wound, then that leaves only one bullet responsible for the seven separate wounds in Kennedy and Connally. According to the Commission this 'magic bullet' entered the president's back at an angle of 17 degrees and was deflected upward and out through the president's neck, then suspended for 1.6 seconds after

> The forensic evidence alone challenges the idea that a single sniper killed President Kennedy

POLICE LINE DO NOT

A model reconstruction to try to determine the path of the gunfire that killed JFK

possible explanation for the number of wounds and their angle of entry is that there were four shots, not three, and that would require at least two marksmen, maybe even a third. A triangulation of fire is standard set-up for a moving target in US 'black operation' assassinations. It establishes a killing zone that reduces the risk of the target escaping alive and is usually indicative of a CIA or military involvement. A ballistics expert who studied the location could see that a single assassin would have had a perfectly clear shot from the rear of the Book Depository as the motorcade passed slowly towards him along Huston and possibly even time for a second shot, whereas the view Oswald is said to have had of the president's car as it turned into Elm Street at the rear of the Depository was obscured by an enormous tree which retains all its foliage in autumn. Clearly someone in the conspiracy did not do their homework and reckoned without the tenacity of those who refused to take the official version at face value.

ANOMALIES AT THE AUTOPSY

At Parkland Hospital, Dallas, where the preliminary autopsy was carried out, no fewer than twenty-six medical personnel were witness to the fact that the back of the president's head had been blown away in a manner which could only have been caused by a shot entering the right side of the head. One of the attending physicians, Dr Peters, later testified that the wound was 7 cm (2¾ in) in diameter and that 'a considerable portion of the brain was

which it turned right and then left and entered the Senator's right armpit. It then headed downwards at an angle of 27 degrees, shattering Connally's fifth rib, and exited from the right side of his chest. We are then asked to believe that the bullet made a right turn and shattered Connally's radius bone in his right wrist, after which it made a U-turn and buried itself in the Senator's left thigh. Incredulity is stretched beyond breaking point by the assertion that this

miraculous projectile then dropped out of the wound unnoticed, only to be later found in pristine condition on a stretcher at Parkland Hospital, where it proved a perfect match for Oswald's weapon.

THREE BULLETS OR FOUR?

The Army wound ballistics experts later fired identical rounds for comparison and all were severely distorted after striking just one bone in a cadaver. Any forensic pathologist would know that the only

'missing'. Another observed that as much as a fifth or even a quarter of the back of the head had been blasted out and that a large fragment of skull remained attached to a flap of skin, the sign of an exit wound.

Incredibly, the pathologist present at the preliminary examination was asked to concentrate exclusively on the head wound and not to dissect the neck, which would have revealed the presence of a second bullet wound. Significantly, all of the civilian doctors who were present regarded the hole in the throat as an entry wound, but it was disregarded by the chief pathologist, Commander Humes, who, under instructions from the military observers, abruptly wound up the examination. Humes is said to have later burned his autopsy notes.

LOST BRAIN

The body was then transferred to a military base, where it was examined by service physicians who would not have been free to publish their findings and who were under orders to prepare a report for the eyes of designated officers only. More revealing and disturbing is the fact that later the same day, President Lyndon B. Johnson ordered the immediate cleaning and repair of the presidential limousine, thus destroying crucial fragments of physical evidence including the bullet holes from which the angles of trajectory could have been calculated.

Many years later, when conspiracy-obsessed New Orleans DA, Jim Garrison, obtained a court order so he could examine the president's remains in the National Archive, he was told by officials that the president's brain had been lost!

The presidential motorcade on an earlier visit to Italy

POLICE LINE DO NOT CROSS

Josef Mengele

Dr Josef Mengele's insatiable appetite for cruelty exceeded that of the most cold-blooded mad doctors of pulp fiction. The murderous Nazi was known as the 'Angel of Death' because of the many sadistic experiments he carried out on the helpless inmates of Auschwitz concentration camp. Mengele selected who was to work and who was to die – he was personally responsible for the murder of 400,000 people, many of them children.

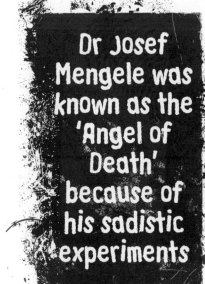

Dr Josef Mengele was known as the 'Angel of Death' because of his sadistic experiments

POLICE LINE DO NOT CROSS

Mengele's name and the enormity of his crimes was unknown to the Allies when they liberated the concentration camps in 1945, allowing the 'Angel' to slip unnoticed through the chaos of post-war Europe and seek asylum in South America. It was only in 1961, after the dramatic arrest and abduction from Argentina of Adolf Eichmann, the architect of the 'Final Solution', to stand trial for war crimes that the search for Mengele was intensified. But it would be another twenty-four years before one of the most notorious mass murderers in history was finally located.

BURIAL SITE

In 1985, impelled by a fresh American initiative to bring Mengele to justice, two German expatriates domiciled in Brazil offered to take investigators to what they claimed was the burial site of the world's most wanted war criminal.

Naturally, both the American and German authorities demanded that their forensic experts be allowed to examine the remains and determine the identity of the man who had been buried under the name of Wolfgang Gerhard. But there was an additional group with claims to a special interest in the outcome – associates of the celebrated Nazi-hunter Simon Wiesenthal, who had himself been an inmate of Auschwitz. Together the three parties assembled a distinguished team of experts who travelled to the remote Brazilian town of Embu on 6 June 1985.

There they exhumed the coffin and examined its contents, which were evidently those of a white, right-handed elderly male between sixty and seventy years of age. These basic facts could be

determined by the narrowness of the pelvis, the shape of the skull, the comparatively longer bones on the right side and the degree of wear of the teeth and specific bones. A more accurate estimate of the age of the skeleton was indicated by the multitude of microscopic canals in the femurs which carry the blood vessels. The amount and condition of these indicated a man in his late sixties, which would correspond to Mengele's age. The length of key bones gave a reliable height for the corpse of 173.5 cm (5 ft 7½ in), half a centimetre short of the height recorded in Mengele's SS file.

But his dental record proved to be of little use as it was hand-drawn and light on detail, although it indicated a gap at the front of the upper palate which resulted in a characteristic gap-tooth grin. An X-ray of the skull confirmed that 'Herr Gerhard' had possessed the very same distinctive feature.

NO DOUBT

In the final stage of the examination the skull provided the conclusive evidence. Using a technique known as video superimposition, the German forensic anthropologist Richard Helmer overlaid a photograph of the skull on to archive photographs of Dr Mengele to reveal thirty key features that were a positive match. Nevertheless, there were those who feared the Angel of Death had eluded them yet again.

Finally, in 1992 the advent of genetic fingerprinting made it possible to compare DNA from the remains in Embu with a sample from one of Mengele's living relatives. There could be no doubt – the bones in Brazil were those of Dr Mengele.

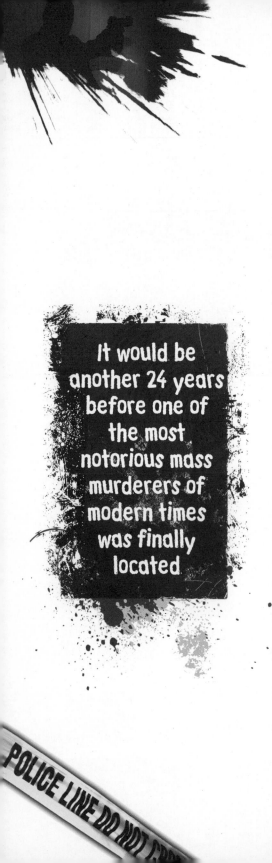

It would be another 24 years before one of the most notorious mass murderers of modern times was finally located

POLICE LINE DO NOT CR

O.J. Simpson

The O.J. Simpson murder trial in 1995 was lost, as the prosecution would see it, through a combination of incompetence and carelessness on behalf of the Los Angeles police, who provided a perfect textbook example of how not to process a crime scene.

The case against the former American football star and one-time TV actor was compelling. His ex-wife Nicole and her friend Ronald Goldman had been brutally murdered at her Brentwood home on the night of 12 June 1994, and there appeared to be plenty of indisputable physical evidence linking O.J. to the crime scene.

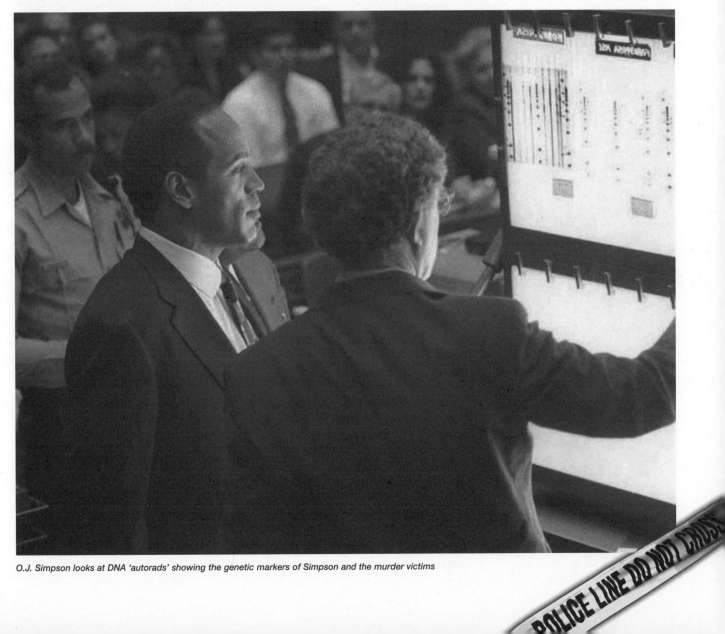

O.J. Simpson looks at DNA 'autorads' showing the genetic markers of Simpson and the murder victims

POLICE LINE DO NOT CROSS

There was a trail of bloody footprints leading away from the scene

Blood covers the path outside the home of Nicole Brown Simpson

POLICE LINE DO NOT CROSS

A bloodied glove found in the grounds appeared to match another recovered from O.J.'s house in Rockingham just five minutes' drive away, together with a sock which also had traces of Nicole's blood. Near the bodies detectives bagged a discarded hat which was later found to have hair and fibres which matched O.J.'s. And most compelling of all, there was a trail of bloody footprints leading away from the scene and bloodstains on the gate. The killer had evidently been wounded in the frenzied knife attack. When detectives called at O.J.'s home they noticed blood on a vehicle parked outside and a trail of blood from the car to the front door. Analysis proved that the blood on the glove found at O.J.'s home and the blood on the car were from three people, the two victims and O.J.

NOT INTERESTED

But O.J. couldn't be questioned. He had taken a flight to Chicago earlier that night and, when interviewed over the phone, appeared curiously uninterested in his ex-wife's death. On his return to LA the next day he was questioned by detectives, who commented on the fact that he had a bandage on his hand which he claimed was the result of having cut it accidentally on a glass in his hotel room.

He was allowed to remain at liberty for the next couple of days while the police concluded their examination of the crime scene, but on 15 June they lost patience with the star, who had gone into seclusion, and issued a warrant for his arrest. It was then that he attempted to evade capture during the now-famous slow-motion freeway chase which was televised live around the world.

It looked like the case against O. J. couldn't be lost. But it was, largely thanks to police failures. O.J. hired a dream team of top-drawer defence attorneys who raised serious doubts as to the validity of the evidence, which they intimated might have been planted by over-eager or even racist detectives to frame their man. They even managed to secure a recording on which Detective Mark Fuhrman was heard to refer to Simpson as a 'nigger' no fewer than forty-one times, which tainted his testimony and the physical evidence he had accumulated. But the defence didn't have to work too hard.

UNDERMINING THE CASE

On the night of the murder the police had failed to secure the scene, allowing numerous personnel to trample through the bloody footprints and carry crucial trace evidence from room to room and out of the house on the soles of their shoes. Video footage of the police walk-through of the scene shows investigators working the scene without protective overalls or gloves and one policeman is actually seen to drop a swab then wipe it clean with his hands. During the trial Detective Philip Vannatrer even proudly asserted that old-school experienced officers of his generation did not wear protective clothing and saw nothing wrong in handling evidence without gloves like a cop in a 1950s TV show.

The prosecution case was still further compromised by Vannatrer and his colleagues' insistence on going straight from the crime scene to O.J.'s home without changing their clothes or processing the evidence from the first location, which could have allowed

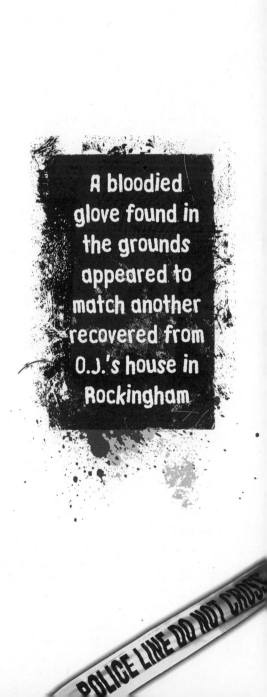

A bloodied glove found in the grounds appeared to match another recovered from O.J.'s house in Rockingham

POLICE LINE DO NOT CROSS

Demonstrating the fatal stab wound in court

transference of trace evidence from the crime scene to the second location.

And then there was the evidence which was captured on film by the police photographer, but which had not been logged in and could not be found in the archive. This included a bloody note seen in one particular shot near Nicole's head. It may have been irrelevant to the case, or it may have been crucial. We shall never know because it was presumably 'tidied away' with whatever else seemed like rubbish at the time and was lost. Incredibly, no photographs were taken inside the house, only of the immediate area where the bodies were found. So there is no record of any signs of a struggle or of any items that were later put back in their place.

ERROR UPON ERROR

More critically, the bodies of the victims were left as they lay for ten hours without being examined by a medical examiner, who would have been able to determine the time of death and recover vital trace evidence from the bodies. But after Nicole's body had been photographed someone had turned her over onto her back, eliminating the blood splatter that can be seen on her skin above her halter top in the official police photographs. It was the coroner's opinion that this splatter came from her assailant who had been injured in the attack, but no swabs were taken before she was turned. After she had been moved it was too late to do so. The coroner is also responsible for making a search of anything at the crime scene which might have a bearing on the cause and time of death. So a dish of melting ice cream in Nicole's house which the police ignored might have provided a vital clue as to the time of death, but no one considered it worth photographing.

CATALOGUE OF BLUNDERS

As if these errors were not enough to compromise the prosecution case, the police also failed to bag the hands of the deceased, they neglected to use a rape kit, and they did not examine or photograph the back gate, which was the likely exit point for the killer. It was only weeks later that blood was found there, prompting accusations that it had been planted, when it had probably been yet another crucial clue that had been overlooked. These errors were compounded after Nicole's body was removed to the morgue. Instead of being examined in detail, it was washed, thereby eliminating the last vestiges of trace evidence that might have given a clue to the identity of her killer. It was only two full days later that an autopsy was performed.

After a protracted nine-month trial O.J. was predictably found not guilty. The jury could have done nothing else, since the police errors cast more than 'reasonable doubt' on the proceedings. But in a subsequent civil case brought by the families of Nicole Simpson and Ronald Goldman the circumstantial evidence was deemed overwhelming. O.J. Simpson was found guilty and ordered to pay $33 million compensation to the bereaved families.

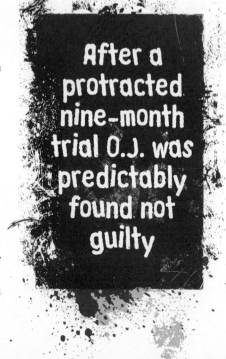

After a protracted nine-month trial O.J. was predictably found not guilty

Gangs, Mobs and Outlaws: Running with the Pack

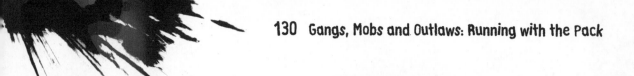

Al Capone

Al Capone, a.k.a. Scarface, is perhaps the most famous of all gangsters. His name sums up an era when organized crime looked set to take over America. This was the 1920s when Prohibition created a huge money-making industry under the control of criminal gangs, giving them unimaginable wealth. Nowhere were this wealth and power more obvious than in Chicago, where the mob's frontman was Al Capone. For many years, he appeared to be above the law, simply murdering his enemies while the police looked the other way. The legend of Scarface became known across the world, and such was his fame that he became the subject of many books and films.

Remarkably, more than half a century after his death, his name remains a byword for the urban gangster, still vividly remembered today while most of his fellow criminals are long forgotten.

The reason? Perhaps it is the mixture of calculation and sheer brutality that he embodied. Al Capone was both a conscientious book-keeper and a man capable of beating another human being to death with a baseball bat: in short, the ultimate gangster.

AN EQUAL OPPORTUNITIES GANGSTER

There was little in Al Capone's childhood to suggest such an outcome. He was born Alphonse Capone in New York on 17 January 1899, the fourth child of Gabriele and Teresina Capone, Italian immigrants from a small town near Naples who had arrived in New York five years earlier. The Capones were hard-working people, and better off than many of their fellow immigrants. Gabriele was a barber by trade and able to read and write: he got a job first as a grocer and then, once he had saved some money, he opened his own barbershop. Soon after Alphonse was born, the family was able to move out of the Italian ghetto where they had initially lived to a more prosperous multi-ethnic area. Growing up in such a neighbourhood was no doubt responsible for the fact that, later on, Capone was unusual among Italian gangsters for his lack of ethnic, or even racial, prejudices.

Al Capone did reasonably well at school until the age of fourteen, when he had a fight with a teacher. He was duly expelled from school and started to hang out on the streets, where he came into the orbit of local gangster John Torrio. Capone joined Torrio's outfit, the James Street Gang, and later went on to become part of the Five Points Gang, along with a childhood friend, and fellow future mob boss, 'Lucky' Luciano.

Torrio moved his operation to Chicago in 1909 and, for a time, Capone worked at regular jobs until Frankie Yale, one of Torrio's friends, offered Capone a job as

The classic look of Al Capone – a mobster who once appeared on the cover of Time *magazine*

bartender in the Harvard Tavern on Coney Island. While working there, Capone got involved in a dispute with a gangster named Frank Gallucio that ended with Capone getting cut three times across the face. These were the wounds that got him his well-known and feared nickname: Scarface.

THE RISE OF SCARFACE

Not long after this incident, Capone met a girl called Mae Coughlan from a middle-class Irish family. In 1918 they had a child, Alphonse Jr (known as Sonny). They married the following year. Once again, Al straightened out and got a job as a bookkeeper in Baltimore. Then, in November 1920, his father Gabriele died, which seemed to prompt Al to give up any pretence of living the straight life.

Capone moved to Chicago and hooked up with Johnny Torrio. The Chicago boss at that time was a man known as Big Jim Colosimo, whose main business was running brothels. Now that Prohibition had come into force, however, Torrio could see that the big money was in illicit liquor. Colosimo was not interested in pursuing this line of business. As far as Torrio and Capone were concerned, this meant that he was in the way. Torrio arranged alibis for himself and Capone, and hired his old friend Frankie Yale from New York to shoot Colosimo down in his own nightclub on 11 May 1920.

As a result of this takeover bid, Torrio was now the big man in the Chicago rackets, with Capone as his right-hand man. Over the next few years, their gang made huge profits through bootlegging, but they also made many enemies among rival mobsters, notably Dion O'Banion,

leader of the Irish North Side Gang. Once again, Torrio and Capone called upon the services of Frankie Yale, who shot O'Banion down in 1924. This inevitably provoked a backlash and, when Torrio himself was badly wounded in an assassination attempt the following year, he decided to give up the life of danger. He passed control of his businesses, which by then amounted to thousands of whorehouses, gambling joints and speakeasies, to his protégé Al Capone.

ST VALENTINE'S DAY MASSACRE

Despite being only twenty-five years old, Capone relished the new responsibility. He was an effective leader, able to build bridges with other gangs thanks to his lack of prejudice against working with Jewish or Irish gangsters. However, those who did try to challenge him paid very high penalties. One such vendetta was with an Irish gang led by Bugs Moran and culminated in the infamous St Valentine's Day Massacre.

Capone's plan was to lure Moran and his gang to a meeting where they expected to make a deal for some bootleg whiskey. Fake police would then show up, disarm the Moran gang and shoot them dead. Everything went according to plan: seven of the Moran gang were tricked by the fake officers, who lined them up against a wall and machine-gunned them, killing six on the spot. The only flaw was that Moran himself arrived late to the meet and thus escaped.

Capone was not personally involved in the massacre but soon after, when two of the gangsters used on that occasion, John Scalise and Albert Anselmi, were suspected

The Capone gang did not disband after Al Capone was jailed; it simply carried on as before under the leadership of the Fischetti brothers, the Guzik clan and Tony Accardo

of changing sides, Capone was very much present at their execution. The two men were invited to a grand banquet in their honour. At the end of the meal, Capone was presented with a gift-wrapped parcel containing a baseball bat. His bodyguards restrained the two men, and Capone used the bat to beat them both to death.

CAUGHT… FOR TAX EVASION

Such excesses could not carry on indefinitely. Up to this point, Capone had avoided

POLICE LINE DO NOT CROSS

Al Capone in custody – the only crime the prosecutors could pin on Capone was tax evasion

prosecution by paying off police and politicians alike. In the Chicago township of Cicero where he lived, he had his men elected to run the place. However, the FBI, now under the direction of the legendary Elliot Ness, had a new weapon that they were starting to use against gangsters: they charged them with tax evasion on their ill-gained funds. Eventually, with the help of informant Frank O'Hare, Ness managed to make a case against Capone. It took years of skirmishes between the two men, but in the end it was Ness and the FBI who won.

In 1931, Capone was convicted of several charges of tax evasion and sentenced to eleven years in prison. He spent much of this sentence in the notorious Alcatraz. By the time he was released in 1939, Capone was a broken man, his health – both physical and mental – ruined by jail and the effects of long-untreated syphilis. Al Capone retired to his Florida mansion, and died on 25 January 1947.

POLICE LINE DO NOT CROSS

George Kelly

George 'Machine Gun' Kelly was one of several celebrity gangsters active during the Prohibition era. An undistinguished man in early life, when he turned to crime he became famous, largely as a result of his wife Kathryn's relentless publicity campaign on his behalf. Kelly committed a series of flamboyant bank robberies before he went on to kidnap a millionaire. This action led to a national manhunt and his eventual capture. He died in 1954, while serving out a sentence of life imprisonment.

Kelly was born George Kelly Barnes on 18 July 1895 in Memphis, Tennessee.

Kelly committed flamboyant bank robberies before kidnapping a millionaire

Behind every great man... Kathryn Thorne was Kelly's unofficial public relations manager, building him a fearsome reputation as a highly skilled machine gunner

POLICE LINE DO NOT CROSS

Unlike most gangsters of the period, he was not tempted into a life of crime through growing up in poverty; on the contrary, his father was an insurance company executive and he came from a wealthy, middle-class family. As a child, Kelly was very fond of his mother, but did not get on with his father. During his teenage years, he found out that his father was having an affair and, when his mother died while he was in high school, he blamed his father for her death.

THE BOOTLEGGING TRADE

After graduating from high school, Kelly enrolled at Mississippi State University to study agriculture. He was not a particularly good student,

Kelly's trial was a high-profile one – and well guarded

and showed no interest in his work. When he met a girl called Geneva Ramsey and fell in love, he decided to quit university and marry her.

The couple went on to have two children, and Kelly had to support his new family. He worked as a cab driver in Memphis for a while, but his meagre earnings were not enough for the three of them, and Kelly soon began to look around for other opportunities. Before long, he met a local gangster and turned to crime, working in the bootlegging trade and changing his name so as not to bring shame on his respectable family.

Kelly was arrested several times as a result of his illegal activities, and each time his wife and other relatives had to bail him out. He began drinking heavily. To get him away from his underground cronies, the family moved to Kansas City, where for a short time Kelly went straight and worked in a grocery store, before his wife found out that he was stealing from the till. Realizing that he was incapable of staying in a straight job, his wife left him, and the couple later divorced.

Now on his own, Kelly stayed in Kansas City and began to build up a bootlegging business there. He gained a reputation in the trade, expanding his operations across several states, but in 1927 he was caught and arrested. The following year, he was sentenced to three years imprisonment for smuggling liquor into an Indian reservation. He then had to serve out another sentence for bootlegging before moving to Oklahoma City, where he met his future partner in crime.

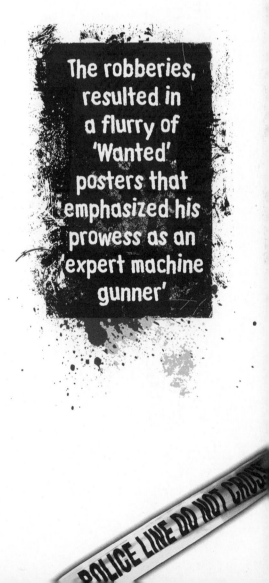

The robberies, resulted in a flurry of 'Wanted' posters that emphasized his prowess as an 'expert machine gunner'

POLICE LINE DO NOT CROSS

THE OUTLAW BRIDE – AND PR GIRL

Kathryn Thorne was the mistress of a bootlegger named Steve Anderson, but she was also a hardened criminal in her own right. She came from a family of outlaws: her mother was a bootlegger, her aunt a prostitute and several other members were known to police for robbery offences. Thorne was also a divorcee who had been married twice, and it was rumoured that she had shot her second husband dead for infidelity.

George Kelly immediately became enamoured of the worldly wise Kathryn Thorne, and the pair were married in 1930. From that time on, Kelly rose from being a small-time criminal to a well-known gangster, reaching a pinnacle of infamy when he became 'Public Enemy Number One'.

SHOOTING SOUVENIRS

Thorne bought her husband his first machine gun and encouraged him to practise shooting it, distributing the used cartridges to the denizens of underground drinking clubs as souvenirs from 'Machine Gun' Kelly. In this way, she built up a reputation for her husband as a cold-blooded killer and an expert gunman. Kelly went on to perform a series of bank robberies, resulting in a flurry of 'Wanted' posters that emphasized his prowess as an 'expert machine gunner'. The public was terrified, while Kelly was pleased to hit the headlines as America's most wanted gangster.

In July 1933, Kelly kidnapped a wealthy oil man, Charles Urschel. He demanded a ransom of $200,000. Once the money was delivered, Urschel was freed. A huge investigation was launched, aided by Urschel, who had carefully laid as many clues as he could during his ordeal. Kelly and his cronies were now on the run.

THE LAW CLOSES IN

The other members of the Kelly gang were soon arrested and charged as accomplices in the kidnap. Meanwhile, Kelly and his wife moved around from state to state, living a life of luxury on the ransom money. However, the police were steadily closing in. When the couple paid a visit to an old friend in Memphis, the FBI managed to catch up with them, surrounding the house and forcing their way in. It was the first major case solved by the FBI. Kelly, unarmed and terrified of being killed, was reported to have pleaded for mercy. The couple were arrested, tried and convicted. It was the first trial after the Lindbergh Law had been passed, which made kidnap a federal offence. They both received life sentences.

Initially, George Kelly was jailed at Leavenworth in Kansas, but while he was there he continually boasted about how he would escape from the prison. His threats were taken seriously, and in 1934 he was transferred to Alcatraz. There, he continued to boast, this time about crimes he had never committed, which irritated his fellow prisoners immensely. However, in most ways he served out his sentence as a model prisoner. In 1951, he was sent back to Leavenworth. Three years later, on 18 July – which happened to be his birthday – he died of a heart attack.

A huge investigation was launched... Kelly and his cronies were now on the run

POLICE LINE DO NOT

John Gotti

The final arrest of John Gotti marked the end of an era in organized crime. He was the last of the old-style Mafia bosses to become a household name. Gotti was the product of a media age in which fascination with the Mafia was at an all-time high, and the media was desperate to find a real-life counterpart to the godfathers of popular films. They eventually hit upon John Gotti, a well-dressed *capo* with a nice repertoire of catchy one-liners.

Gotti was born on 27 October 1940. He was the fifth of eleven children born to John Gotti Sr and his wife, Fannie. At the time of John's birth, the family lived in the poverty-stricken South Bronx. By the time he was ten, they managed to move to Sheepshead Bay

Every inch the old-style Mafia boss, Gotti rarely lost his composure, even when sentenced to a term in a prison with a notoriously harsh regime

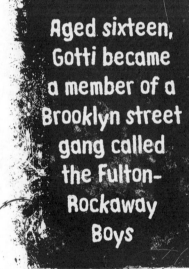

Aged sixteen, Gotti became a member of a Brooklyn street gang called the Fulton-Rockaway Boys

POLICE LINE DO NOT CROSS

POLICE LINE DO NOT CROSS

in Brooklyn, and then, a year or so later, to another Brooklyn neighbourhood, East New York.

THE FULTON-ROCKAWAY BOYS

While growing up, Gotti was drawn to the criminal lifestyle he saw around him. By the time he was twelve, he was running errands for local mobsters, forming a gang with his brothers Peter and Richard. John soon quit going to school and concentrated on getting into trouble instead. When he was fourteen, he crushed his toes while stealing a cement mixer and spent several months in hospital. He was released with a limp he would have for the rest of his life.

Aged sixteen, Gotti became a member of a Brooklyn street gang called the Fulton-Rockaway Boys, who prided themselves on being serious criminals. They stole cars and fenced stolen goods. Other members of the gang included two associates who would stay with Gotti through most of his career, Angelo Ruggiero and Wilfred 'Willie Boy' Johnson. Between 1957 and 1961, Gotti was arrested five times, but managed to avoid prison each time.

In 1960, when he was twenty, Gotti met Victoria Di Giorgio. They had their first child, Angela, a year later, and got married the following year on 6 March 1962. The couple remained together until Gotti died, and had five children, but, although long-lasting, the marriage proved to be a stormy one, with many fights and periods of separation.

The 'Teflon Don' possessed the silver tongue of a politician – perhaps a role he could have played had he not chosen a life of crime instead

CIGARETTES AND STOCKINGS

Following his marriage, Gotti briefly tried his hand at legitimate employment, working for a trucking company, before opting instead for a full-time life of crime. He served a brief jail sentence in 1963 when he was caught with Salvatore Ruggiero, Angelo's younger brother, in a stolen car. This was followed by another short jail sentence in 1966, this time for robbery. That same year, Gotti joined a Mafia gang operating out of a club in Queens. This gang was part of the Gambino family, controlled by Carlo Gambino and his underboss, Aniello Dellacroce.

Gotti's particular role in the organization was as a hijacker, specializing in stealing loads from John F. Kennedy airport. Several more arrests followed as Gotti was caught with truckloads of women's clothing and cigarettes. Eventually, he spent three years in the federal penitentiary in Lewisburg for hijacking. When he was released in January 1972, he immediately returned to the Bergin gang. Soon he became the effective *capo* of the crew, with the approval of Dellacroce. Times were changing and, despite the Mafia's previous policy of having nothing to do with selling drugs, it was becoming increasingly clear that there was big money to be made in this area – much more than in smuggling.

Gotti's next step up the ladder came as the result of a spate of kidnappings that broke out among Mafiosi during the early 1970s. In one incident, Carlo Gambino's nephew was kidnapped and murdered. A known kidnapper, James McBratney, was suspected. Soon

Gangster John Gotti was arrested five times, but managed to avoid prison each time

POLICE LINE DO NOT CROSS

afterwards, Gotti was one of three men who burst into a Staten Island diner where McBratney was enjoying a meal and gunned him down.

SHOOT-OUT AT THE STEAKHOUSE

Gotti was identified by witnesses, but the charge was bargained down to manslaughter. He served only two years for it. While Gotti was in prison, Carlo Gambino died, leaving another mobster named Paul Castellano in his place, while Dellacroce remained as the underboss.

> He acquired a series of nicknames. First he was called 'The Dapper Don' in honour of his sharp suits, then 'The Teflon Don'

Gotti became disenchanted with the leadership of the remote Castellano. He agitated for Dellacroce to take on the job instead, but Dellacroce, who was by now suffering from cancer, counselled Gotti to have patience. Meanwhile, in 1980, personal tragedy struck the Gotti family; a neighbour, John Favara, accidently ran over and killed the Gottis' 12-year-old son, Frank. Four months later, following a series of death threats, Favara was abducted by four men and never seen again, though rumours as to his fate abounded.

FBI surveillance of the Gambino family intensified during the 1980s, and tensions between rival leaders increased as a result. In 1985, Dellacroce finally died of cancer. Gotti was hoping to be made the new underboss by Castellano. When it became clear that Castellano intended to promote Thomas Bilotti instead, Gotti decided it was time to act. He assembled a team of hit men and, on 16 December 1985, Paul Castellano was assassinated as he left a Manhattan steakhouse. Afterwards, Gotti moved quickly to take his position at the head of the Gambino family.

THE TEFLON DON

Following this sensational murder, reminiscent of the old days of Mafia feuds, Gotti became a kind of alternative celebrity. Time and again the FBI would arrest Gotti on one charge or another, and time and again he would appear in court in an immaculately tailored suit and beat the rap. During this period, he acquired a series of nicknames. First he was called 'The Dapper Don' in honour of his sharp suits, then 'The Teflon Don'

in recognition of the FBI's seeming inability to lay a glove on him despite near-constant surveillance. Gotti became well known for conducting meetings while walking down the street or playing recordings of white noise to prevent any bugs from working. However, by now the FBI were locked in a battle they could not be seen to lose. In 1992, they once again brought racketeering charges against Gotti under the RICO legislation, and this time they found a weak point.

Gotti's underboss was a notoriously brutal mobster named Sammy 'The Bull' Gravano, a man believed to be responsible for at least nineteen murders. So desperate were the FBI to convict Gotti that they offered Gravano, a known killer, a virtual free pass in return for testifying against his boss. To secure the deal, they played tapes of Gotti making disparaging remarks about him to Gravano. A livid Gravano agreed to testify against his boss, making him one of the highest-ranking mobsters ever to turn informer.

THE DON GOES DOWN

Gravano's testimony was sufficient to see Gotti finally put behind bars. He was convicted on 2 April 1992 for fourteen counts of murder, conspiracy to commit murder, loan sharking, racketeering, obstruction of justice, illegal gambling and tax evasion. To punish this highly public criminal even more, he was sent to the federal penitentiary in Marion, Illinois, where he was kept in solitary confinement for twenty-three hours a day until his death from cancer on 10 June 2002. Sammy 'The Bull' Gravano, meanwhile, enjoys the safety of the witness protection programme to this day.

Lucky Luciano

One of the most influential Mafia bosses of the 20th century, 'Lucky' Luciano almost single-handedly transformed the world of organized crime from a few warring Italian families to a large number of affiliated ethnic groups running criminal activities on a grand scale. A vicious killer who was finally jailed for running one of the biggest prostitution rings of all time in the United States, he was also an intelligent and able businessman, and a patriotic American to boot. The contradictions of his life were such that, while serving a prison sentence for his crimes, he also helped the government in the war effort during the Second World War.

Lucky Luciano was born Salvatore Lucania in Lercara Friddi, a village near Corleone in Sicily. When he was ten years old, he moved with his family to the United States. He began his career of crime early, demanding that younger children playing on the streets pay him a cent a day to protect them from older ones. Children who refused to pay were given a sound thrashing. One of those who refused protection was the young Meyer Lansky, who put up a good fight when Luciano attacked him. Lansky went on in later years to become a top Mafia boss like Luciano, and the pair became good friends.

THROAT CUT

As a young man, Luciano joined a team of thugs known as the Five Points Gang, headed by John Torrio. Members of the gang were suspected by local police of being involved in many different crimes, including murder. Luciano specialized in pimping and in protection rackets; he also dealt heroin on the streets. It was not long before his ruthless spirit of enterprise attracted the attention of the most influential mobsters in New York, such as Vito Genovese and Frank Costello. He began working for them, and soon became a leading member of one of the biggest Mafia families in the United States, the Masserias, organizing prostitution, bootlegging, drug trafficking and other criminal activities.

At the end of the 1920s, Joe 'The Boss' Masseria became embroiled in

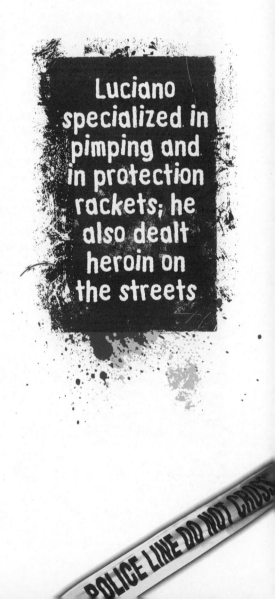

Luciano specialized in pimping and in protection rackets; he also dealt heroin on the streets

POLICE LINE DO NOT CROSS

a gang war with Salvatore Maranzano, leader of another important Italian mobster family. During this period, Luciano was captured by Maranzano's men as he waited for a shipment of drugs at the docks in New York. His mouth was taped shut and he was driven out to Staten Island. There, the gangsters cut his throat and threw him in a ditch, thinking that he was dying or dead. Amazingly, he survived, and was known by the nickname of 'Lucky' for the rest of his life.

DEAD MEN'S SHOES

The incident prompted Luciano to become even more ambitious. Already, he had broken with several of the traditional ways of doing business among the Mafia. For example, he associated openly with gangsters from other ethnic groups, an innovation to which his boss Masseria was deeply opposed. Luciano had close links with two major Jewish gangsters, Meyer Lansky and 'Bugsy' Siegel; later, this threesome was to form the National Crime Syndicate, with Luciano as the originator, Lansky as the brains and Siegel as the brawn.

For now, however, Luciano had to operate within the constraints of the old-time Mafia bosses. The only way to change the situation, he realized, was to kill off the top men. When Maranzano began to gain the upper hand in the turf war, he switched sides and, together with Siegel, arranged for Masseria's murder. Within six months, however, he

Surviving a murder attempt when young, Luciano was indeed lucky – dying of natural causes is a rare way for a Mafia mobster to go

was plotting against his new boss, Maranzano. Maranzano was duly dispatched with ruthless efficiency. Now, with both the big men out of the way, the field was clear for Luciano and his men to take the lead.

Luciano went on to head the Mafia and then to restructure the world of organized crime. Instead of continuing with the old gang wars, he divided up different areas of crime between the major families, including families who were not of Italian origin. He then developed a system where, when problems arose, he could balance the interests of all concerned. Luciano was one of the first Mafia bosses to realize the obvious fact that, at the end of the day, all criminals have one common interest: to make the maximum amount of money in the shortest time possible, whatever the means might be.

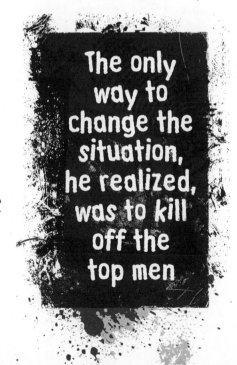

The only way to change the situation, he realized, was to kill off the top men

POLICE LINE DO NOT CROSS

Charles Floyd

Oklahoma's 'Pretty Boy' Floyd provides the link between the semi-legendary outlaws of the Old West – Jesse James, Wild Bill Hickok to name but two – and the gangsters of the early 20th century; Al Capone and Dutch Schulz, for example. Essentially, Pretty Boy Floyd was an outlaw who simply found cars more efficient than horses when it came to running from the law.

Charles Arthur Floyd was born in Bartow County, Georgia, on 3 February 1904, the fourth of eight children born to Walter Lee and Minnie Floyd, hard-working rural Baptists. In 1911, when Charles was seven, Walter Lee decided to move the family to Oklahoma, where he had heard there was work in the cotton fields. The family settled there in the Cookson Hills and became tenant farmers. Through immensely hard work they prospered. Walter eventually opened a general store in the town of Akins. At first Charles seemed to be one more hard-working member of the family, leaving school after the sixth grade to help out with the business.

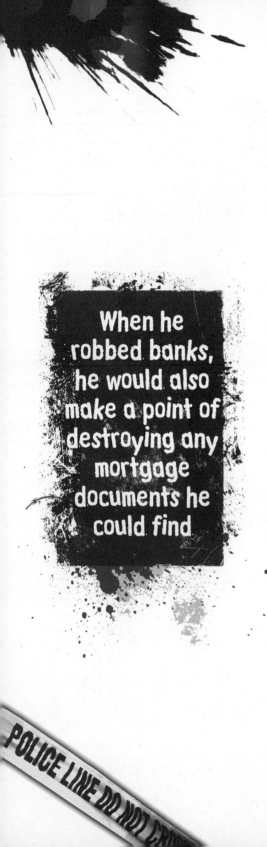

When he robbed banks, he would also make a point of destroying any mortgage documents he could find

A CHANGED MAN

All this changed in 1919, when Charles set off to the harvest fields of Kansas and Oklahoma to make some money. Working in the fields, he fell in with a rough crowd of drifters and vagabonds. When he returned he was a changed man. He started getting into fights and hanging around the local pool hall. He then met his wife, Ruby, and appeared to go straight for a while, but it was not to last. The couple set up home and had a baby, Charles Dempsey Floyd, and Charles Sr went back to working in the fields, but with an increasing sense of dissatisfaction. He met a petty criminal called John Hilderbrand, who told him how he had successfully robbed a manufacturing company in St Louis of $1,900. Hilderbrand encouraged Charles to join him in carrying out future raids. In August 1925, Charles decided to give it a try. He left home and carried out several successful robberies.

Unfortunately, the duo then made the classic mistake of inexperienced crooks. They bought an expensive car, a new Studebaker, and cruised around the streets of Fort Smith, Arkansas. This soon attracted the suspicion of the police and, before long, Charles was arrested, found guilty of a variety of robberies and sentenced to three years in prison. At his trial the clerk to the court described Charles as 'a mere boy – a pretty boy with apple cheeks' – and a nickname was born, no matter that Charles himself absolutely hated it.

RESTROOM ESCAPE

In prison Charles met many more experienced criminals, who urged him to come in with them when he was released. At first Charles wavered, but when he learned that his wife had divorced him, his mind was made up. On release he headed straight for Kansas City, then a mecca for criminals of all descriptions. He stayed in a boarding house popular with those on the wrong side of the law, where he met Beulah 'Juanita' Baird, who became his girlfriend. Before long he had hooked up with the

POLICE LINE DO NOT CR

Pretty Boy Floyd's apple cheeks belied a criminal mind, but his destruction of banks' paperwork did mean he had more of a claim to the Robin Hood legend than most

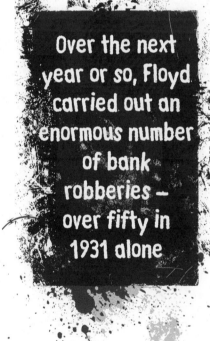

Over the next year or so, Floyd carried out an enormous number of bank robberies — over fifty in 1931 alone

Jim Bradley Gang and joined them in a series of raids on banks across Ohio.

At first they were successful, but on 8 March 1930, their luck ran out and they were arrested by the cops in Akron, Ohio, following a gun battle. This time

Floyd was sentenced to fifteen years in prison. However, en route to the penitentiary at Columbus, he performed one of the stunts that were to make his name. During a pit-stop on the journey, Floyd talked his guards into uncuffing

POLICE LINE DO NOT CROSS

him so that he could use the restroom. He smashed the window, jumped out and escaped, then managed to make it all the way back to Kansas City.

There he found a new partner, William Miller (a.k.a. Billy the Baby Face Killer). The two of them, along with Juanita, set off to rob banks across the east and south. Once again, though, Floyd met his comeuppance in Ohio. The law caught up with them and there was a shoot-out. Miller was killed and Juanita injured, but Pretty Boy Floyd himself again managed to escape.

FOLK HERO

He returned to the Cookson Hills, where folk had little love for the law and would protect him. Over the next year or so, Floyd carried out an enormous number of bank robberies – over fifty in 1931 alone. These were the exploits that made him a folk hero, because when he robbed banks, he would also make a point of destroying any mortgage documents he could find. This made him very popular with local farmers as, during these hard Depression years, the banks were busily foreclosing on mortgages.

During this time, Floyd also reunited himself with his wife and son. She had remarried but fell in love with Floyd once more, and left her husband to live as a family with Floyd in Fort Smith, Arkansas, where they adopted the alias of Mr and Mrs Charles Douglas.

This was to be an unusually happy and contented period in Floyd's life. However, after only six months, Ruby suggested that they move to Tulsa, Oklahoma, and there they were turned over to the police by informants eager

for the reward money placed on Floyd's head. Once again, however, Floyd managed to escape the arm of the law by the narrowest of margins. He returned to the hills and soon became confident enough to give an interview to a reporter, one that helped to ensure that Pretty Boy Floyd would become a legend.

FBI PURSUIT

In 1933, Floyd decided to get back into big-time crime and headed for Kansas City with his new crime partner, Adam Richetti. While he was there, on 17 June 1933, an incident known as the Kansas City Massacre took place. This was a gun battle between mobsters and the FBI, in which several FBI agents were shot dead. It is very doubtful that Floyd was actually there, but the FBI chief J. Edgar Hoover claimed that he had been, and from this point on Floyd was a major target for the FBI.

He fled to Buffalo, New York. In October 1934, following the death of John Dillinger, Floyd was officially named 'Public Enemy Number One'. The FBI agent who shot Dillinger, Melvin Purvis, was set on his trail.

Floyd decided to flee to Mexico. On the way there, passing through Ohio on 18 October, his car crashed into a ditch. The police stumbled on the car and Floyd fled on foot into a nearby forest. Purvis was notified immediately and FBI agents combed the area. After four days on the run, Purvis finally tracked Floyd down and shot him dead as he tried to escape. After his death, Pretty Boy Floyd's body was shipped to the Cookson Hills where more than 20,000 people attended his funeral.

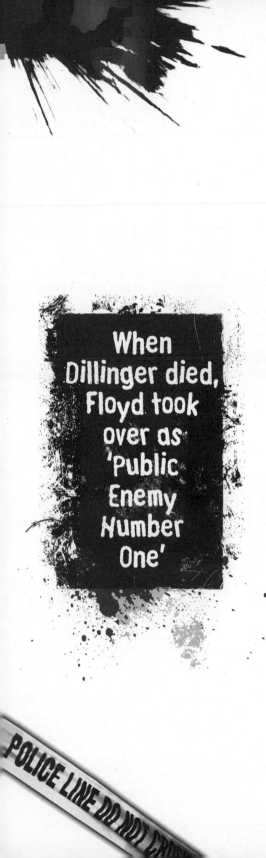

When Dillinger died, Floyd took over as 'Public Enemy Number One'

POLICE LINE DO NOT CROSS

The Kray Twins

The Kray Twins masterminded the world of organized crime in London's East End during the 1960s. Their fearsome reputation for ruthless violence protected them from the law for many years, but in the end they were arrested, convicted of murder and sentenced to life imprisonment. Both of them later died while serving their sentences. Although the twins were both vicious criminals, they have often been depicted as 'rough diamonds', essentially good-hearted cockney characters who kept a certain degree of law and order in the East End underworld – but it was their law and their order. The final demise of their reign of terror coincided with the fragmenting of the close-knit, colourful East End community at the end of the 1960s, which perhaps explains why these legendary and ruthless villains have been sentimentalized to such a degree by the popular media, both in Britain and internationally.

Ronnie and Reggie, with their beloved mum, Violet

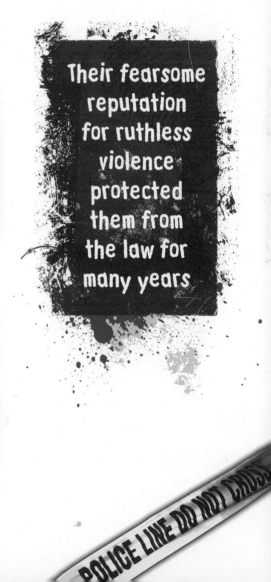

Their fearsome reputation for ruthless violence protected them from the law for many years

POLICE LINE DO NOT CROSS

DODGING THE DRAFT

Ronald and Reginald, or Ronnie and Reggie as they were known, were born in 1933. Their father, Charlie, was seldom at home, but travelled the country as a trader, knocking at people's doors to buy and sell goods. Although he was a hard drinker and gambler, he earned a good living, and made sure that his family lived well. His wife, Violet, and his children were always comfortably housed, well clothed and well fed, and the children were surrounded by a close network of relatives and neighbours. As well as the twin boys Ronnie and Reggie, there was an older brother, Charlie, who often took on the responsibility for his younger brothers in the absence of their father.

When Charlie Snr was called up to fight in the Second World War, he repeatedly dodged the draft, which meant that military police often called at his home to find him. This situation gave the brothers a lifelong hatred of authority that was later to become a hallmark of their criminal behaviour.

ARMED ROBBERIES AND ARSON ATTACKS

- In their early days at school, both twins were co-operative pupils. Encouraged by their grandfather, Jimmy 'Cannonball' Lee, they took up amateur boxing and did well at it. However, the pastime spurred them to fight constantly on the streets, and they became known as notorious bullies among the youth of the East End. In 1951, the pair were called up for state military training, or National Service as it was called, but like their father, they were unwilling to become soldiers. They both escaped from army camp several times,

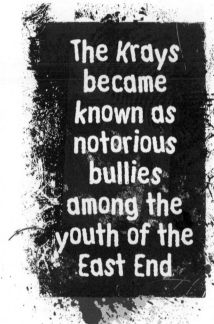

The Krays became known as notorious bullies among the youth of the East End

and eventually ended up in military prison for assaulting a police officer who noticed that they were on the run and tried to arrest them. They were imprisoned for the assault, but behaved so badly that eventually they were given a dishonourable discharge from the army instead.

As a result of their anti-social behaviour, the twins now had few career options. They bought a nightclub in Bethnal Green, in the East End, and from there ran a variety of criminal enterprises, including protection rackets, armed robberies and arson attacks for insurance claims. The operation expanded quickly, and more gang members were brought in. However, as it transpired later during their trial, their empire could have been much bigger and more efficient had they not argued with each other constantly.

A REIGN OF TERROR

Even so, through their many nefarious activities the Krays became rich, and went on to acquire several more nightclubs. The clubs became part of the newly emerging 'swinging London' scene of the 1960s. Ronnie in particular enjoyed having his photo taken with celebrities of the day, and in this way the twins started to become famous within the East End and beyond. As a homosexual, Ronnie made friends with several high-profile figures of the day, including Lord Boothby, a high-ranking Conservative, who was the centre of a scandal at that time when a tabloid paper named him as homosexual.

As the Krays' fame and fortune increased, so did their criminal activities.

The picture of a close-knit family – Reggie, Charles Jr and Ronnie Kray

POLICE LINE DO NOT CRO

However, it was difficult for the police to persuade witnesses to testify against the brothers, because of their increasing reputation for violence. Ronnie in particular was feared by everyone in the East End. He was by this time suffering from mental illness, and was brutally savage in his attacks on rival gangsters, informers and others. It was only when the pair started to turn on their own followers that the law was at last able to catch up with them.

STABBED TO DEATH

In 1967, Reggie killed a member of the Kray gang, Jack 'The Hat' McVitie, so called because he always wore a hat to cover a bald patch in the middle of his head. A minor player in the Krays' gang, McVitie was a seedy drunkard who often criticized the twins, disobeyed orders and generally refused to be intimidated by his bosses. To punish him, members of the gang lured him to a house in the East End, where they stabbed him to death.

Inspector Leonard 'Nipper' Read of Scotland Yard had been trying to bring down the Kray twins for several years, but only now did he begin to obtain incriminating statements from witnesses about the brothers' activities. In 1968, Scotland Yard managed to build up enough evidence to arrest the twins and several important members of 'The Firm', as their gang was known. As the police had hoped, once the Krays and their henchmen were in custody, many more witnesses were ready to come forward to testify against them.

Savile Row-suited London gangsters Ronnie and Reggie Kray walking along an East End street, London, 1965

PSYCHOTIC CRUELTY

After a long trial at the Old Bailey in London, the twins were both convicted of murder and given life sentences. Several other men from 'The Firm' were also found guilty of murder: John 'Ian' Barrie, Tony Lambrianou, Christopher Lambrianou and Ronnie Bender. The Krays' elder brother Charlie and two other men were found guilty of the lesser crime of being accessories to the murder of Jack McVitie.

During the trial, the psychotic cruelty of the twins came to light. As well as the murder of McVitie, Ronnie had shot dead a man named George Cornell at the Blind Beggar public house in the East End, in full view of all the customers, for calling him 'a fat poof'. (No witnesses to this murder ever came forward until the twins were in custody, so terrified were they of the potential consequences.) His brother Reggie was also shown to be an extremely violent man, though most often committing his crimes as a result of Ronnie's influence. In the McVitie murder, Reggie had repeatedly stabbed the victim in the face, neck and stomach, while being urged on by Ronnie, who was holding the victim down.

THE DEATH OF THE KRAYS

Ronald Kray died in 1995 in a mental institution, having been certified insane. Reginald Kray was let out of prison in 2002 on compassionate grounds because he had terminal cancer, but he was to die in the same year. Thus the criminal career of the Kray twins, once feared throughout the London underworld, finally came to an ignominious end.

It was difficult for the police to get witnesses to testify against the brothers

POLICE LINE DO NOT CROSS

John Dillinger

The bank robber John Dillinger was the original 'Public Enemy Number One', the first man to be branded by the FBI as America's most dangerous criminal. However, while the state regarded him as a menace, there were many who saw him as a hero, a latter-day Robin Hood. This dual reputation was a result of the times in which he lived. In the early 1930s, the United States was going through the Depression. Many banks had gone bust, taking people's hard-earned savings with them. Others were busy foreclosing on small debtors and taking their houses. People no longer trusted the banking system and when outlaws robbed the banks, many found it hard to condemn the criminals.

CELEBRITY CULTURE

Furthermore, the golden age of mass communications had dawned. Radio and newsreels transported stories around the States in a flash. One side-effect of this was the beginning of the culture of celebrity. John Dillinger was among the first of the celebrity criminals, his exploits followed as keenly as those of any Hollywood film star.

John Herbert Dillinger was born in Indianapolis, Indiana, on 22 June 1903 and grew up in the middle-class Oak Hill neighbourhood. His father, John Wilson Dillinger, was a hard-working grocer. His mother died of a stroke when he was only three years old. His 16-year-old sister Audrey took over the running of the family for a while, and later John Sr remarried. Much of John's upbringing, however, was left to his father, who would alternate between being a strict disciplinarian and spoiling his son rotten with expensive toys.

GANG RAPE

This confusing combination may well have been a factor in John Jr growing up to be a difficult, rebellious child. He formed his own gang of local kids, known as the Dirty Dozen. They stole coal from passing freight trains and got into trouble. A more dangerous side to the young Dillinger's nature emerged when he and another boy tied a friend down in a nearby wood mill and turned on the circular saw. Dillinger stopped the saw only when it was close to cutting into his friend's body. Aged thirteen, Dillinger and some friends then went on to gang-rape a local girl.

Dillinger left school aged sixteen and got a job as a mechanic, leading a wild lifestyle when he was not at work. His father had tried hard to make him toe the line. Now he thought it was time for drastic action: he sold up and moved the whole family to a farm near Mooresville, Indiana. However, his son reacted no better to rural life than he had to the city and soon got into trouble again.

Dillinger was arrested for stealing a car and decided to avoid prosecution by joining the navy. This only lasted a matter of months, however, before he deserted his ship when it docked in Boston. Returning to Mooresville, he married 16-year-old Beryl Hovius in 1924. He then became friends with

Dillinger's court case was followed by millions of Americans as it was reported on the new and immensely popular invention: the radio

> Dillinger formed his own gang of local kids, aka the Dirty Dozen, who stole from freight trains

a man named Ed Singleton, the town pool shark. Together they tried to rob a Mooresville grocer, but were caught in the act. Singleton pleaded not guilty, stood trial and was sentenced to two years. Dillinger, following his father's advice, confessed and ended up being sentenced to 10–20 years in the Indiana State Prison. The harshness of the sentence seems to have turned Dillinger against society once and for all.

ESCAPE AND CAPTURE

While inside, Dillinger made repeated attempts to escape. He also met up with several more experienced criminals who would have a big influence on his subsequent career. Chief among them were two bank robbers, Harry Pierpoint and Homer Van Meter. Much of their time was spent discussing means of escape. They found a corrupt guard: all they needed was for someone on the outside to bribe the guard to bring some guns into the prison.

The chance came when Dillinger was suddenly and unexpectedly paroled ahead of time on 10 May 1933, the reason being that his stepmother was desperately ill. On the outside, Dillinger laid plans to spring his friends from jail. However, a few days before the planned jailbreak, he robbed a bank in Bluffton, Ohio. He was arrested and sent back to jail in Lima, Ohio, to await trial.

While he was in jail the police searched him and found a document that seemed to be a plan for a prison break. Dillinger denied it and, before the police could get to the bottom of it, eight of Dillinger's friends escaped from

John Dillinger, shown here under heavy police escort, en route to Indiana by air, where he was wanted to answer charges of murdering a policeman in a hold-up

POLICE LINE DO NOT CROSS

the Indiana State Prison, using the guns that had been smuggled into their cells. During their escape, they shot two guards. On 12 October, three of the escaped prisoners repaid the favour and busted Dillinger out of prison, shooting a sheriff in the process.

Now the Dillinger gang swung into action with a vengeance. They pulled several bank robberies. They raided the police arsenals at Auburn, Indiana, and Peru, Indiana, stealing several machine guns, rifles, ammunition and bulletproof vests. Their robberies became ever more high-profile. Then, during a raid on a Chicago bank that December, a police officer was killed. Every cop in the country was now on the lookout for the Dillinger gang, but they had plenty of money and headed to Florida for Christmas and New Year.

WEAPONS ARSENAL

Next, the gangsters decided to head west to Tucson, Arizona. On the way, however, Dillinger could not resist robbing a bank in Gary, Indiana. This time Dillinger himself shot and killed a policeman as he made his getaway. When they arrived in Tucson, the gang found that they were not as anonymous as they had hoped. A local fireman identified them and soon they were arrested. They were found in possession of three Thompson submachine guns, two Winchester rifles mounted as machine guns, five bulletproof vests and the vast sum of more than $25,000 in cash, part of their ill-gotten gains from the Chicago robbery.

Dillinger was taken back east to the county jail in Crown Point, Indiana, to await trial for the murder of the police officer. The jail was said to be 'escape proof'. However, on 3 March 1934, Dillinger demonstrated that, as long as it has human beings running it, no jail is truly escape proof. He made a replica gun out of wood, then coloured it black with boot polish. He then used the replica gun to force a prison officer to give him a real gun. With the help of another inmate, he took several hostages and drove out of the prison in the governor's own car.

This sensational sting made Dillinger an even bigger hero in the public eye. It also made J. Edgar Hoover's newly formed FBI ever more determined to catch him. A nationwide manhunt began. Pierpoint had been arrested in Tucson and subsequently executed. However, Van Meter was still on the loose and Dillinger teamed up with him. They formed a new gang featuring the murderous talents of Lester Gillis a.k.a. Baby Face Nelson, a man never happier than with a machine gun in his hand. They continued where the old gang had left off, robbing a series of banks, and engaging in another shoot-out with the FBI, this time in St Paul, Minnesota.

THE GAME IS UP

Following the shoot-out, in which Dillinger was wounded, the gang went on the run again. They robbed a police station of guns and bulletproof vests before heading to a resort lodge called Little Bohemia, near Rhinelander, Wisconsin, where they planned to hide out for a while. However, the FBI received a tip-off and arrived en masse at Little Bohemia. Once again, it looked

Dillinger demonstrated that, as long as human beings run it, no jail is truly escape-proof

POLICE LINE DO NOT CROSS

A relaxed John Dillinger in prison, surrounded by people eager to appear in a photograph with him. The gangster's celebrity was never in doubt

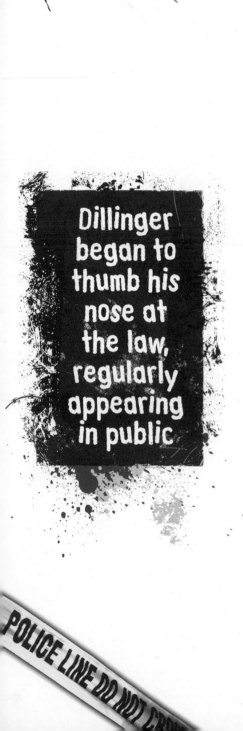

Dillinger began to thumb his nose at the law, regularly appearing in public

as if the game was up for Dillinger. However, it all went disastrously wrong. The FBI killed an innocent bystander, Baby Face Nelson killed an FBI agent and all the gangsters got away.

Dillinger's fame was now at its zenith. Perhaps beginning to believe his own publicity, he returned to Chicago, had some minor plastic surgery and began to thumb his nose at the law, regularly appearing in public to watch the Chicago Cubs play baseball, or to visit nightclubs. Finally, however, he fell victim not to FBI ingenuity but to the greed of his

fellow criminal. A brothel-keeper named Anna Sage, a friend of Dillinger's new girlfriend Polly Hamilton, sold him out.

On the night of Sunday, 22 July, FBI agents were waiting as Dillinger, with Sage and Hamilton on either side, walked out of a theatre. Dillinger quickly realized what was happening and grabbed a pistol from his right trouser pocket as he ran towards the alley. Five shots were fired from the guns of three FBI agents. Three of the shots hit Dillinger and he fell face down on the pavement, dead at last.

POLICE LINE DO NOT CROSS

Bonnie and Clyde

Bonnie Parker and Clyde Barrow were among the first celebrity criminals of the 20th century. During the years of the Depression in the 1930s, they shocked America with a series of murders, kidnaps, bank robberies and hold-ups, leaving a trail of devastation wherever they went. The pair are known to have committed at least thirteen murders during their career. Barrow was renowned as a cold-blooded killer, though some allege that Parker herself was not, and that she left her lover to do the dirty work. However, the truth will never be known, because Bonnie and Clyde weren't taken alive. After being hotly pursued by police for several years, they finally died in an ambush when their car was pumped full of bullets.

LOVE TATTOO

Bonnie Parker was born in Rowena, Texas, in 1910. At sixteen, she married a man named Ray Thornton. The young woman was madly in love with Thornton and had two intertwined hearts with both their names tattooed on the inside of her thigh. However, shortly after they were married, Thornton received a long prison sentence for murder. With her husband incarcerated for the foreseeable future, Parker was forced to take a waitressing job and wait for him. She did not wait very long.

Clyde Barrow was a year older than Bonnie, and had grown up on a farm in Telico, Texas. He was one of many children in a large, poverty-stricken family. In 1926, he was arrested for

Publicity-loving Bonnie and Clyde posing with the tools of their trade – guns and a getaway car

POLICE LINE DO NOT CROSS

car theft, but continued his life of crime, committing a string of robberies in the Dallas area. Four years later, by now a hardened criminal, he met Bonnie. However, not long after their meeting, Clyde was jailed. He made an escape, helped by Bonnie, but was apprehended after only a week, and remained in jail for the following two years.

THE GANG IS FORMED

When Clyde got out of jail, he and Bonnie teamed up and stole a car in Texas. A chase ensued, and this time it was Bonnie who was arrested and sent to jail. Clyde waited for her – her sentence was only a few months – and when she was released, the pair began their career of crime in earnest. They formed a group of like-minded criminals around them, initially travelling with a young gunman named Raymond Hamilton, who then dropped out and was replaced by a man called William Daniel Jones. The gang also included Clyde's brother Ivan, known as

Buck, and Buck's wife Blanche. The group became known as the Barrow Gang, and became notorious for a series of murders, kidnaps, armed robberies, burglaries and car thefts around the country.

By 1933, police were hot on the trail of the gang, having stumbled across a piece of evidence that revealed to them who the culprits were. The Bureau of Investigation, which later became the FBI, had been notified of a Ford automobile stolen in Illinois and abandoned at Pawhuska, Florida. The search of the car netted a medicine bottle and, when special agents called at the drugstore where it was bought, the prescription was found to have been filled in by a relative of Clyde Barrow. After further investigation, it became clear that the occupants of the stolen car had been Bonnie, Clyde and Clyde's brother. A warrant was issued for their arrest, and the hunt began in earnest.

HUNTING DOWN THE KILLERS

On 29 July 1933, police officers caught up with the outlaws in Iowa. During the subsequent shoot-out, Buck was killed and Blanche was arrested. A few months later, William Daniel Jones was captured, this time in Houston, Texas. Undeterred by danger, Bonnie and Clyde carried on by themselves. By this time, they were well known to the public. The Barrow Gang's cavalier attitude towards killing their victims had struck fear into the hearts of people, and their crimes had been reported in the most sensational terms in the national press.

A glamorous Bonnie – she had an addiction to bad men and fast living that was to prove her downfall

Clyde Barrow – a sharp-suited and ruthless sharpshooter

Bonnie had had a poem, 'The Story of Bonnie and Clyde', published in several newspapers

Bonnie and Clyde's flamboyant reputation had also been enhanced by various publicity stunts. The Ford Motor Company had advertised their automobiles with a letter signed 'Clyde Champion Barrow', alleged to have been written by the gangster. In it, Barrow praised Ford cars as 'dandy'. In addition, Bonnie had had a poem called 'The Story of Bonnie and Clyde' published in several popular newspapers, showing her to be quite a talented wordsmith.

On 22 November 1933, the police set a trap for the couple in Grand Prairie, Texas. However, Bonnie and Clyde managed to escape, holding up and stealing a passing car. They later abandoned it in Oklahoma. The following year, in January, they

POLICE LINE DO NOT CROSS

Bonnie and Clyde's days were numbered as soon as they became killers in earnest. In 1934 they shot two highway patrolmen, seemingly in cold blood

The increased efforts to apprehend the pair paid off, and the trail grew hot when an FBI agent found out that they had been visiting the home of the Methvin family in a remote area of Louisiana. Henry Methvin was one of the prisoners whom Bonnie and Clyde had helped to escape from the Texas jail. Police were tipped off that the pair had held a party in Black Lake, Louisiana, on 21 May and were due to return two days later.

AMBUSHED

On the morning of 23 May, a posse of police officers hid in the bushes on the highway near Sailes, Bienville Parish, Lousiana, and managed to ambush the outlaws. In early daylight, the car appeared and, before it could drive away, the police opened fire. They took no chances, and fired round after round of bullets into the car, which became spattered with holes. The couple, who were riding in the front, died instantly.

Despite the fact that Bonnie and Clyde were responsible for more than a dozen murders, and that Clyde was known to be a highly violent man, their glamorous reputation lived on for many years. Several movies were made about their lives, including *You Only Live Once* (1937), *The Bonnie Parker Story* (1958) and – most memorably – *Bonnie and Clyde* (1967), directed by Arthur Penn and starring Warren Beatty and Faye Dunaway. Despite the deaths they caused and the havoc they wreaked, their spirited attempt to break away from poverty and live a free life outside the conventions of society continues to hold a romantic appeal.

helped five prisoners make a daring escape from a jail in Waldo, Texas. During the escape, two prison guards were shot.

COLD-BLOODED MURDER

In 1934, the pair hit the headlines once more when they killed two young highway patrolmen in Texas before the officers could reach for their guns. Five days later came the news of another police officer killed in Oklahoma. Not long after, Bonnie and Clyde abducted and wounded a police chief. By this time, the law enforcement authorities were absolutely determined to catch the killers, posting 'wanted' signs all over the country, and distributing the outlaws' photographs, fingerprints and other data to all their officers.

Final ride – the bullet-riddled car of Bonnie and Clyde

POLICE LINE DO NOT CROSS

Ned Kelly

Ned Kelly is perhaps the most famous folk hero of Australia. A bushranger, he rose from poverty during the late 19th century to become a thorn in the side of the police. His career of crime, and his letters to the press explaining his actions, drew the general public's attention to the authorities' persecution of the country's poorest farming families, who were trying to scratch a living in the harsh conditions of the Australian outback at the time.

Kelly was born near Melbourne in Beveridge, Victoria, in 1854. His parents, John and Ellen, were Irish immigrants; his father was an ex-convict, now doing his best to go straight. Ned was the eldest boy, and the third of eight children. As a child, he once saved a schoolmate from drowning, and for his bravery he was awarded a green sash, which he later proudly wore under his armour when he clashed with police.

THE OUTLAW CLAN

When Ned was twelve years old, his father died, and the family moved to Glenrowan in Victoria, which today is known as 'Kelly Country'. Ned was forced to leave school to provide for his large family. The family became 'selectors', landless farmers who were allowed to live on small, often barren areas of land set aside by the government. The idea was that the selectors could improve the property and buy the land bit by bit, but inevitably, these families were too poor to make the necessary improvements, and often the land was taken back from them. Faced with ruin,

the selectors sometimes took to stealing livestock from richer farmers, and then escaping into the bush and living as 'bushrangers' – bandits and cattle rustlers.

As the 12-year-old head of the family, Ned was faced with an impossible task. He did his best, struggling to earn a living in the harsh weather conditions of the country. As well as the poverty, the Kelly family had to endure persecution from the police, because their mother, Ellen Quinn, came from an extended family of outlaws that had a reputation in the area. The Kellys were constantly being charged with one offence or another, although often when the cases came to court the charges did not stick.

THE BATTLE OF STRINGY BARK CREEK

At the age of fourteen, Ned was arrested for assaulting a pig farmer, but found not guilty. The following year, he was again arrested for assault, and this time he was sentenced to six months' hard labour. After he was released, he was arrested again for being in possession of a stolen horse, although it seems that he did not know the horse was stolen. This time, he was sentenced to three years in prison.

In 1878, a policeman, Constable Alexander Fitzpatrick, assaulted Kelly's sister, Ellen, at the family's home. Fitzpatrick then accused Kelly of trying to murder him. Kelly fled with his brother Dan into the bush. Some months later, they and their friends Joe Byrne and Steve Hart came across police camped at a place called Stringy Bark Creek. A fight ensued and, during the course of it, Kelly shot dead three policemen. From that time on, Kelly was a fully fledged outlaw,

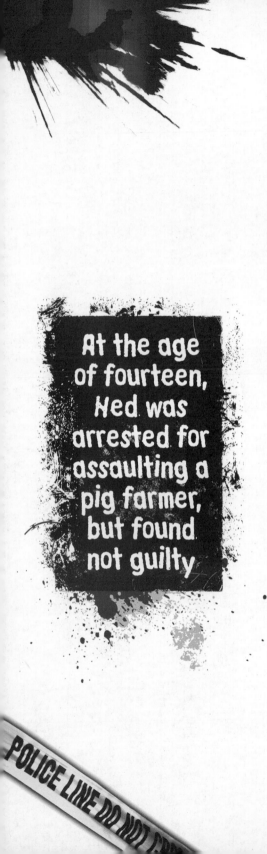

At the age of fourteen, Ned was arrested for assaulting a pig farmer, but found not guilty

Ned Kelly was Australia's best-known outlaw. This picture was taken the day before he was hanged at the Old Melbourne Jail, in November 1880, aged just twenty-five years

As a child, Ned saved a schoolmate from drowning, and for his bravery was awarded a green sash

POLICE LINE DO NOT CROSS

constantly on the run. Police put up a huge reward for his capture, but the Kelly Gang, as they had become known, had many friends in the area, and nobody stooped to turning them in.

HOME-MADE ARMOUR
In 1879, having run short of funds, Kelly robbed a bank at Euroa. The same year, he also committed a bank robbery at Jerilderie. He then composed a long letter to the press, which became known as the 'Jerilderie Letter'. It set out his views on the police and the way they had treated his family, and listed the way in which Protestant police ill-treated Catholic families in Australia. It also predicted uprisings in Australia, Ireland and the United States against the unjust persecution that he felt the Catholics had suffered at the hands of the authorities.

In 1880, Kelly and his men came back to Glenrowan, bringing armour that they had fashioned themselves. The armour had been made out of various agricultural machinery parts, and weighed about 36 kg (80 lb) per suit. The gang held about sixty hostages prisoner in a local inn, and then attempted to derail a police train. The plan was foiled by a hostage, schoolmaster Thomas Curnow, who stood on the rails waving a red scarf and holding a lighted candle to warn away the train.

Ned Kelly's infamous armour was made from beaten-out farm implements

AN ALMIGHTY SHOOT-OUT
When police caught up with the Kelly Gang at Glenrowan, there was an almighty shoot-out, in which Kelly himself was shot many times in the legs, the only part of him not protected by his body armour. Other gang members, namely Dan Kelly, Joe Byrne and Steve Hart, died at the inn. Ned managed to survive his injuries long enough to stand trial, and was later sentenced to death. A petition was signed by over 30,000 people, asking for his sentence to be repealed, but to no avail. The flamboyant Ned Kelly was hanged on 11 November 1880, at the age of twenty-five.

During his life, Kelly had developed a reputation as a polite man who treated his neighbours well. The hounding of his family by the police had attracted a great deal of sympathy from the public. The outcry that accompanied his hanging eventually caused the authorities to launch an enquiry, and as a result all the police officers connected with the case were either dismissed or demoted.

After his death, Kelly became a folk hero in his native land, and eventually around the world. Peter Carey's novel, *The True History of the Kelly Gang*, was published in 2000 to great acclaim.

FREEDOM FIGHTER... OR COMMON CRIMINAL?
Today, Kelly is a controversial figure. Some see him as a common criminal who robbed and murdered for his own gain; but to others, he is a romantic figure who embodied the Australian settlers' values of self-reliance, independence and freedom from persecution in a land of opportunity.

A mock-up of the Kelly Gang's last stand still draws crowds of interested tourists each year, proving the enduring appeal of this gang of Australian desperadoes

POLICE LINE DO NOT CROSS

Fraudsters and Spies: White-Collar Crime

Frank Abagnale

Frank Abagnale Jr is one of the most outrageous conmen of all time. During his career of crime, he impersonated a Pan Am pilot and flew around the world, enjoying the high life, before posing as a paediatrician and finding a senior job in a Georgia hospital. As if that were not enough, he then found employment as a bogus lawyer in the office of the state attorney general, before going on to claim he had a degree in sociology and become a university lecturer. Yet, amazingly, Abagnale was in fact a high-school dropout with no qualifications whatsoever to his name; and even more unbelievably, all this took place before he was twenty-one years of age. However, he did end up with a high degree of knowledge in one particular field: today, he is an expert on counterfeiting.

Frank Abagnale Jr was born in 1948. His early family life was uncomplicated, but when he was a teenager, his parents divorced. He took to spending money on his father's credit cards, running up huge bills as he tried to impress young women with his lavish lifestyle. His father, who ran a stationery store, was kind and patient with his son but nevertheless soon faced financial ruin. At this point, Abagnale ran away from home.

Looking more like someone's uncle than a highly successful fraudster, Abagnale helped the US authorities uncover many cases of fraud while he was in prison

'THE SKYWAYMAN'

At the age of sixteen, Abagnale found himself in New York City, looking for a job. Luckily for him, he looked older than he really was – in fact, his hair was already beginning to turn grey – and so found it easy to pretend that he was about ten years older than his actual age. This, of course, involved altering his driving licence. After that, he realized the potential of counterfeiting, and he was never to look back.

His first target was his bank account. He changed numbers on deposit slips in the bank, so that money went into his account every time a customer made a deposit at the bank. He also wrote hundreds of bad cheques himself and overdrew massively on his account. In this way, he made and spent thousands of dollars. His next fraudulent move was to impersonate a Pan Am pilot using a uniform he acquired by phoning an outfitter's, telling them that he had lost his uniform, and charging the account to a fictitious employee of the company. He got a special pass by contacting the company who made the passes for Pan Am and telling them he needed a sample. He added his own logo to the pass by taking one from a model aeroplane kit.

POLICE LINE DO NOT CROSS

Abagnale then turned up at airports and asked for a free ride on TWA aeroplanes, having found out through extensive study of the aviation industry about a practice known as 'deadheading', in which airlines helped each other out by carrying pilots from other companies in available remaining seats. Each time he flew, his expenses would be billed to Pan Am. When his ruse was discovered, he became known as 'The Skywayman'.

THE FAKE MEDIC

During the 1960s, when Abagnale was masquerading as a pilot, the aviation industry was held in high esteem. With his uniform and his passes (which even included a pilot's licence that he had forged), Abagnale found that he was able to cash cheques anywhere, and that people immediately trusted and respected him. He also became very popular with women, most of them air hostesses a good deal older than himself. However, despite the thousands of dollars he amassed, and the exciting life of travel and adventure that he was leading, he later admitted to being quite lonely at this point, since he was always on the run from the police and could confide in no one.

He decided to change tack, and settled for a while in Georgia, where he pretended to be a doctor in order to rent an apartment more easily. He soon became acquainted with a 'fellow' doctor, who asked him to help out temporarily at his hospital. Amazingly enough, given the fact that he did not even have a high-school diploma, let alone a qualification in medicine, nobody noticed Abagnale's lack of

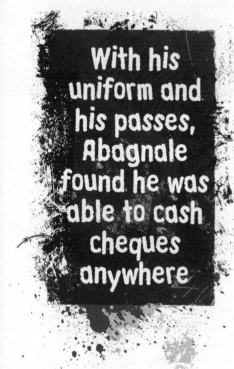

knowledge. He often covered his ignorance by joking with staff, who warmed to his jovial manner, and accepted his authority completely.

CHANGING IDENTITIES

Realizing that his cover would soon be blown, and that he was in danger of causing his patients real damage, Abagnale moved on, this time to Louisiana. He forged documents to show that he was a lawyer, and even passed exams. He enjoyed his new job, before realizing that it was only a matter of time before his deception would be discovered, so he left and took up a new career – this time as a sociology lecturer. This pattern of change continued until he finally returned to his old role as an airline pilot – this time with a crew of beautiful young 'air hostesses' to assist him. In all, he changed his identity many times, becoming a series of different people with different aliases. He also became extremely adept at forging cheques, and amassed millions of dollars in this way.

It was not long, of course, before Abagnale was being seriously pursued by international law enforcement agencies across the world. He was wanted in all American states and in twenty-six countries worldwide. However, his extraordinary career of deception and fraud finally came to an end when, at the age of twenty-one, he was arrested as he attempted to board an Air France aeroplane. He was tried and convicted in France, and spent several years in prison in Europe before returning to the United States, where he was sentenced to a further term of imprisonment.

Perhaps crime can pay? Frank Abagnale Jr with director Steven Spielberg at the premiere of the film made of his life, Catch Me If You Can

THE MODEL BUSINESSMAN

As Abagnale was serving out his prison sentence, the US government approached him and asked him to help them solve some of their many fraud cases, by showing them the workings of this kind of crime from the inside. Abagnale agreed, and was duly released. He then set up a company, paid off all his debts, married and had a family, and since that time he has used his remarkable skills to catch other criminals.

In 1980, Abagnale co-wrote the story of his life, entitled *Catch Me If You Can*. Within weeks it topped the bestseller lists, and was hugely popular around the world. The book later became the basis of a film, directed by Steven Spielberg and starring Leonardo diCaprio.

Aldrich Ames

Aldrich Ames, a CIA official, was one of the most damaging spies ever to work at the agency. In order to fund his lavish lifestyle, he sold secrets to the Soviet Union, which resulted in the arrest and execution of many of his colleagues by the KGB. After thirty-one years with the CIA, during which time he spent almost ten years spying for the Russians, he was eventually caught. In 1994, he received a life sentence, while his Colombian-born second wife, Maria del Rosario, was sentenced to five years in prison.

Ames was born in 1941 in Wisconsin. His mother, Rachel, was a high-school teacher. While he was growing up, his father, Carleton Ames, secretly worked for the CIA. The family lived in Burma in the early 1950s, and then returned to the United States to live in Washington DC. Aldrich, known as Rick, attended Langley High School, and was especially keen on drama. During his teenage years, he got a summer job working for the CIA, making fake money for use in training exercises.

RECRUITING SPIES

Rick then went on to attend Chicago University, but did not finish his degree because of his drama activities. His father came to the rescue, getting him a job with the CIA in 1962. He began working for a secret branch of the CIA that trained employees to recruit spies. Ames was then sent to Ankara in Turkey to find spies for the agency, posing as an army officer. His acting skills came in handy for the job, but he failed to recruit any spies.

Next, the CIA sent him abroad to study Russian, at which he proved more successful. He went on to work in Moscow, New York and Mexico City for the CIA. He began to deal with top-level Russian spies who had defected, and became a high-ranking CIA official. However, by this time he had begun to drink heavily, and had quarrelled with his wife, Nan, who had remained in the United States when he was posted to Mexico. Moreover, he was having strong doubts about the policies the CIA were adopting at that period. Contrary to the government's propaganda, he believed that the threat to the United States from the Soviet Union was, in fact, non-existent, and that the CIA's involvement in Nicaragua, trying to crush the Sandinista rebels, was entirely wrong.

LOVE AND BETRAYAL

In Mexico City, he met Maria del Rosario Casas Dupuy, who worked as the cultural attaché for the Colombian embassy there. Ames and Rosario began to go out together and soon fell in love. However, in 1983 he was called back to New York with a promotion, as head of counter-intelligence in Soviet operations.

Once in the job, Ames began to realize the extent of the States' espionage system in the Soviet Union. He had information on every aspect of it, including the many Russian operatives who secretly worked for the CIA. With his faith in the agency gone, and with mounting personal pressures – Rosario had followed him to New York and he was negotiating a divorce with his first wife – he began to think about ways in which he could make extra money. His new girlfriend was a

> In order to fund his lavish lifestyle, he sold secrets to the Soviet Union

POLICE LINE DO NOT CROSS

I AM READY TO MEET
AT B ON 1 OCT.
    I CANNOT READ
NORTH 13-19 SEPT.
    IF YOU <u>WILL</u>
<u>MEET</u> AT B ON 1 OCT.
PLS SIGNAL NORTH u
OF 20 SEPT TO CONFI.
<u>NO</u> MESSAGE AT PIPE.
    IF YOU <u>CANNOT</u> MEE.
1 OCT, SIGNAL NORTH AFTER
27 SEPT WITH MESSAGE AT
PIPE.

Once they suspected him, the CIA enlisted the help of the FBI. This note, concerning a meeting with his KGB contact in Bogotá, Colombia, was found by the FBI in Aldrich Ames' rubbish bin in 1993

Over a period of several years he received as much as two and a half million dollars from the KGB

spendthrift, and he was having trouble keeping up with her extravagant ways; additionally, his wife had kept many of their joint assets, and he owed her money as part of the divorce settlement.

Ames now began to sell the names of Russians spying for the CIA to the KGB.

Over several years he received as much as two and a half million dollars in return for information on more than a hundred US intelligence operations. The most shocking aspect of this betrayal was that it led to the execution of at least ten of his CIA colleagues in the Soviet Union.

POLICE LINE DO NOT CROSS

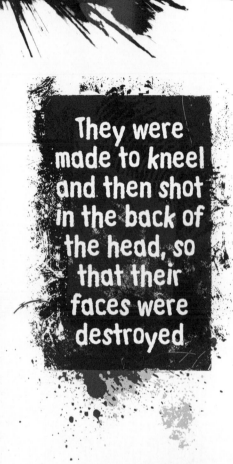

They were made to kneel and then shot in the back of the head, so that their faces were destroyed

SHOT IN THE HEAD

Of the twenty-five 'sources' that Ames named, ten were sentenced to what the Russians called *vyshaya mera* ('the highest measure of punishment'). They were taken to a cell, made to kneel and then shot in the back of the head so that their faces were completely destroyed. Afterwards, they were buried in unmarked graves, so that their relatives could not mourn them properly.

Most of the Russian operatives were not personally known to Ames, but there was one old friend whom he betrayed – not once, but twice. This was Sergey Fedorenko, who had known Ames since

his days in New York. Fedorenko knew that the KGB suspected him of spying (the result of Ames' tip-off), and so he contacted his friend and asked for help in defecting to the United States. At a secret meeting between the two, Ames promised he would do his best, but immediately afterwards telephoned his superiors and told them what had happened.

SMELLING A RAT

Meanwhile, the CIA was beginning to realize that something was wrong in the organization. As ever more operations failed, it soon became clear that someone in the know was selling their secrets to the Russians. However, it took a long time for the searchlight to fall on Ames, even though it was clear that his lifestyle was way above what his salary could pay for. Instead of looking at their personnel, the CIA concentrated on technical problems, such as code breaking, to explain what had gone wrong. It was not until the FBI were called in that Ames became a prime suspect. The FBI put him under constant surveillance, and just before he and Rosario, now his wife, were due to fly to Moscow, they arrested the pair and charged them with providing classified information to the KGB.

Both pleaded guilty and, at their trial, Ames was sentenced to life incarceration without parole, while Rosario received a sentence of sixty-three months. Today, Ames continues to serve out his sentence, while Rosario, after serving hers, returned to live in Colombia.

Not caring who he hurt – American or Russian, friend or foe – Ames found spying the most lucrative way to fund his and his partner's lavish lifestyle

POLICE LINE DO NOT CROSS

Han van Meegeren

The story of master art forger Han van Meegeren is an extraordinary one. It is likely that his forgeries would never have been discovered until after his death, had it not been for the fact that he once sold a painting – apparently by Vermeer – to the Nazi Reichsmarshall Hermann Göring during the Second World War (this was during the period when Holland was occupied by the Germans). The Dutch authorities accused van Meegeren of being a Nazi collaborator and arrested him, but he then revealed that the painting was a forgery, and that he had duped Göring into buying it. At first no one believed him, but when he managed to prove his case, he was hailed as a national hero for tricking the Nazis instead of a traitor to his country.

Henricus Antonius van Meegeren was born in Deventer, Holland, in 1899. His parents were Roman Catholics, and he was the third child in the family. As a young man, Henricus studied art and architecture, much to the annoyance of his father who did not approve of his son's choice of career, but van Meegeren was determined to follow in the footsteps of the classic Dutch painters – and so he did, but not in the way that he expected.

OUT OF FASHION

Unfortunately for van Meegeren, who had developed considerable skills as a painter in the classic style, the fashion of his day was for modern art. It became clear that unless he changed his direction,

He decided to paint a fake Vermeer, watch the art world rave over it and then reveal that it was his own work

he was never going to be taken seriously by the critics. Indeed, when he exhibited his paintings, his work was quite often ridiculed. To get back at his critics, he conceived a plan that would show them up for what they were in his eyes: shallow, ignorant slaves to fashion who knew nothing about 'real' art. He decided to paint a fake Vermeer, watch the art world rave over it and then reveal that it was his own work. Therefore, it can be argued, that when he first took to forgery, his aim was not to make money but to show his critics his skills and techniques, thus proving what a fine painter he was.

THE FAKE VERMEER

In 1936, Han van Meegeren painted a picture of Christ at Emmaus, and passed it off as an early, unknown Vermeer. He worked very carefully, copying every aspect of Vermeer's style of painting, and using paints specially mixed according to the formulas of the period. He applied techniques that he had developed himself to glaze, harden and bake the paintings so that they appeared crackled and old, rubbing dirt into the cracks to complete the effect of an 'Old Master'.

Today, scientific procedures can date a painting accurately, however authentic it may look. However, at that time, no such methods existed, and paintings had to be judged on the basis of how they appeared to the naked eye. Van Meegeren's very skilfully forged Vermeer fooled the Dutch art world completely, in particular the art critic Dr Abraham Bredius, whom van Meegeren loathed. Much to van Meegeren's glee, Bredius declared the painting a genuine masterpiece. Van Meegeren's trick had worked.

POLICE LINE DO NOT CR

To save his life – by getting the charge of treason against him changed to forgery – van Meegeren was forced to reveal his fraudulent skills to the authorities

from then on, until 1945, he painted forgeries. His fake paintings by Dutch masters such as Vermeer, Pieter de Hooch and Frans Hals fetched the equivalent of millions of dollars. His forgeries remained undetected for years, and he made a great deal of money. The war raging in Europe helped cover his tracks: there was a lot of secret trafficking in great works of art at the time, and his activities were not as carefully monitored as they might have been in peace time.

Van Meegeren's paintings sold for higher and higher sums. One of them cost over a million Dutch guilders, and became the most expensive painting ever sold at the time. As a result, he became used to living the high life, as one of the richest men in Holland's art world. Yet he was a difficult, unhappy man with a turbulent personal life. At heart, despite his wealth, he was extremely bitter about his lack of success as a creative artist.

FOOLING THE NAZIS

The last fake Vermeer that van Meegeren painted, *Christ and the Adultress*, was sold to Hermann Göring in 1943, during the Nazi occupation of Holland, for a huge sum. Two years later, at the end of the war, the painting was found in Göring's vast collection, and traced back to van Meegeren. Van Meegeren was arrested and charged with collaborating with the Nazis, a treasonous offence punishable by death at the time. While he was being held in prison, van Meegeren confessed that the painting, along with several others, had been forged by him. The authorities did not believe him, so to prove it, he

THE BLACK MARKET

At this point, when van Meegeren had planned to reveal all, it became clear to him just how much money he could make by producing these fake paintings. He sold *Christ at Emmaus* for a huge sum;

Van Meegeren painted 'Jesus Among the Doctors' in the style of Vermeer under supervision to prove his skill as a forger. His life of crime came to an abrupt end when his fakes were found in Hermann Göring's collection

offered to paint another fake, this time under police surveillance.

To everyone's amazement, van Meegeren was able to show that he could paint like Vermeer. He took as his subject 'Jesus Among the Doctors', and created a painting that was obviously the work of a master forger. He was duly charged with forgery rather than treason. However, van Meegeren was so annoyed by this that he refused to finish the fake painting. At his trial, he was sentenced to prison for one year.

By this time, van Meegeren had become something of a national hero as the man who had outwitted the Nazis and divested Hermann Göring of large sums of money (in actual fact, it was later found that Göring had himself duped the forger and had paid for the painting in fake currency). However, van Meegeren was not able to enjoy his moment of fame: by now he was extremely sick. Over the years, he had used his money to indulge himself, and had abused drink and drugs to such a degree that he had completely ruined his health. Instead of going to prison for his crimes, he was therefore admitted to hospital, where he died on 30 December 1947. Thus ended the bizarre career of one of the greatest master forgers in history.

Mark Hofmann

Mark Hofmann has been called 'one of the most chillingly compelling criminals the world has ever known'. In 1997 he forged a poem, supposedly by the 19th-century American poet Emily Dickinson, which completely fooled the literary world. However, his greed got the better of him; to finance his lifestyle, Hofmann borrowed some money to create yet more forgeries to sell and, when he could not pay back the money, ended up murdering two people. When eventually he was arrested, Hofmann confessed to many forgeries, as well as the murders, and at his trial he received a life sentence. Today, he remains incarcerated in the Utah State Correctional Facility.

Hofmann was born in 1954 and grew up in a devout Mormon family, living in the suburbs of Salt Lake City. As a child, he was interested in chemistry and in performing magic tricks. At the age of fourteen, he managed to electroplate an 'antique' coin in such a proficient way that the US Treasury department declared it to be genuine. These childhood hobbies would serve him well in his later career as a master forger.

THE SALAMANDER LETTER

Early on, Hofmann began to doubt his family's faith. He came to believe that the founder of the Mormon religion, Joseph Smith, was a fraud. Smith had claimed that his teachings, compiled as *The Book of Mormon*, were given to him by an angel called Moroni, and that he, Smith, had transcribed them from a set of golden plates using 'magic goggles'. To suggest

A typical Mormon image by C.C.A. Christensen showing the angel Moroni – and not a salamander – revealing the word of God to Joseph Smith

POLICE LINE DO NOT CROSS

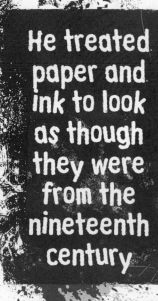

He treated paper and ink to look as though they were from the nineteenth century

One of Joseph Smith's genuine diaries. Forging similar documents would have taken a lot of painstaking work

POLICE LINE DO NOT CRO

that these claims were false, Hofmann set about re-creating a page of Smith's work. He treated paper and ink to look as though they were from the 19th century, adding every detail expected of an old book. Later, when the forgery was tested, the page was declared genuine.

Hofmann then continued to create forgeries that would cast further doubt on the Mormon religion, such as a letter from Joseph Smith, which he called 'The Salamander Letter'. In this, Smith apparently admitted that he had been shown *The Book of Mormon* by a salamander, and not the angel Moroni. In order to protect themselves and the religious beliefs of fellow Mormons, elders of the Mormon faith began to buy Hofmann's fake documents. From this point on, Hofmann realized that he could make a lot of money from his forgeries, and began his new career in earnest.

FOOLING THE EXPERTS

Hofmann had an extraordinary ability to adopt the writing style of just about any historical figure he wanted to, from George Washington to Mark Twain. He developed a method of hypnotizing himself before writing, so that he could transport himself into each character, identifying himself completely with his chosen subject.

One of Hofmann's most notorious stunts was to forge a poem purporting to be by the reclusive 19th-century poet Emily Dickinson. Amazingly, he wrote a new poem in her unique literary style, reproducing her handwriting exactly. Through meticulous historical research, as well as self-hypnosis, he managed to see into her mind and produce

a remarkable new piece of writing. Not only the words of the poem itself, but his painstaking attention to technical detail ensured that the manuscript he created fooled the greatest poetry experts in the country. The poem thrilled the literary world, and was pronounced genuine. It was bought by the library at Amhurst, Dickinson's home town, for a sum of more than $20,000.

AN ENDURING MYSTERY

Hofmann's downfall came about when he began to get entangled in money problems. To complete more forgeries, he borrowed half a million dollars that he could not pay back. He was also an avid collector of first editions of children's books – an expensive hobby. The volume of 'finds' he was making began to cause suspicion and his (forged) documents were subjected to closer and closer public scrutiny.

As his creditors began to pursue him, Hofmann resorted to planting bombs. He murdered document collector Steven Christensen, who owned a forged document that he had bought from Hofmann for one million dollars, and he also killed the wife of Christensen's employer. When another bomb went off prematurely and wounded Hofmann himself, an investigation was launched, which soon led to the discovery of forgery equipment in his basement.

Hofmann was arrested and charged. He pleaded guilty to lesser charges in order to escape the death sentence and received a life sentence. His ability to create works of some of the greatest figures in American history led to feats unsurpassed in audacity to this day.

Hofmann had an extraordinary ability to adopt the writing style of just about any historical figure

POLICE LINE DO NOT CROSS

C. Boyce and A.D. Lee

Christopher Boyce was a CIA employee who had access to highly classified information from the Pine Gap spy satellite, which was based in Australia. He was caught selling secrets to the Russians, and received a forty-year prison sentence. His defence was from an apparently moral standpoint – that the US government was not sharing secret information with the Australian government, which they had signed an agreement to do. He also believed that the CIA wanted to destabilize the socialist government of Australian prime minister Gough Whitlam.

However, during his trial it emerged that Boyce's real reasons for spying were somewhat less transparent. Although he despised the US government, he was not politically involved with any particular group or party; nor did he make a great deal of money from his spying activities. It seems possible that, ultimately, his career as a spy was motivated by nothing more than a lust for adventure.

THE YOUNG DAREDEVIL

Christopher Boyce was born in 1953 in Santa Monica, California. His father Charles had at one time been an FBI agent, but was now working in the aircraft industry. His mother Noreen was a devout Catholic who did not believe in contraception, and so the couple went on to have eight more children. Christopher was brought up in a strongly moral and religious atmosphere and was taught to be a patriotic, all-American boy.

The young Christopher did well in school, and became an altar boy at church. He loved the outdoor life, and was well known to everyone locally for his daredevil exploits. He turned into a good-looking teenager, and was generally popular.

Christopher met his friend Andrew Daulton Lee at church, where the pair served as altar boys. They spent a lot of time together, and attended the same high school. They took up falconry, developing a passion for training birds. Lee was also enjoying woodwork at school, and becoming an excellent carpenter. However, despite his talent, Lee felt inferior: he was short, he had a face covered in acne and he thought himself unattractive to girls.

GOVERNMENT SECRETS

As teenagers, Boyce and Lee both began to lose interest in school work. Boyce also started to lose his Catholic faith and to question his patriotism. Lee took to selling drugs, supplying marijuana and cocaine to girls in exchange for sex. When the boys left high school, Lee stepped up his drug dealing, especially in cocaine, and became known as 'The Snowman'. Boyce enrolled in college, but kept dropping out.

At this point, Charles Boyce intervened on behalf of his son, getting a friend to hire him at an aerospace company called TWR. This was a private company

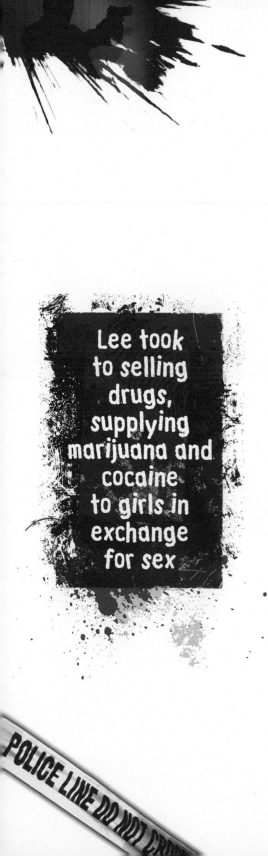

Lee took to selling drugs, supplying marijuana and cocaine to girls in exchange for sex

Christopher Boyce – denied the freedom he so loved, as exemplified by his passion for falconry

POLICE LINE DO NOT CROSS

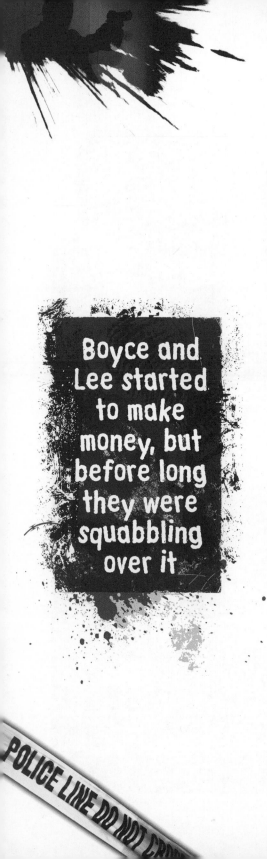

Boyce and Lee started to make money, but before long they were squabbling over it

that was involved in operating US spy satellites. Boyce became a general clerk in the company, dealing with classified information. An intelligent young man who actually read the material carefully, he was disgusted to find that the US government was withholding information gathered from spy satellites; in particular, they had signed an agreement with the Australian government, and were not passing on vital data.

According to Boyce, this was because the Australian government was headed by a socialist, Gough Whitlam. Boyce was even more enraged when he found out that the CIA was infiltrating the Australian labour unions. However, rather than showing his disapproval through legal protest, Boyce decided on another course of action. He would sell the secrets of the United States to the Russians. That way, he would not only salve his political conscience, but he would also make some money.

LUST FOR ADVENTURE
Boyce discussed his plans with Lee, who by that time was getting into a great deal of trouble because of his drug-dealing activities. Lee had been in prison, and was frightened of returning there. He needed another line of business fast. The pair hatched a plot together whereby Lee would travel to the Soviet embassy in Mexico City and tell them about Boyce's access to highly classified information. This Lee did, showing evidence of his friend's employment.

The Soviets immediately showed an interest, and within a short time Lee was dropping off information for them and receiving packets of money for his friend Boyce, who now became known as 'The Falcon'. Lee met a Soviet official in public, using passwords and designated drop-off points. Boyce and Lee started to make money, but before long they were squabbling over it.

Lee had by now become a heroin addict, and Boyce suspected that he was not getting his fair share of the cash. Boyce was getting tired of the whole business of selling secrets, and was planning to leave TWR to go to college. In the meantime, he gave Lee some photographs of a new satellite, the Pyramider, that the United States was planning to build.

DOWN MEXICO WAY
When Lee took the photos down to Mexico City, trouble ensued. Lee was arrested by Mexican police and charged with murdering a policeman. After a harrowing experience in a Mexican jail, Lee was handed over to the FBI, where his story – that he was working for the CIA – began to seriously unravel.

Not long afterwards, Christopher Boyce was also arrested. He was brought to trial, and told the jury the truth about his spying activities. He added that he had never told Lee that they were working for the CIA. Boyce was given a forty-year sentence. Lee was tried separately, and was sentenced to life imprisonment.

In 1980, Boyce managed to escape and went on the run, living free for over a year. He was working at a tree nursery before he started committing a series of bank robberies. He was eventually caught and sent back to prison. Lee was paroled in 1998, and Boyce in 2003.

Sean Penn (left) and Timothy Hutton in the film *The Falcon and the Snowman* – the story of Boyce and Lee

POLICE LINE DO NOT CROSS

Klaus Fuchs

Klaus Fuchs was a German-born physicist who was hounded by the Nazis during the 1930s because of his communist beliefs. He left Germany to live in Britain and the United States, where he worked on the development of the atom bomb. On the face of it, he posed as an impartial scientist, but unbeknown to his colleagues, he was passing highly sensitive information to the Soviet Union, at a time when the race was on to develop the atom bomb as the ultimate war weapon. In 1945, the United States won the race, detonating the bomb with horrific consequences on Hiroshima.

To this day, no one knows exactly how much Fuchs influenced the outcome of the arms race. Edward Teller, one of the principal figures in developing the hydrogen bomb, believed that Fuchs gave away major secrets, and that he saved the Russians about ten years of their own research as a result. Other commentators, such as the CIA, thought that the time saved was probably much less, perhaps only one or two years. It seems likely, in hindsight, that Fuchs confirmed what the Russians were already working towards, rather than that he gave them entirely new information.

FLEEING THE NAZIS

Emil Julius Klaus Fuchs was born in Rüsselsheim, Germany, in 1911, one of four children. The whole family was intensely political but somewhat mentally unstable. His father was a Quaker and took great care in the moral education of his children, but he was not an affectionate man. His mother committed

In 1933, the Nazis gained power in Germany, forcing Klaus Fuchs to flee the country

suicide when Fuchs was at college. His sister Elisabeth became a radical activist and met her death by jumping into the path of an oncoming train while being pursued by the Gestapo. His brother Gerhard was also an activist, and was expelled from law school and imprisoned several times. His younger sister Kristel left Germany and studied in the United States, where she was diagnosed as a schizophrenic during her college years.

Fuchs later believed himself to be suffering from what he called a 'controlled' form of schizophrenia, and some believe that this condition may have been a factor in his ability to 'compartmentalize' his feelings, such as loyalty to his colleagues, in his work as a spy.

Klaus began his career at Leipzig University, where he studied physics and mathematics. He took a keen interest in politics and joined the Communist Party. In 1933, the Nazis gained power in Germany and began to round up and imprison German communists, forcing Klaus to flee the country. He escaped to Britain and continued his studies there, gaining a doctorate in physics from Bristol University in 1937. He then went on to further study at Edinburgh University.

THE TRINITY TEST

At the outbreak of the Second World War, German citizens living in Britain were sent to internment camps, to be held there until the war ended. Fuchs was taken to a camp in Quebec, Canada, but a colleague intervened to persuade the authorities that he was doing important work that would be useful in the war effort, and he was set free. He went to work at the British atomic bomb centre in

Birmingham, on a project known as 'tube alloys'. Here, he conducted research with another German physicist who had fled his homeland, Rudolf Peierls.

In 1942, Fuchs became a British citizen. The following year, he went to the United States to work at Columbia University in New York, on the atom bomb research programme there, the Manhattan Project. From New York, he was sent to another research centre, Los Alamos in New Mexico, where he was involved in developing and testing the atom bomb. He was present at the first atomic bomb test, the Trinity test. At the end of the war, Fuchs returned to Britain and worked in nuclear research at the centre in Harwell.

SOVIET SPY

It was during his time at 'tube alloys' in Birmingham, England, that Fuchs began to pass information about his work on the project to the Soviet Union. He was contacted by a female Russian spy, known only as 'the girl from Banbury', and in brief meetings with her, gave her research papers to look at. At this stage, he is thought to have communicated only his own research information. When he moved to New York and started work on the Manhattan Project, he began to give detailed information on the programme in general to Harry Gold, a Soviet spy who worked under the name 'Raymond'. This was not discovered until several

Atom spy Dr Klaus Fuchs checks his ticket with an air hostess at London Airport, in June 1959. Fuchs was released from jail in England after serving nine years of his fourteen-year prison sentence for spying

186 Fraudsters and Spies: White-Collar Crime

After his release Fuchs departed to East Germany, where he was met by his nephew Klaus Kittowski (right) at an airport in East Berlin.

years later, when intelligence officers managed to crack Soviet codes in an operation known as the Venona Project. A message was deciphered, reporting on the progress of the atom bomb in the West. It was unclear whether or not Fuchs himself had written the document, but there was now no doubt that the Russians had infiltrated the Manhattan Project and had known all along what was being developed.

DEFECTING TO THE EAST

Suspicion soon fell on Klaus Fuchs, and he was investigated by the FBI. At first he denied any involvement, but after a series of interviews he confessed. He was duly brought to trial. In 1950, he was found guilty of passing secrets to the Soviet Union, and received a prison sentence of fourteen years. After nine years, he was released, and went to work in communist East Germany, at the Institute for Nuclear Physics near Dresden. He married, lived a quiet life with his wife and worked hard as a scientist. In 1979, he was honoured for his life's work with the Order of Karl Marx. He died in 1988.

POLICE LINE DO NOT CROSS

Victor Lustig

Known as 'the man who sold the Eiffel Tower – twice!', Count Victor Lustig has gone down in history as one of the greatest conmen of all time. A charming yet completely corrupt swindler, he spoke five languages, went under scores of different names and was arrested many times before he was finally caught and sent to prison for good.

Victor Lustig was born in Bohemia, now the Czech Republic, on 4 January 1890. When he was nineteen, he got into a fight with a man over a girl. The man slashed his face, leaving him with a large scar that ran from his eye to his ear. When he later took to a life of crime, this was to prove a distinguishing feature.

As soon as he could, Victor left home and headed towards the bright lights of Paris. His intelligence and wit, not to mention his charm and his mastery of several languages, made it easy for him to make friends among the wealthy upper classes of Parisian society. His skill at cards led him to become a professional gambler, making a living by working on luxury ocean liners crossing from Paris to New York City. However, with the onset of the First World War, pleasure cruises like these became a thing of the past, and Lustig had to find another way to make money and finance his lifestyle. He decided to travel to the United States and develop other lines of business.

CONMAN EXTRAORDINAIRE

His first major con in the United States was in 1922, when he bought a dilapidated farm in Missouri, offering the bank Liberty bonds for it. The bank was only too glad to oblige, since the farm was not worth much at all, and showed its gratitude by cashing an extra $10,000 of bonds for him. During the transaction, Lustig managed to switch the envelopes containing the bonds and the cash, and stole both. He was later caught, but – unbelievably – managed to persuade the bank to let him off. Not only that, but he also kept the $10,000.

His next con took place in Montreal, Canada, where he stole the wallet of a banker named Linus Merton, and then returned it to him intact, saying that he had found it. This ploy gained the banker's confidence, so Lustig told his new friend of a scheme to make money by betting on horses. In those days, racing results were wired ahead to the bookmakers several minutes before the betting was closed. Lustig told Merton that, by intercepting the wire, one could find out the winner and place a bet. He claimed that his cousin worked in the bookmaking industry and had access to this information, and that a very large bet placed on a horse at the last minute could thus be guaranteed to win. In this way, Lustig obtained £30,000 from Merton to put on a horse. Needless to say, Lustig's story was complete fiction, and once he had Merton's money he immediately made off with it. Once again, he got away with this audacious swindle, and Merton never saw Lustig – or his money – again.

AN AUDACIOUS SCAM

Lustig's third con was his most outrageous. He read a newspaper article about the Eiffel Tower being so badly in need of repair that the authorities were thinking

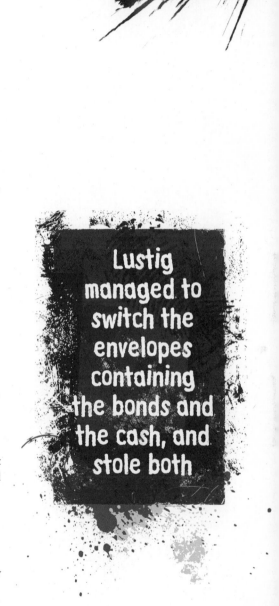

Lustig managed to switch the envelopes containing the bonds and the cash, and stole both

POLICE LINE DO NOT CROSS

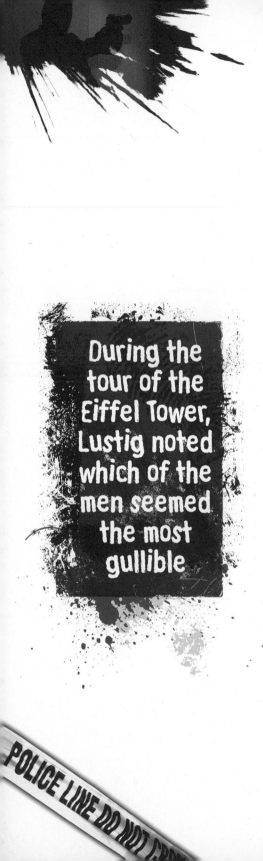

During the
tour of the
Eiffel Tower,
Lustig noted
which of the
men seemed
the most
gullible

of destroying it. Pretending to be from a government department, he sent 'official' letters to the directors of several scrap iron companies, and met with them at the Hotel de Crillon on Place de la Concorde. The Crillon was one of the best hotels in Paris, and a popular meeting place for top-level government officials. Once the gentlemen were assembled, he introduced himself as the deputy Director General of the Ministry of Posts and Telegraphs. He announced that the government had decided that the upkeep of the Eiffel Tower was too expensive and that they were going to demolish it. He said that in order to secure the iron from the tower, the dealers first needed to bid for the rights to it. He then took the men for a trip around the tower, which was indeed in a bad state of repair at the time. It had never been built as a permanent structure, but as a display of engineering skill for the 1889 Paris Exposition.

GULLIBLE DIRECTORS

During the tour, Lustig noted which of the men seemed the most gullible. Afterwards, he asked that the men put forward their bids the next day, and told them to keep the project secret, since the idea of tearing down the Eiffel Tower was a very controversial one and had not been made known to the public.

Accordingly, the following day each of the companies submitted a bid for the tower. Lustig selected one of the directors, an unfortunate man named André Poisson, as the winner. He encouraged Poisson to bribe him, and then accepted Poisson's

A surprisingly jaunty Lustig, given that he had just been sentenced to a long spell in prison

Victor Lustig was as genuine a count as he was a French government minister. The title was to lend gravitas to his scams

bid. As soon as Lustig had the money, he went to Austria where he enjoyed the high life in the best hotels and restaurants. He read the French newspapers every day, expecting them to report the incident and for the police to come after him, but they never did – as it turned out, Poisson was so embarrassed by his own gullibility that he didn't go to the police, and the whole affair was covered up.

PUSHING HIS LUCK

Encouraged by getting away with such an audacious scam, Lustig went back to Paris. He mounted exactly the same con all over again, with five new scrap iron dealers. However, this time he pushed his luck too far. The victim of the scam went straight to the police, and the story was soon reported in all the newspapers. However, the police did not manage to catch up with Lustig at the time.

Lustig spent the remainder of his life in the United States, where he posed as a European aristocrat, calling himself 'count'. He continued to come up with a series of amazing scams, until he was finally caught, tried and sent to prison. He managed to make a dramatic escape, but was recaptured only twenty-seven days later and was sentenced to twenty years at Alcatraz. The 'count' died of pneumonia in 1947, at the age of fifty-seven.

POLICE LINE DO NOT CROSS

The Cambridge Four

During the years of the Cold War, the fraught ideological battle between the western democracies and the communist states was conducted in secret by an army of spies trading in information. Not only that, at the end of the war many agents were revealed to have been working for both sides. Their motives varied: some were engaged in this dangerous game for money; others had strong political convictions; and yet others – in a milieu where the ends always justified the means – had lost sight of their moral code altogether. Among the most prominent of these double agents were four young Englishmen recruited from the social elite at Cambridge University. Their names were Kim Philby, Guy Burgess, Donald Maclean and Anthony Blunt.

THE 'OLD BOY' NETWORK

The four met as students during the 1930s, at a time when the Depression was causing mass unemployment in the West. In this context, the rise of fascism in Germany and Italy was extremely menacing: Hitler and Mussolini were rapidly mobilizing support among a working-class population suffering poverty and social fragmentation in the aftermath of the First World War. In British academic circles, it was widely believed that the western democracies would not provide strong anti-fascist leadership against these demagogues; in fact, it was well known that among the anti-semitic British upper classes there was a good deal of sympathy for the Nazis. Thus, a rising generation of intellectuals looked to the Soviet Union as a bulwark against fascism.

At the same time, the Soviet Union's intelligence agency, the KGB, conceived the plan of recruiting at Britain's most respected universities. They knew that the British establishment operated on an 'old boy' network, in which the children of the upper classes went to fee-paying 'public' schools, then to one or other of the two top universities in the country, Oxford and Cambridge, and from there into high-level jobs in politics, the civil service, the law and so on. In this way, the KGB planned to recruit agents who would be working at the heart of government. Their plan paid off: with the Cambridge spies, they managed to recruit young men who would become important establishment figures with easy access to extremely sensitive information. Moreover, the 'old boy' network ensured that, for many years, their activities as double agents were never discovered: so snobbish and cliquey was the British establishment that it simply could not bring itself to suspect its own members.

DEBONAIR, CHARMING – YET DEADLY

The most infamous of the four men was Harold Philby, nicknamed 'Kim' after a character in Rudyard Kipling's *Jungle Book*. Philby was highly intelligent, and could be debonair and charming, yet few claim to have really known him well. On graduating from Cambridge, he became a newspaper reporter and then went on

The KGB knew that the British establishment operated on an 'old boy' network

POLICE LINE DO NOT CROSS

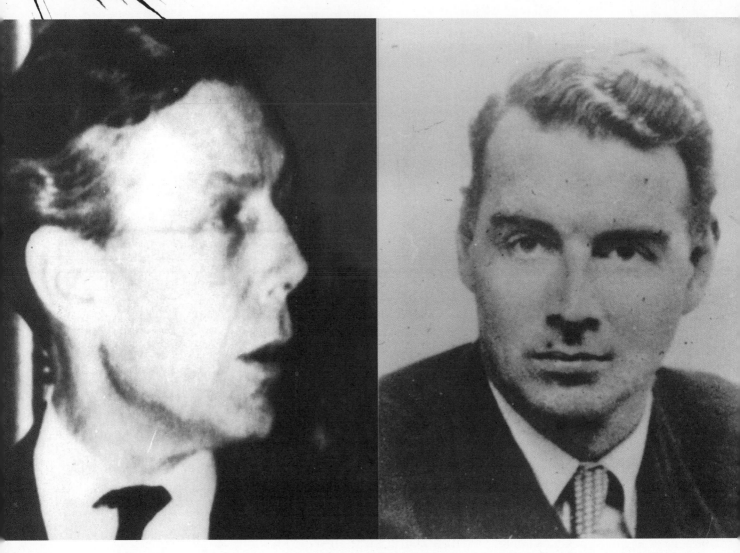

to work for the British Secret Intelligence Service, where he eventually headed the anti-Soviet section. All the time, he was reporting back to the KGB, resulting in the execution of some British spies in the Soviet Union and contributing to damaging the Allies' military efforts during the Second World War.

Blunt was another enigmatic figure. Unlike Philby, who was known as a womanizer, Blunt was a homosexual. It is thought that he was recruited by the KGB on a trip to Russia in 1933, and that he recruited the other agents on his return. An art historian, Blunt became director of the Courtauld Institute and art adviser to the Queen,

both extremely respected positions. In 1956, he was knighted for his espionage services for MI5.

Guy Burgess was also a homosexual, and at one time had a sexual relationship with Blunt. A flamboyant character, he was intelligent and charming, but had a serious flaw that made him deeply unreliable: he was an alcoholic. Burgess

became a BBC broadcaster and a senior
civil servant at the Foreign Office, which
gave him access to extremely important
people and crucial information.

The fourth spy, Donald Maclean,
was a high-level diplomat at the British
Embassy in Washington DC, and during
the war became one of Stalin's chief
informants. His work as a spy helped the

Soviets build the atom bomb and assess
their capability in the nuclear arms race.
He was a tense, nervous man – also an
alcoholic – who became a worry to his
colleagues Blunt and Philby because
they thought that given his unstable
mental state, he would probably crack
if interrogated by the British secret
services, and land them all in trouble.

*Anthony Blunt, Guy Burgess, Kim Philby and Donald
Maclean – the idealistic Cambridge spies at the
height of their activities*

The spies' activities were not discovered until the FBI broke a secret code in 1949

DEFECTING TO THE USSR

For many years, the spies' activities were not discovered. Then, in 1949, Robert Lamphere of the FBI found out, through breaking a secret code, that a member of the British embassy was sending messages to the Russians. With pressure mounting, Burgess and Maclean unexpectedly defected to the Soviet Union, leaving Philby to pick up the pieces. Philby remained stoical under British intelligence questioning, but was forced to resign from his job. He later also defected to the USSR.

Anthony Blunt remained in the country and, in 1964, confessed to his part in the spying operation. However, he was given immunity from prosecution, largely to protect the reputation of British intelligence and the British royal family. Many years later, in 1979, Blunt was publicly stripped of his honours, including his knighthood. Even then, he continued to live quietly in England, where he died in 1983.

MORAL MELTDOWN

Today, many questions still remain unanswered about the Cambridge spies. It is clear that they did not become traitors to their country for money: none of them appears to have been paid a great deal for his services. At the same time, their political convictions are somewhat unclear; they may have begun their careers as staunch communists, but at the least, one can say that the Cold War was an extremely complex business, and so was their response to it. Recent information from the disbanded Soviet Union has indicated that the Cambridge spies may in fact have been triple agents: that is, British spies working as informers for the Russians, but secretly infiltrating the KGB and reporting back to British intelligence.

Whatever the truth, it seems that ultimately, the deviations and counter-deviations of the Cold War became so tortuous that in the end, a kind of moral meltdown took place. In this context, notions of truth, justice and the greater good appeared to have become simplistic and meaningless to many, and it was no longer clear who a person with humanist convictions should feel loyal to – at least this was the case with the Cambridge spies, who were at the heart of the ideological battle between western democracy and eastern-bloc communism.

POLICE LINE DO NOT CROSS

Martin Frankel

Martin Frankel conducted one of the most far-reaching series of frauds in the history of the US financial world. With no formal qualifications and a string of failed business ventures behind him, he managed to pose as an investment specialist and persuade several skilled, intelligent people to part with their money and involve themselves in his scams. He showed no moral scruples whatsoever, and for many years got away with his crimes. However, his insecurity and paranoia finally got the better of him, and he was eventually brought to justice when his trail of lies was uncovered.

A SOCIAL MISFIT
Born in Toledo, Ohio, in 1954, Frankel was the son of was a well-respected Lucas County judge, Leon Frankel. Martin was the second child of the family. He was a bright pupil at school and did well at his studies, but socially he was a misfit. After leaving high school, he went on to study at the University of Toledo, but dropped out of his course before finishing it. He had developed a crippling fear of taking tests, and was also completely unable to discipline himself to work. It seems that his early success had been achieved without trying very hard, and he had later become anxious about any situation in which he had to make an effort, or in which there was a chance of being seen to fail.

After dropping out of college, Frankel began to take an interest in the world of finance. He believed that by researching and playing the securities market, he could earn a great deal of money very

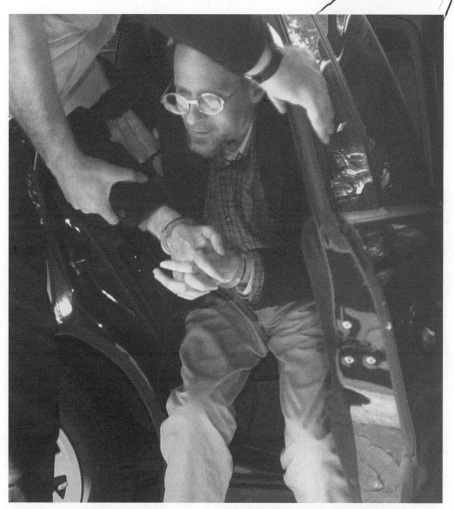

Martin Frankel is helped out of a car on the way to his trial in Hamburg. Having had the potential for a glittering future, his choice to go down the path of criminality was a particularly poor one

quickly – which, fortunately, proved to be the case. Unfortunately, however, he did not also take into account that he could also lose it just as quickly.

FEAR OF FAILURE
Frankel took to hanging around brokerage houses, learning as much as he could

about the finance business. He took a particular interest in big fraud cases, such as that of Robert Vesco, who had masterminded one of the largest swindles in US history. He met many business people, befriending a couple named John and

In 1997, one of the young women living in the house of orgies hanged herself

Sonia Schulte, who owned a securities business affiliated to the New York company of Dominick & Dominick. Frankel impressed the couple with his knowledge of the market and with a scheme that he claimed could help him predict which stocks would yield a great deal of money in future.

Sonia Schulte persuaded her husband to take Frankel on as a consultant analyst, but it was not long before John Schulte regretted his decision. Frankel was not a good employee. He refused to conform to the company's dress code, turning up for work in jeans rather than a suit and tie. His money-making scheme was also failing to yield any good results. One of the problems was that, although Frankel knew how to analyse the market, he did not actually have the confidence to trade. As with taking tests at school, he feared that he would be seen to fail.

The final straw for Schulte was when Frankel posed as an agent working for the larger affiliated firm of Dominick & Dominick, a move that could have put his boss out of business for good. Schulte lost patience with his useless new employee and fired him. However, that was by no means the end of his relationship with Frankel: for, by this time, Frankel had become Sonia's lover.

THE VATICAN FRAUD

Now unemployed and living at his parents' house, Frankel set up his own bogus investment business, which he named Winthrop Capital. He advertised in the Yellow Pages, and gained the trust of several clients, telling all sorts of lies to do so. However, his investments were not sound, and he lost a great deal of money

on his clients' behalf. Undeterred, he set up another business, Creative Partners Fund LP. He was joined by Sonia Schulte, who by this time had left her husband. Together, the pair set up another company, Thunor Trust, and began buying failing insurance companies, doing shady deals to fund their ever more lavish lifestyle.

Frankel's next, and most bizarre, scam was to mastermind a fraudulent charity scheme with links to the Vatican. Posing as a wealthy philanthropist, he set up a body called the St Francis of Assisi Foundation, and made several important contacts: with Thomas Bolan, founder of the Conservative Party of New York; and with two well-known New York priests, Peter Jacobs and Emilio Colagiovanni. It was a complicated fraud, involving the buying and selling of insurance companies with funds that were certified to belong to the Vatican, but the lure for all parties was a simple one: money.

SADOMASOCHISTIC ORGIES

By 1998, Frankel's assets were over four million dollars. He and Sonia moved to a large, lavish mansion in Greenwich, Connecticut, together with Sonia's two daughters. However, the new family home was not a happy one. Frankel began to show a greedy sexual appetite and a cruel streak, surrounding himself with young women and hosting sadomasochistic orgies in the house. Sonia soon left with her daughters. In 1997, one of the young women living in the house of orgies, who had apparently been rejected by Frankel, hanged herself there.

By 1999, Frankel's many nefarious dealings were finally attracting the

POLICE LINE DO NOT CROSS

Martin Frankel's luxury house in Greenwich, Connecticut – just one of the assets he had to give up when arrested and found guilty of fraud and racketeering

attention of the police authorities. All his companies were put under state supervision, and it now seemed only a matter of time before his rackets would be revealed for what they were. Martin Frankel became extremely anxious and decided to make a run for it. He assumed several false identities and hired a private jet to fly him to Europe, taking with him millions of dollars' worth of diamonds. He also took with him two of his girlfriends, who later baled out and were replaced as companions by an employee called Cynthia Allison. He hid out until he was finally found, along with Cynthia, in one of the most luxurious hotels in Hamburg, Germany. He was immediately arrested.

INDICTED FOR FRAUD

Frankel was indicted by the US federal government for frauds worth over two million dollars. The German authorities also accused him of using a false passport and smuggling quantities of diamonds into the country. He pleaded guilty to the German charges, but came up with several far-fetched excuses, including the bogus claim that he had smuggled in the diamonds so that he could feed the poor and hungry of the world. Not surprisingly, the German courts were not impressed with this story, and at his trial Frankel received a three-year sentence.

While serving out his sentence, he attempted to escape from prison, but failed. Eventually he was extradited, and in 2002, Frankel was charged with twenty-four federal counts of fraud and racketeering in the United States, and sentenced to more than sixteen years in prison.

POLICE LINE DO NOT CROSS

Elmyr de Hory

Elmyr de Hory was one of the most talented art forgers of the 20th century. For over two decades, his forgeries of masters such as Picasso, Matisse and Modigliani sold in their hundreds across the United States and Europe, fooling some of the greatest experts in the art world. When his fraud was discovered, the FBI and Interpol pursued him, but he managed to evade capture for most of his career. However, his life ended tragically when he committed suicide in 1976.

He was born Elmyr Dory-Boutin in 1906 to a Jewish Hungarian family. His father was a diplomat, but although well-to-do, the family was an unhappy one. Elmyr spent a lot of time away from his parents, being cared for by a succession of governesses. His parents finally divorced when he was sixteen years old.

PRISON CAMP NIGHTMARE

De Hory moved to Budapest, living among a bohemian community of artists. It was here that he began to discover his homosexual nature. When he was eighteen, he moved to Munich, Germany, enrolling in art school to study classical painting. He found that he had a real talent for the work, and went on to study in Paris under the painter Fernand Léger.

On his return to Hungary, de Hory began a relationship with a British journalist who was suspected by the Hungarian government of being a spy.

Elmyr de Hory in 1972. Forging great works of art gave him the comfortable lifestyle that his own paintings could not buy

As a result of this connection, de Hory ended up in prison in the Carpathian Mountains. There, he experienced terrible conditions that were only slightly improved when he painted the portrait of a senior camp officer. Eventually, de Hory was released, but by this time the German Nazis were in control of Hungary.

As a Jew, de Hory was sent to a German concentration camp, where he was beaten so badly that he had to be transferred to a hospital. From there, he managed to escape, even though he had a broken leg. He then made his way back to Hungary, only to find that both his parents had been killed and that most of the family estate had been taken away.

LIVING THE HIGH LIFE

De Hory managed to escape from Hungary to France, where he tried to start a new life. He soon found out that he had a knack for reproducing the styles of others and, in order to survive, began to sell these works. In 1946, he sold his first forgery, a Picasso, and realized that he had found a way to make a profitable living. He began to make and sell more forgeries, claiming that the artworks had been in his family's collection.

He found a sympathetic art dealer, Jacques Chamberlin, and together the pair toured Europe, selling forged paintings. During this period, they lived the high life, making huge profits. However, de Hory soon discovered that Chamberlin was keeping most of the money for himself, so he ended the partnership. Alone, he visited the United States, and decided to stay and ply his trade there.

At times, de Hory tired of his cheating way of life and attempted to go straight, trying to sell his own paintings. However, there was little or no market for these, and he could not make a living from his own work. The temptation of earning thousands of dollars by forging the works of others was too much for him. By now, his repertoire of forgeries had expanded to include works by Renoir, Modigliani and Matisse. He began to work in the medium of oil, which also brought him larger sums for his paintings.

SUICIDE ATTEMPT

In the 1950s, de Hory decided to settle in Miami. From there, he sold his work by mail order so that he would not be traced. However, in 1955, one of his forgeries, a Matisse, was sold to the prestigious Fogg Art Museum, whose experts discovered that it was a fake and notified the police. During the same period, a Chicago art dealer called Joseph Faulkner found out that the works sold to him were fakes, and began a court case against de Hory. De Hory fled to Mexico City, using false papers. Here, he was unfairly jailed for the murder of a British homosexual, a crime he had not committed. After a great deal of wrangling, he was set free and returned to the United States.

Back in the States, de Hory discovered that his forgeries were selling for a lot more than he had been paid by the art galleries who bought them. He also became aware that his style of work was being recognized as fake, and worried that his source of income would soon dry up. Moreover, he was frightened of getting caught and being imprisoned again. He became very depressed and took an overdose of sleeping pills. Luckily, the forger was discovered before he died and

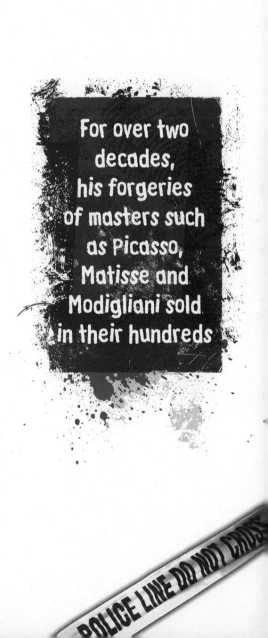

For over two decades, his forgeries of masters such as Picasso, Matisse and Modigliani sold in their hundreds

POLICE LINE DO NOT CROSS

taken to hospital. On his recovery, de Hory returned to Miami and there struck up a relationship with a man named Ferdinand Legros, who became his art dealer. Legros had a talent for selling, but he was dishonest, and kept most of the money from the paintings he sold. Tired of his art dealer's company, de Hory left to return to Europe.

ON THE RUN

After several years, de Hory found that he could not make enough money on his own, and began to do business with Legros again. Legros built de Hory a splendid home on the island of Ibiza, Spain, where he could live quietly and paint in peace. However, Legros also continued to swindle de Hory who, away from city life, was becoming bored. He started to produce substandard paintings and so it was not long before the paintings were detected as fakes. The police embarked on the men's trails and De Hory fled to Australia, but later returned to his home on Ibiza.

In 1966, Legros managed to sell over fifty paintings to one client, a Texas oil magnate, who later discovered that most of them were fakes. To escape the law, Legros went to Ibiza, turning de Hory out of the house. Shortly afterwards, Legros was arrested.

THE FINAL END

After trying to work in Europe, de Hory decided to give up his fugitive lifestyle and go back to Ibiza. There, the Spanish authorities charged de Hory with homosexuality and consorting with criminals but they could not prove that

On hearing the French authorities were to extradite him, de Hory ended the struggle that was his turbulent life, and committed suicide. After his death, his paintings became valuable collectibles

he had made the forgeries on Spanish soil. De Hory spent two months in prison, and was afterwards expelled from Ibiza, though a year later he returned. By that time he was a celebrity, having appeared on television and in an Orson Welles' movie, and having collaborated on a biography with writer Clifford Irving.

With his new-found fame, de Hory relaunched his career, this time selling his own paintings. However, in 1976, he found out that the French authorities planned to extradite him. On 11 December 1976 de Hory committed suicide by taking an overdose of sleeping pills, bringing his turbulent career to a final, tragic end.

POLICE LINE DO NOT CROSS

Drug Barons: Dealing with Death

Pablo Escobar

During the 1970s and 1980s, the illegal drugs industry expanded massively. What had once been a very marginal industry, selling only to those on the fringes of society, now became a multi-billion dollar business selling to everyone from bankers and politicians to suburban teenagers. The drug at the heart of this expansion was cocaine. The marijuana industry remained small in comparison, due to the ease of growing and preparing the product. Cocaine, however, is the product of a particular climate and needs a larger scale production system to process it.

The prime sources of the coca leaf are in South America. For years, cocaine had been manufactured in small quantities and sold at a high price. During the 1970s, however, demand began to build and a few criminal masterminds in South America saw that there were huge profits to be made if they began to control not just the growing, but also the refinement, distribution and sale of cocaine on a much larger scale than ever before. Chief among these criminals was a Colombian called Pablo Escobar, who in little more than a decade would become the first of the billionaire drug dealers.

THE MEDELLIN CARTEL

Escobar was born on a small farm in Rionegra, near Medellin in Colombia, on 12 January 1949. In his teens he gravitated towards petty crime. He began by stealing gravestones, of all the unlikely commodities, for resale. He also helped steal cars. Before long, he became involved with a small Mafia-run cocaine-producing operation, and then developed his own small business. He soon became aware that this was a business with an almost limitless market. He approached other cocaine growers in the Medellin area and offered to pay them double what they were receiving for their crop from the Mafia, who were their main buyers. They agreed. He used friends and relatives to take the drugs into the United States and establish distribution networks.

Escobar's cocaine business grew with extraordinary speed. His business plan mimicked that of legitimate multinational companies. There was a whole host of separately run cocaine operations – a sort of franchise scheme – all manufacturing and distributing cocaine, and all wired into a network that was organized by Escobar to give him a handsome share of their profits. The organization became known as the Medellin cartel, with Pablo Escobar its CEO.

To ensure his continued dominance in an incredibly competitive and murderous world – a big business regulated not by law but by machine guns – Escobar used an individual mixture of extreme brutality and surprising philanthropy.

THE COLOMBIAN NECKTIE

Escobar himself was a hands-on leader who carried out many murders personally. He was even credited with inventing the 'Colombian necktie' – this referred to his predilection for cutting his victims' throats, then pulling their tongues through the open wound. At the same

Pablo Escobar began by stealing gravestones, before joining a Mafia-run cocaine operation

Escobar took on the Mafia and won, building a huge cocaine-based empire in little more than a decade. He is shown here attending a soccer game in 1983, in Medellin, where he sponsored a team

POLICE LINE DO NOT CROSS

time as terrorizing his enemies, Escobar ploughed a lot of his ill-gotten money into social improvements. He built sports facilities and new housing, and even created Colombia's first-ever welfare programme in his home town. These charitable acts made him an enormously popular figure in Medellin. He was even elected to a seat in Congress in 1982. A useful side-effect was that his popularity made it very difficult for rival cartels to assassinate him.

His political career did not last long, but his criminal career continued to flourish. The US appetite for cocaine continued to grow, entirely unaffected by Nancy Reagan's 'Just Say No' campaign. By the late 1980s, *Forbes* magazine ranked Escobar the seventh-richest man in the world, worth in total over three billion dollars.

ASSASSINATION ATTEMPTS

By 1989, however, the United States started to put extreme pressure on the Colombian government to clamp down on the cocaine moguls; the billions at stake also meant that there were other criminal gangs – in particular the Cali cartel – determined to murder Escobar and take his business.

After several near-miss assassination attempts, Escobar decided on a novel survival plan. In 1990 he turned himself in to the government and agreed to plead guilty to a relatively minor drug-dealing charge for which he would receive an agreed sentence of nine years. What Escobar was able to demand in return for this is remarkable. First, he

received a guarantee that he would not be extradited to the United States as the US government wanted. Secondly, he would build his own private prison in which to serve his time. The prison itself, nicknamed the 'Cathedral', was a luxurious fortified abode designed less to imprison Escobar than to keep his enemies out.

WALKING OUT OF JAIL

After a year, Escobar began to tire of his imprisonment. He was worried that changes in the government might alter his terms of imprisonment, and his erstwhile minions were taking advantage of his absence to siphon off huge amounts of money. And so, in 1991, Escobar went back to running his organization from a succession of safe houses.

Escobar had been right to fear the change in government policy. For the first time, the authorities began to make serious attempts to put an end to his reign. On 2 December 1993, he was trapped in a Medellin apartment block by the secret police, who killed him during a rooftop gun battle. However, his legacy remained: the worldwide trafficking of cocaine continued to expand at full speed.

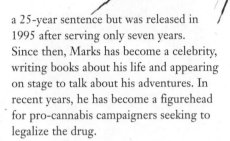

Howard Marks

Howard Marks is one of the most audacious drug traffickers of all time. An intelligent, charming man, he managed to import huge amounts of cannabis into the United States and Britain, and to elude the authorities while doing so for over twenty years. However, his luck came to an end when Craig Lovato, an agent of the US Drug Enforcement Administration, took it upon himself to bring the elusive Marks to justice. After a long chase, he was finally caught and arrested, and was convicted of drug smuggling. He received a 25-year sentence but was released in 1995 after serving only seven years. Since then, Marks has become a celebrity, writing books about his life and appearing on stage to talk about his adventures. In recent years, he has become a figurehead for pro-cannabis campaigners seeking to legalize the drug.

A CHARMED LIFE

Marks was born in Britain in 1945, in Port Talbot, Wales, an industrial town dominated by a huge steelworks. In later years, he liked to represent himself as an illiterate miner's son who walked barefoot to school and whose parents kept coal in the bath, but in actual fact his background was fairly comfortable. Howard did well at school, and went on to study at Balliol College, Oxford, arriving there at a time when the 1960s counter-culture was in full swing. He took to supplying cannabis for his friends to enjoy at parties; he attests, however, that he always steered clear of hard drugs such as heroin, especially after a fellow student, Joshua Macmillan (the grandson of the British prime minister), died after an overdose.

On leaving Oxford, Marks began to smuggle drugs, using his sharp wits to come up with clever schemes to evade the authorities. He loved the life, travelling to exotic places and continuing, everywhere he went, to be the life and soul of the party. He began to make a lot of money selling drugs, covering his tracks by opening a boutique in Oxford so that he could pretend his income came from selling clothes. Although he was known by police to be smuggling cannabis, they were unable

Howard Marks – 'chilled' even when in hot water

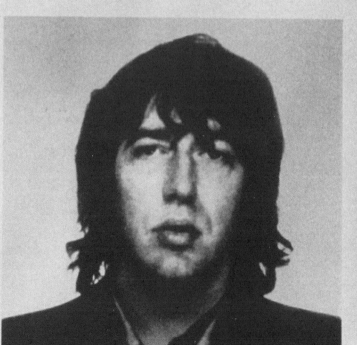

POLICE LINE DO NOT CROSS

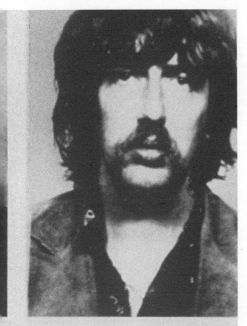

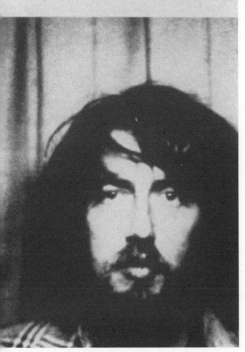

to catch him; he was too smart for the authorities, and soon he gained the reputation of being 'untouchable'.

However, by the 1970s, Marks was beginning to get into trouble. He was shipping tons of cannabis across many miles and continents, using a number of different names and money-laundering businesses to evade detection. When he was finally charged with smuggling cannabis, he managed to skip bail and go on the run. This did not prevent him from enjoying himself: occasionally, he would show up at parties in New York or London and then, mysteriously, disappear.

THE LONG ARM OF THE LAW

Marks' next audacious scam landed him in even more trouble. He was accused of shipping fifteen tons of Colombian marijuana into Britain – an enormous, unprecedented amount. However, to everyone's astonishment, at his trial he somehow managed to get off. Marks' criminal activities continued; although during the 1980s he was, on the face of it, living quietly in Spain with his family, he was in fact masterminding cannabis smuggling all over the world. At this time, he is thought to have had about forty-three aliases, twenty-five businesses and ninety phone lines.

Marks continued to outwit the authorities until US drug enforcement agent Craig Lovato decided that enough was enough. Lovato doggedly set out to gather evidence against him, tapping Marks' phone lines and breaking his coded messages to his associates. He

The many faces and disguises of Howard Marks

During the 1980s, he is thought to have had 43 aliases, 25 businesses and 90 phone lines

POLICE LINE DO NOT CROSS

found out, for example, that 'Your dog is sick' meant 'Your phone is bugged', and that 'champagne' meant 'marijuana'. Lovato kept a detailed record of Marks' drug-dealing activities and eventually built up a strong case against him. The final piece fell into place when a business associate and friend of Marks, a rich, decadent aristocrat named Lord Moynihan, informed on him, taping conversations that incriminated Marks and many of his cronies. Marks and twenty-two of his associates were arrested.

PEACE, LOVE AND CANNABIS

Marks received a long prison sentence, but only served seven years in jail. He remained unrepentant about his crimes, arguing that cannabis should be legalized, and that he had done nothing wrong. Lovato, for his part, pointed out that Marks had made a great deal of money from his drug-running activities, and that, in the process, he had ruined many of his associates' lives.

Today, Howard Marks has become something of an icon of the 1960s, and continues to argue his values of peace, love and cannabis to an admiring younger generation, all the while maintaining that his aim was to provide what he saw as a positive, life-enhancing drug to as many people as possible, rather than to amass a fortune for himself and his friends. Whatever his aim, he showed remarkable business acumen, far removed from the hippy image he cultivated.

Still living with the hippy values of peace, love and getting stoned, Howard Marks in the mud at the Glastonbury Festival

POLICE LINE DO NOT CROSS

George Jung

The story of George Jung is a fascinating one. It is the story of how the hippy idealism of the 1960s, based on love, peace and cannabis, slowly developed into a violent culture based on greed, guns and cocaine. The man in the middle of it all was George Jung, who became almost single-handedly responsible for flooding the United States with cocaine in the 1970s. Along the way, Jung lost his ideals, his family and his freedom, and today serves out his sentence in a prison cell.

George Jung grew up in the 1960s in Massachusetts. His father was an honest, hard-working man; and his mother was a dissatisfied woman, who constantly berated her husband for not earning enough money. The young George left home with a burning desire, above all else, to be rich – an aim he soon achieved. He began by selling marijuana to students in the northeast, before realizing the financial potential of buying it cheap in southern California and Mexico and then transporting it to the east coast of the United States, where the street price was much higher. His operation expanded rapidly, until finally one day he was caught. He was tried and sentenced to prison.

'WHITE-COLLAR CRIMINALS'

It was in prison that Jung met the men who were later to become his partners in the cocaine trade. At the time, cocaine was a little-known drug in the United States, hardly used at all. However, from his cellmate, an English-speaking Colombian named Carlos Lehder, Jung learned that cocaine was available cheaply in Colombia and could fetch a very high price in the United States. Together, the pair devised a plan for smuggling cocaine from South America into the States. In pursuit of this aim, they met with a number of other prisoners – 'white-collar criminals', as Jung called them – including lawyers and bankers. From a drug smuggler they learned everything they could about navigation, and from a banker, they found out about money laundering.

Once they were released from prison, Lehder and Jung used their new contacts to build up a massive cocaine-trafficking operation. They and the members of their Medellin cartel became responsible for introducing an astonishing eighty-five per cent of the entire amount of cocaine smuggled into the United States from the late 1970s to the early 1980s.

ADDICTED TO FEAR

By this point, Jung was living a life of luxury, having amassed over a hundred million dollars. His money, and his glamorous lifestyle, attracted many female admirers. He met and married a beautiful woman named Mirtha, and the couple had a baby daughter. On a financial and social level, Jung had achieved more than he could ever have hoped for. However, in the process, he had completely lost control of his life. He was addicted to cocaine. He was also addicted, as he later put it, to fear: the constant fear of getting caught provided an adrenaline rush that he could not do without, even though he knew that his illegal activities were a threat to his family.

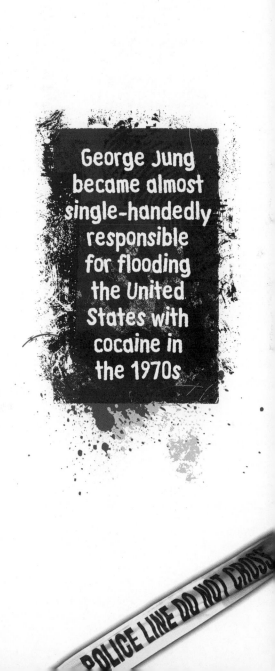

George Jung became almost single-handedly responsible for flooding the United States with cocaine in the 1970s

POLICE LINE DO NOT CROSS

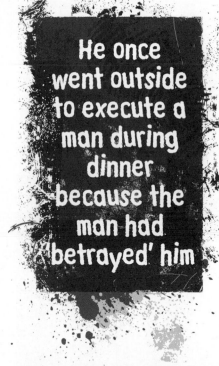

He once went outside to execute a man during dinner because the man had 'betrayed' him

George Jung went from being a small-time pot dealer in California to amassing a million-dollar fortune from the cocaine industry. His story was made into the film Blow, starring Johnny Depp (left)

Jung was also fearful about the company he was keeping: by now, he was surrounded by violent criminals such as Pablo Escobar, who supplied the cocaine from Colombia. Escobar not only carried guns but thought nothing of using them: he once went outside to execute a man during dinner, because the man had 'betrayed' him. He then continued his dinner. It was incidents like these that made Jung realize that the hippy ideals of love and peace he had started out with had long since vanished, and in their place was a terrifying, evil world of greed, paranoia and violence.

As the cocaine operation became bigger, the risks also grew. Eventually, Jung was arrested. He managed to escape, but was then caught again. His wife left him, taking their baby daughter with her, and he ended up serving a long prison sentence. Everything that he had built up collapsed. Jung had never been a violent man, and was known for his kindness and straight dealing, yet he had become part of a world that had absolutely no moral scruples whatsoever.

A VICIOUS CIRCLE

Jung's story was later told in a movie, *Blow*. Unusually, the film tried to avoid the stereotype of drug dealers as sleazy lowlifes, and instead portrayed the main characters as dynamic, intelligent men trying to make a success of their lives but eventually succumbing, through greed, to violence and corruption. Like many of his contemporaries, Jung started out with the idea that the government and corporate America were so corrupt that the laws of the land meant nothing; and that drugs such as cannabis and cocaine could be a liberating force for an alternative lifestyle.

Yet, through dealing drugs on such a massive scale, and making a personal fortune, Jung fell prey to exactly the same kind of corruption as the establishment. In the process, he introduced future generations to one of the most widely used, destructive and addictive drugs in the United States today: cocaine.

POLICE LINE DO NOT CROSS

Arellano-Felix Brothers

The brothers Benjamin and Ramon Arellano-Felix jointly led one of the most successful and bloodthirsty criminal organizations of all time. During the 1990s, they came to dominate the enormously lucrative trade in smuggling drugs – primarily cocaine but also marijuana and amphetamines – into the United States.

Mexico has long been a crucial staging point for drug traffickers thanks to its geographical position. To the south lie the drug-producing countries – particularly the cocaine mecca that is Colombia – while to the north there are 1,600 km (1,000 miles) of borderland with the target market, the United States. This proximity had long led to any number of small-scale smuggling operations. In the 1990s, however, these organizations came under centralized control, dominated by drug-smuggling cartels. The Arellano-Felix organization became the most brutal and feared of all these cartels.

EL MIN AND EL MON
The Arellano-Felix brothers grew up in the coastal province of Sinaloa, near Mazatlan. Their uncle, Miguel Angel Felix Gallardo, ran a drug-trafficking business out of Tijuana, further up the west coast, next to the US border. Before long, the four Arellano-Felix brothers – Benjamin, Ramon, Eduardo and Javier – headed north to work for their uncle. They began by smuggling electronic goods – televisions and so forth – and

soon graduated to narcotics. In 1989, Gallardo was arrested and the brothers quickly took over the drug route.

Now that they were in charge, the brothers – in particular Benjamin, the oldest and the natural leader – saw the opportunity for all-out expansion. Their skills were a classic mix for Latin American drug barons – a lethal mixture of ingenuity and brutality. Benjamin was the brains of the operation, a mild-mannered man who could pass for an accountant. His youngest brother, Ramon, was unquestionably the leader when it came to brutality. The two brothers nicknamed each other El Min (Benjamin) and El Mon (Ramon).

The organization the Arellano-Felix brothers built up was known locally as the Tijuana cartel, after the dangerous border town in which they were based. However, the field of operation soon expanded to cover a 160 km (100 mile) stretch of the border between Tijuana and Mexicali. The brothers would send their drugs by boat or by car. They also used a secret tunnel. At one stage, the US authorities, acting on a tip-off, searched a farmhouse on the American side of the border. Inside they found an empty safe that concealed the entrance to a wide, well-lit tunnel that ran for nearly 1.6 km (1 mile) under the border – a pipeline for drugs trafficking.

MASSACRE AND MUTILATION
The Tijuana cartel's reputation grew to such a degree that the Drug Enforcement Administration in the United States declared it 'one of the most powerful, violent and aggressive drug-trafficking organizations in the world'. Despite the cartel's increasing notoriety, however, the

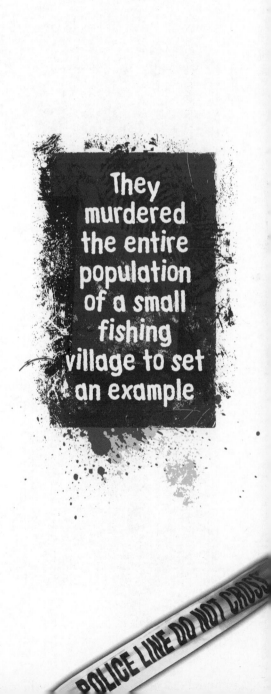

They murdered the entire population of a small fishing village to set an example

POLICE LINE DO NOT CROSS

The brains and the brawn behind the Tijuana cartel;
'El Min' (left) and 'El Mon' (right)

brothers were able to carry on without being arrested for thirteen years. To remain free, they spent an estimated million dollars a week on bribing politicians and policemen. Those who held out, or who were not important enough to need bribing in the first place, were simply killed. The brothers murdered hundreds of their enemies – estimates range between 300 and over 1,000 victims. They killed witnesses, bystanders, policemen, two police chiefs, several federal police commanders, judges and even a Roman Catholic cardinal, Juan Jesus Posadas Ocampo. He was gunned down at the airport in Guadalajara when members of the gang mistook his car for that of a rival drug baron. This extraordinary piece of misjudgement led them to lower their profile for a little while, but otherwise traffic and terror went on unabated.

FAST CARS AND FUR

Ramon, in particular, became a notorious figure around Tijuana, driving around in a red Porsche, sporting a mink jacket and heavy gold jewellery. He started to recruit a new type of gangster to the business. These were the so-called 'narco-juniors', rich kids who became hitmen for fun rather than profit.

Meanwhile, the brothers' brutality became ever more extreme. In 1998, they murdered the entire population of a small fishing village to set an example. Torture and mutilation became part of their way of working as well. A Tijuana prosecutor named Jose Patino Moreno was kidnapped along with two aides. When their bodies were found, they were unrecognizable. Almost every bone in their bodies had been broken and their heads had been crushed in a vice. Intimidated by the drug traffickers, local police officers claimed that the three men had lost their lives in 'a lamentable traffic incident'. Years later, two policemen would be convicted of involvement in the killings.

THE DAY OF RECKONING

Very few drug dealers live to enjoy the fruits of their crimes for very long and the Arellano-Felix brothers were no exception. The flamboyant Ramon was the first to go. He got caught up in a shoot-out with a rival drugs gang in Mazatlan, back in Sinaloa province. After the gun battle the police found three corpses, one of which carried ID in the name of Jorge Lopez. Soon afterwards, the body was removed from the undertakers by people claiming to be relatives of the late Mr Lopez. It was only afterwards that the police examined photos of the dead man and identified him as Ramon.

With Ramon's death, the gang's aura of invincibility was shattered. Soon afterwards, Benjamin Arellano-Felix was arrested at a house in the town of Puebla, his bags packed and ready for flight. However, the younger brothers remain at large, and the rise of other drug lords like them has ensured that the multi-million dollar drug-trafficking industry has been barely affected by the fate of the Arellano-Felix brothers.

POLICE LINE DO NOT CROSS

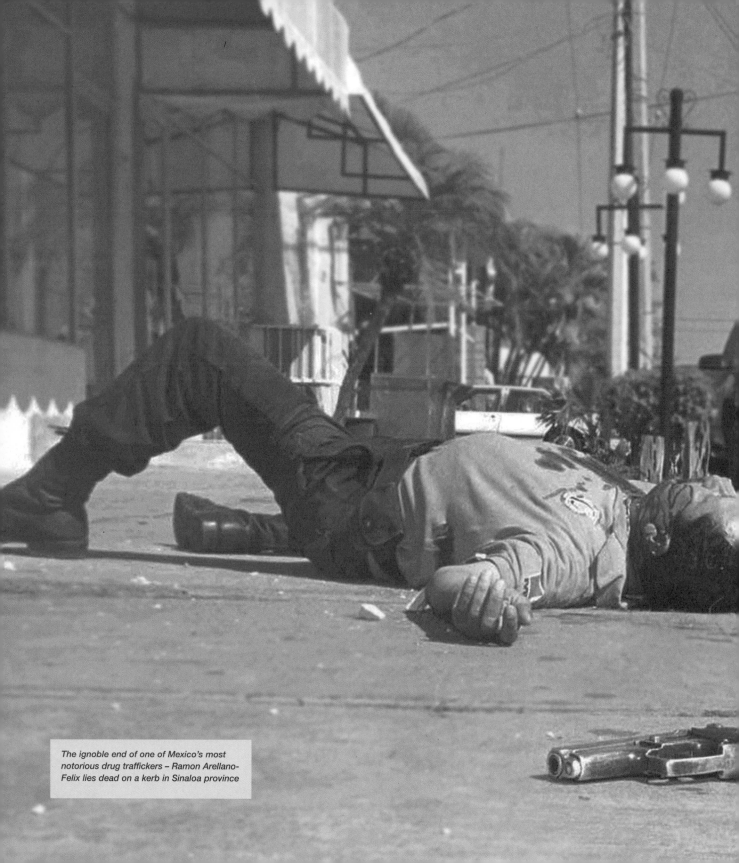

The ignoble end of one of Mexico's most
notorious drug traffickers – Ramon Arellano-
Felix lies dead on a kerb in Sinaloa province

Meyer Lansky

Meyer Lansky was one of the principal figures in the formation of the US Mafia, responsible for transforming black-market activities such as bootlegging, prostitution and narcotics trafficking into an organized crime syndicate spanning America. He is credited with the boastful remark that the National Crime Syndicate, as it became known, was 'bigger than US Steel'. Many commentators have speculated that, had Lansky had a conventional career, he would have ended up as boss of a large corporation, such was his talent for business and management. Unlike many of his mobster colleagues, he was level-headed, rational and extremely intelligent, never letting his passions dictate his actions. Throughout most of his career, he managed to evade the law, only serving a short time in prison towards the end of it, and died a rich old man in Florida in 1983. He left behind a vast fortune of over 400 million dollars.

ROUGH NEIGHBOURHOOD

Lansky was born Majer Suchowlinski in Grodno, Poland, in 1902. His parents were Jewish, and while he was still a boy, the family emigrated to the United States. They Americanized their name to Lansky, settling in New York, where ten-year-old Meyer, as he was now called, was captivated by the vibrant street life of the big city. However, as a small, foreign boy in a rough neighbourhood he quickly had to develop survival skills, and became tough. While he was in school, he came up against the Sicilian street gang led by Lucky Luciano who demanded protection money from him. Lansky refused to pay and, although he was much smaller in stature than his opponents, put up a spirited fight. Luciano was impressed, and the pair became firm friends.

THE BRAINS AND THE BRAWN

Growing up in a tough area of Brooklyn, Lansky soon realized that the only way to make big money was to become involved in the various street enterprises that he saw around him. His hard-working father, a garment presser in the clothing industry, had sunk into depression as a result of his family's poverty, and Meyer had no intention of following the same path. He began to join in street gambling games and, with his good head for figures, he often won, hiding his increasingly large bankroll of money in a hole in his mattress. At fifteen, he left school, and his father found him a job as an apprentice toolmaker. However, the job did not last long; by this time, he was becoming involved in all sorts of unsavoury street scams. In 1920, the Volstead Act had brought in Prohibition, providing a new opening for young men like Lansky in buying and selling illegal liquor. The following year, Lansky quit his job and never looked back.

He hooked up with a friend, 'Bugsy' Siegel, and together the pair formed a notorious gang that took on anything from protection rackets to car-jacking and armed robbery. They then moved on to work for Arnold Rothstein, the 'Mr Big' of New York crime, bootlegging scotch and running gambling houses and brothels. Lansky and Siegel were like chalk and cheese: where Lansky always tried to figure out the most effective way

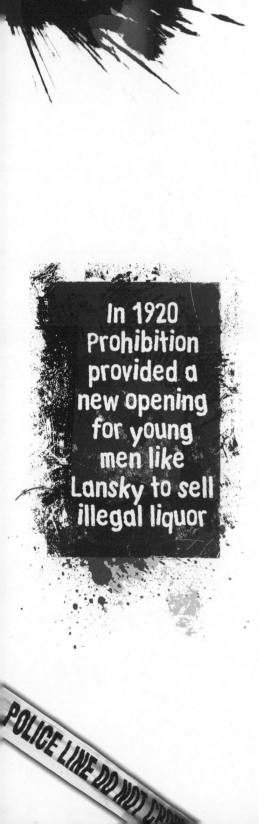

In 1920 Prohibition provided a new opening for young men like Lansky to sell illegal liquor

POLICE LINE DO NOT CROSS

With an ill-gotten fortune of over four hundred million dollars, Lansky certainly had something to smile about

By the 1930s, Lansky was involved in running 'carpet joints' and paying off 'tame' politicians

POLICE LINE DO NOT CROSS

to handle a situation, Siegel on the other hand was hotheaded and trigger-happy to the point of being psychotic. Despite their differences, the two of them were very close, and many believed that Lansky was the only person who could control Siegel's violent streak. In turn, Siegel offered Lansky the protection he needed to pursue his various illegal business activities, and many times saved his friend's life. As a business team, the pair were formidable: Lansky was the brains, and Siegel the brawn. The partnership lasted for many years until Siegel's reckless behaviour got the better of him.

BETRAYING BUGSY

Along with Siegel, Lansky joined up with his old sparring partner Lucky Luciano to become part of the notorious New York mobsters the Five Points Gang. Early in his career, Lansky helped Luciano bump off Mafia bosses Joe Masseria and Salvatore Maranzano, although as a Jew he was forced to take a back seat in the conflict between the Italian overlords. Luciano then took over 'The Firm', as he called it, and partly because of his close relationship with Lansky, threw the field open to Jewish and other ethnic groups, instead of limiting it to those of Sicilian origin, as his previous bosses had done. His equal opportunities policy was highly successful, and soon the Italian and Jewish gangs were operating an international crime network that boasted all kinds of criminal activities, from gambling and prostitution to drug smuggling and extortion.

By the 1930s, Lansky was a very rich man, despite the fact that Prohibition had now come to an end. He was involved in

One of the most important Mafia godfathers of the twentieth century

running illegal casinos across the country, known as 'carpet joints', and had evolved a complex system of paying off politicians to allow him to do so. He then expanded the operation to Cuba. Meanwhile, his old friend and partner, Bugsy Siegel, was in charge of construction projects in Las Vegas. However, Bugsy Siegel was no businessman and had begun to overrun building and decorating costs by millions of dollars. Luciano and other members of the syndicate were convinced that Siegel and his girlfriend, Virginia Hill, were skimming money, and threatened to have Siegel killed. Lansky pleaded for mercy for his friend, and asked for more time so that the casino could turn a profit. Eventually, it did, but by that time it was too late: Siegel was brutally gunned down in his apartment in Beverly Hills. Lansky always claimed that he knew nothing about the killing, but it may have been the case that he was forced to order it.

THE FINAL YEARS

Lansky continued to run the syndicate until late in life, expanding into legal areas of business such as investment in hotels and golf courses. In his later years, he was accused of tax evasion, and decided to retire to Israel. However, Israel was not prepared to take a mob boss wanted by the FBI, so he eventually returned to Florida where he was arrested and charged. He served a short prison sentence. Afterwards, Lansky settled in Florida and died of lung cancer in 1983. Thus ended the career of Meyer Lansky, a man who had never sought the limelight, or attracted a great deal of media attention, yet who was one of the most important Mafia godfathers of the 20th century.

Assassinations: Proving a Point

Martin Luther King

The assassination of Martin Luther King on 4 April 1968 marked a turning point in the history of America. On that day, the country's leading civil rights activist was shot dead on the balcony of a motel in Memphis, Tennessee. At the time he died, King's campaign to bring equal rights for black people had achieved an extraordinary change of heart among the mass of Americans, and the day before, he had made a rousing speech to an ecstatic crowd of thousands. During the speech, King had referred to the constant threats that were being made on his life, and had predicted that he himself might not live to see the time when America became a 'Promised Land' of people united in peace, freedom and justice.

Sadly, he was proved right when, the following evening, he was shot dead. The person convicted of his murder was James Earl Ray, an ex-convict and open racist. However, there were some – including members of King's family – who did not believe that Ray was responsible, and suspected that the FBI and CIA were behind the killing. Whatever the truth, King's death spelled the end of an optimistic period in American society, in which people began to hope that the racial discrimination and economic inequality which had for so long divided the country would come to an end.

BUS BOYCOTT

Michael King was born in Atlanta, Georgia, the son of a Baptist minister and a teacher.

His parents later changed his name to Martin. As a young man, King followed his father into a career in the church. After studying for several years, he received a doctorate and then went to work as a minister in Montgomery, Alabama. King married Coretta Scott in 1953, and the couple went on to have four children, all of whom eventually became civil rights workers.

King quickly attracted a large congregation and became an important spokesperson for black people in the area. He was vociferous in his condemnation of the racist laws of the South, which required black people to live separately from, and take second place to, the white population. A staunch supporter of desegregation, he made his views widely known, even though he knew that there would definitely be retaliation from white separatists. In 1955, after the famous incident in which Rosa Parks, a black woman, refused to give up her seat to a white man on the bus, he helped to organize a boycott of the buses in Montgomery. Soon the bus company was ordered to change its rules.

CIVIL DISOBEDIENCE

In the years that followed, King became a leading proponent of the growing US civil rights movement. Taking Mahatma Gandhi as his example, he began to lead protests in the southern city of Birmingham, Alabama, putting forward a policy of civil disobedience and stressing that all direct action should be non-

The 1960s were a momentous decade for US civil rights: here two leading lights Martin Luther King and Malcolm X are seen together

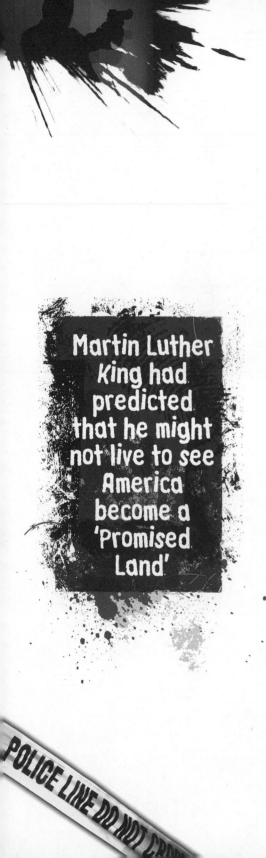

Martin Luther King had predicted that he might not live to see America become a 'Promised Land'

POLICE LINE DO NOT CROSS

violent. Nonetheless, he was imprisoned for his activities. Also, a number of bomb attacks were made on the civil rights campaigners' headquarters, in an attempt to intimidate the activists. However, King and his followers were not deterred, and went on to assist in organizing the huge civil rights march on Washington in 1963. This was the event where King chose to deliver his famous speech about his dream of a united America, where black people could live side by side with white people in peace and equality.

In 1964, King received the Nobel Peace Prize, and went on to campaign successfully for black people's voting rights. He then began to agitate against the US war in Vietnam, which made him new enemies in the government and the media. He also brought people's attention to the extreme poverty in which many Americans, both black and white, were forced to live, which was another issue that the authorities would have preferred him to ignore and keep quiet about.

DEATH THREATS

During this period, King was under constant surveillance from the FBI. Yet despite the fact that there were daily threats on his life, the US intelligence forces did not offer him a great deal of protection. It was this lack of enthusiasm for ensuring the security of one of America's leading political figures that caused rumours to spread when King was later assassinated.

At 6 pm on the evening of 4 April 1968, King was standing on the balcony

Witnessed by a crowd of tens of thousands of mourners, King's coffin went through Atlanta on a wooden farm wagon drawn by two mules

of the Lorraine Motel in Memphis, Tennessee. Without warning, a lone gunman hidden in the bushes below shot him at close range. King was wounded in the jaw, collapsed and was rushed to hospital, where he died a few hours later.

The police seemed unable to find out anything about King's assassin, and came under a great deal of pressure to do so. However, it was not until two months later that an escaped prisoner named James Earl Ray was picked up in Britain. He had been travelling under a false passport. The British police arrested him, interrogated him and extradited him to Tennessee to face charges. There, on 10 March 1969, Ray confessed to the murder of Martin Luther King. He was charged, tried, convicted and sentenced to a prison term of ninety-nine years.

WAS THE KILLER FRAMED?

Later, Ray took back his confession, alleging that he had only pleaded guilty to escape the death penalty, on the advice of his attorney. He also said that his attorney had pressurized him because he wanted to make money from a movie deal. Ray accused his brother, Johnny, and a Canadian smuggler named 'Raoul' for the murder, but his account was full of inconsistencies. In 1994, investigators found a retired auto worker in upstate New York who matched a photo of 'Raoul' given to them by Ray. The man was cleared of involvement, but sadly, the accusation ruined his life, and he never managed to shake off the stigma. The questions about King's death remained unanswered until, in 1997, a House Select Committee finally concluded that there may have been a conspiracy, but that Ray

had definitely shot King. Ray continued to maintain that he had not, until his death in prison on 23 April 1998.

Because of the establishment's ambivalent attitude towards Martin Luther King, rumours about his assassination still persisted. King's son, Dexter King, was convinced that his father had been killed by FBI agents and made strenuous efforts to prove his theory. He pointed out that there were various items of evidence at the scene of the crime, and findings from the investigation, that cast doubt on Ray's guilt. For example, ballistic tests conducted after the assassination could not prove that the

Without warning, a lone gunman hidden in the bushes below shot him at close range

POLICE LINE DO NOT CROSS

rifle was the murder weapon. In addition, Ray's personal history showed that although he was a burglar he had no previous record of violence. It was also doubtful that he was a good enough marksman to hit his target. In fact, Ray's record showed that as a criminal he was not very able, and would not have had the intelligence or the courage to pull off the assassination.

HITMAN FROM THE FBI OR PETTY CRIMINAL?

Other theories were that Ray had acted as a hit man for the FBI, under the direction of assistant director Cartha DeLoach, who had masterminded the plot. According to this theory, Ray had travelled to Memphis to take part in a bank robbery while King was in town. Ray had just happened to be staying in a rooming house next door to King's hotel on the evening when King was shot by an FBI gunman hiding in the shrubbery nearby. Afterward, the FBI had planted the murder weapon, a Remington rifle, in Ray's car and framed him for the murder.

In the years after King's assassination, his family went on to advance their theory that the FBI was responsible for murdering him. Martin Luther's son, Dexter King, publicly met Ray in 1997, shook the prisoner's hand, and pledged support for his campaign for a trial. Two years later, Coretta Scott King launched a civil trial against Memphis bar owner Lloyd Jowers and 'other unknown conspirators' who were thought to have committed the assassination. Jowers was found guilty on that occasion, but the King family were only awarded a symbolic sum of $100, and a later

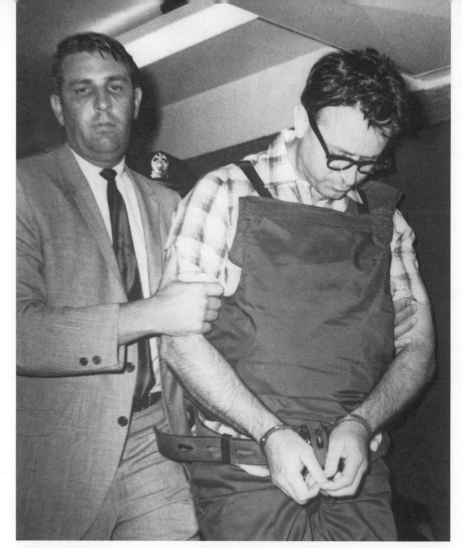

Head bowed and hands manacled, James Earl Ray was charged with killing Martin Luther King and led to his cell in Memphis, Tennessee

investigation found no evidence of Jowers' involvement in any plot.

To date, it also appears that no hard evidence can be found to link the US security services to the assassination of the civil rights campaigner. However, there remain important questions about the FBI's attitude towards King when he was alive. In particular its attempts to smear King as a communist, and its constant, intrusive surveillance of his daily activities, have undoubtedly caused some to question their claim that King was shot

by a petty criminal. Whoever did the deed, and whatever the truth of the matter, there is no doubt that the assassination of Martin Luther King traumatized the American nation, in much the same way that the killing of John F. Kennedy did. King's courageous campaign, in the face of so much vocal opposition, had brought genuine hope for peace, justice and equality to a divided nation; and for many of his followers, when King was assassinated, his vision of a united America also died.

POLICE LINE DO NOT CROSS

John Lennon

The assassination of John Lennon on
8 December 1980 shocked his many fans
worldwide, and turned the former Beatle
into an icon – or even a saint – almost
overnight. Despite the fact that, by the
time he was murdered, the reclusive star
had undergone long periods of creative
inactivity, and was reported at various
times to have been violent, drug-addicted,
alcoholic and mentally unbalanced, after
his death his reputation grew until he
became not only one of the seminal
figures of popular music during the
twentieth century but a figurehead
for peace and love, attracting a loyal
following among generations of new
fans which continues to this day.

'BIGGER THAN JESUS'
Born in Liverpool on 9 October 1940,
John Lennon was the son of a merchant
seaman and grew up in a working-class
area of the city. His parents, Julia and
Alf, split up when he was five, his father
abandoning the family. Julia was left to
cope on her own and found herself unable
to, so John was sent to live with his aunt
Mimi. He continued to see his mother
Julia, with whom he had a troubled
relationship. She taught him to play the
banjo, which gave him a distinctive style
when he later picked up the guitar.

When Lennon was seventeen, Julia
was killed in a car accident and he was
obliged to go to the morgue to identify
her body, an incident which scarred him
emotionally for life. As a young man,
Lennon went to art school but dropped
out, instead forming a band called the

Silver Beetles with Paul McCartney
and George Harrison. In 1962, Lennon
married his girlfriend Cynthia Powell and
became the father of a son, Julian.

The band, whose name was soon
altered to the Beatles, went on to tour
Germany, and achieved worldwide
success. Crucial to their popularity were
the songs of Lennon and McCartney,
which developed from the bright, melodic
pop of the early 1960s to the introspective
psychedelia of their later period.

The Beatles became one of the most
influential bands of their time, not only
musically but in terms of the new 1960s
counterculture in general, and their
opinions were asked on every question
under the sun. Lennon took the
opportunities offered to him by his fame
to express his often controversial beliefs,
sometimes adding ironic comments that
people took seriously, such as that the
Beatles were 'more popular than Jesus'.
This particular remark infuriated the
Christian church, and Lennon was
roundly condemned by many members
of the establishment.

LOVE AND PEACE
Lennon's personal life also became the
subject of controversy after he divorced
his wife Cynthia and married the
conceptual artist Yoko Ono. Together,
the pair recorded experimental albums
and conducted a series of attention-
grabbing public protests, including lying
in bed surrounded by posters for peace
and receiving members of the press for
interviews. Because of stunts such as
these, certain sections of the media
presented Lennon and Yoko as laughably
eccentric, but in retrospect, there is no

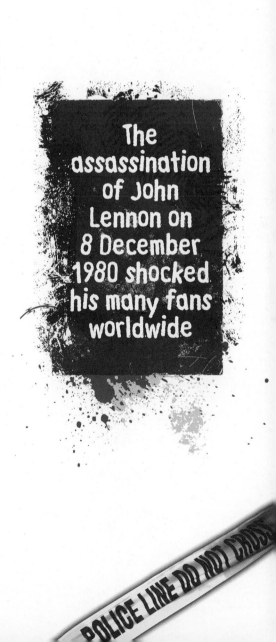

The
assassination
of John
Lennon on
8 December
1980 shocked
his many fans
worldwide

POLICE LINE DO NOT CROSS

doubt that they drew attention to several important political causes at the time, such as the war in Vietnam.

ACRIMONIOUS DISPUTES

As well as the establishment and the media, there were many fans of the Beatles who felt that Ono's influence on Lennon was a negative one. Lennon began to include his wife in every aspect of the band's recording work, and she became a constant presence everywhere he went. Ono's influence, and other issues to do with leadership of the group, eventually caused Lennon's relationship with the Beatles to break down. There followed a series of acrimonious disputes with Paul McCartney and the other Beatles, after which Lennon recorded as a solo artist and with Ono, until his retirement in 1975 following the birth of his second son, Sean. In 1980, Lennon returned to the studio, recording an album, *Double Fantasy*. At this time, shortly before his murder, he appeared to have come out of a fallow creative period in his life, to the delight of his fans.

During the 1960s, Lennon had once been asked how he thought he would die, and had replied that he expected to be 'popped off by some loony'. He had also expressed anxiety, in later years, that he was being stalked. (In part this was based on a well-founded belief that the FBI were harassing him, in order to bar him from living in the United States because of his political activities; and there were, of course, numerous fans who followed him everywhere, making security a constant issue for him.) As it turned out, these words, delivered in his humorous, offhand way, eventually proved prophetic.

THE KILLER

On Saturday, 6 December 1980, a young man named Mark Chapman checked into the YMCA on 63rd Street, just off Central Park West in New York City. A drifter, Chapman had been born in Texas on 10 May 1955. He had grown up in Georgia, an overweight child who was unpopular at school. In his teens he became a committed Christian and youth worker. In despair after a failed relationship, he moved to Hawaii where he planned to kill himself. When his suicide attempt failed, he found a renewed appetite for life. He met and married his Japanese-American wife, Gloria, and things went well for a couple of years.

Gradually, however, Chapman's behaviour became increasingly eccentric and he developed an obsession with John Lennon. Strangely, he was also obsessed with the J.D. Salinger novel, *The Catcher in the Rye*. When Chapman heard that John Lennon had a new record out he felt compelled to meet his idol.

That Saturday, Chapman spent several long hours outside the Dakota building, clutching a copy of *Double Fantasy*, and waiting for Lennon to appear. When he did not, Chapman retreated to the YMCA for the night. Next day, he moved to the nearby Sheraton Hotel and returned to his vigil. Once again Lennon failed to show, and Chapman contented himself with buying a copy of *Playboy* featuring a John Lennon interview. That night he called an escort agency, but when the call girl arrived he told her he merely wanted to talk to her, just as Holden Caulfield, the hero of *The Catcher in the Rye*, had done in a similar situation. He paid her $190 when she left at 3 am.

Strangely, Chapman was also obsessed with the J.D. Salinger novel, The Catcher in the Rye

The iconic image of John Lennon and his wife, Yoko Ono, during their famous 'make love not war' protest in 1969

POLICE LINE DO NOT CROSS

The next morning he woke up at 10.30 am, took out the hotel Bible, opened it at the beginning of the St John Gospel, and wrote in the word 'Lennon' after 'John'. Then he picked up his copy of *Double Fantasy* and his gun, and headed off to the Dakota building, picking up a copy of *The Catcher in the Rye* from a bookstore on the way.

AUTOGRAPH

Once at the Dakota building Chapman became so engrossed in the book that he did not even notice Lennon entering the building. He continued to wait and chatted with other Lennon fans. Soon after lunchtime a fellow fan spotted five-year-old Sean Lennon coming out with his nanny. Chapman shook the child's hand. During the course of the afternoon he saw other celebrities including Lauren Bacall and Paul Simon coming and going. Finally, around 6 pm, John Lennon came out with Yoko Ono, heading for a recording studio. Chapman offered him the record to sign and Lennon did so graciously, asking him, 'Is that all you want?'

Part of him, Chapman said later, was satisfied with this, wanted to take his autograph and go home to Hawaii and get on with his life. Another part of him, however, had a much darker purpose in mind, and that part won out.

Chapman continued to wait outside the Dakota building. At around 10.50 pm John and Yoko returned from their visit to the recording studio. Yoko Ono got out of the white limousine first. This is what happened next, by Chapman's own account, as given to the police a few hours later: 'He walked past me, and then a voice in my head said, "Do it, do it, do it," over and over again, saying "Do it, do it, do it, do it," like that. I pulled the gun out of my pocket. I handed it over to my left hand. I don't remember aiming. I must have done it, but I don't remember drawing the bead or whatever you call it. And I just pulled the trigger steady five times.'

Lennon tried to get away from the gun and the assassin, but four of Chapman's five bullets hit him. Even so he managed to run up six steps into the concierge's station. There he said the words, 'I'm shot', then fell face down.

DEAD ON ARRIVAL

Chapman, meanwhile, just stayed exactly where he was. He got out his copy of *The Catcher in the Rye* and started reading, waiting for the police to arrive. Then he put his hands in the air and surrendered immediately, saying, 'I acted alone.' Lennon was rushed in a police car to St Luke's Roosevelt Hospital, but died soon after his arrival. Within hours there was a crowd of thousands of people outside the hospital. The following day the whole world seemed to be united in mourning of a kind not seen since the Kennedy assassination.

Mark Chapman was arrested, brought to trial and pleaded guilty to murder. He was convicted and sentenced to a term of life imprisonment in Attica State Prison, near Buffalo in New York. He is still serving his sentence, despite several parole hearings, at least in part because the authorities firmly believe it to be highly likely that Chapman would himself be murdered by enraged fans were he ever to be released.

Mark Chapman being interviewed by Barbara Walters on the US TV show 20/20 in 1980

POLICE LINE DO NOT CRO

Mohandas Gandhi

Mohandas Karamchad Gandhi has a permanent place in history as one of the greatest leaders of the 20th century. His aim was to seek independence for his country, India, from its British colonial rulers through a committed campaign of non-violence. During his lifetime, he set an example to his people by pursuing a highly principled, moral way of life, dressing in the clothes of an Indian peasant and eschewing the trappings of luxury. As well as advocating non-violence, Gandhi also believed that people of all religious persuasions should have equal rights, and that Hindus were no more important than Muslims, which made him many enemies among radical Hindu political factions in India. On 30 January 1948, Gandhi was assassinated at the hands of a Hindu fanatic, Nathuram Godse, who shot and killed him as he walked through the streets to attend a prayer meeting in New Delhi. At his funeral, the nation mourned the loss of the man they called 'Mahatma', or 'great soul', and the prime minister of the newly independent India announced, 'the light has gone out of our lives'.

NON-VIOLENT PROTEST
Born in 1869 in Porbander, western India, Gandhi travelled to London, England, as a young man and studied law there. He began his career as a lawyer in Bombay, but soon moved to South Africa, where he took part in non-violent protests against the government, in support of Indian

Here, in a civil disobedience demonstration, Gandhi marches to the shore at Dandi to collect salt in defiance of the law

POLICE LINE DO NOT CROSS

immigrants' rights there. On his return
to India in 1915, he became involved in
politics, and began to campaign on behalf
of the Indian National Congress against
the British government, encouraging
Indians to buy Indian rather than British
goods. He consistently advocated non-
violent protest, but even so, he was
imprisoned several times for his activities.
He became a thorn in the side of the
British authorities, showing up their
hypocritical attitudes, and attracting
attention wherever he went. In 1931, he
famously attended a political conference
in Britain dressed only in the simple
clothes of an Indian peasant, once again
reminding the world of the harsh poverty
in which many of his countrymen lived.

A DREAM COMES TRUE

After many years of political campaigning,
Gandhi began to see his dream of a free,
independent India become a reality.
However, there were other problems on
the horizon that threatened to destroy
India's peaceful transition to independence,
in particular the deep antagonism that
existed between Indian Hindus and
Muslims. Having co-operated with the
British, Gandhi was accused of helping to
partition the country, a step that by all
accounts he fundamentally opposed.
He was also criticized for weakening the
Hindus' political power through his belief
in the equality of all religious faiths.

Despite the criticisms, Gandhi continued
to be regarded by most Indian people as
the father of Indian independence, and as

*Gandhi at No 10 Downing Street.
He dressed like a simple peasant,
jogging the world's memory
about India's terrible poverty*

POLICE LINE DO NOT CROSS

Some of the fanatics accused of assassinating Gandhi: (l to r) Godse, Apte, Krishna and Badge (bearded in the second row)

such became, by the end of his life, one of the most famous, well-loved and inspirational figures in the country.

ASSASSINATION ATTEMPTS

On 20 January 1948, there was an assassination attempt on Gandhi, but it failed. Ten days later, an assassin struck again, and this time was successful. Gandhi was on his way to a prayer meeting at Birla House, the home of a prominent industrialist where he often stayed during his visits to New Delhi.

At about 5 pm, people began to gather for the meeting. According to witnesses, Gandhi arrived for the meeting at about 5.12 pm, dressed in his customary garb, though wearing a homespun shawl over his loincloth because it was a cold evening. As he walked across the grass, accompanied by various followers, including some young women, onlookers knelt down or bowed their heads before him. Then, suddenly, several shots rang out. Gandhi fell to the ground, mortally wounded, his loincloth heavily stained

with blood. A doctor rushed to the scene, but it was too late to save the victim. As Gandhi lay dying, the police took charge, dispersing the weeping crowds and carrying the body away.

At 6 pm on All India Radio, it was announced that a lone gunman had shot Gandhi on his way to Birla House. He had been killed by three pistol shots in his chest. The killer was Nathuram Godse, a Hindu activitist who was thought to be

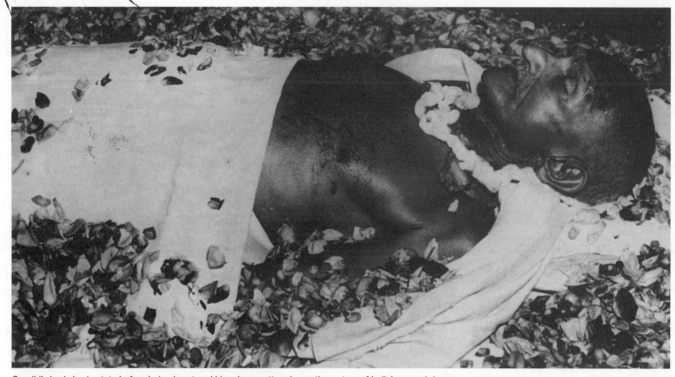

Gandhi's body lay in state before being burnt and his ashes scattered over the waters of India's sacred rivers

connected to the Hindu organization Mahasabha. Godse was immediately taken into custody and was tried and convicted. He received a death sentence and was hanged on 15 November 1949. Four other conspirators, including Godse's brother Gopal, were given life sentences. The president of the Mahasabha, Vinayak Damodar Savarkar, was also thought to be behind the assassination, but there was not enough evidence to link him to it.

GANDHI'S LAST WORDS

Not surprisingly, given the confusion of the assassination events, accounts differ as to what Gandhi actually said as he lay dying. Some attest that his last words were 'He Ram!' (Oh God!), which may have expressed his strong spiritual commitment to God, or – as some commentators have pointed out – could just be the normal expression of surprise and shock on being attacked. Whatever the truth, these are the words that are inscribed on Gandhi's memorial tomb in New Delhi. Others believe that the Mahatma exclaimed 'Rama Rama' and that as he fell, he put his hands together in the gesture of 'namaste', a religious gesture symbolizing love, respect and connection to others.

After his death, Gandhi was cremated on a funeral pyre as is the Hindu custom, and his ashes were collected in twenty urns. These were taken around India, and the ashes scattered among the waters of the country's great rivers, in accordance with Gandhi's wishes.

Today, Gandhi is remembered in India as the architect of independence, and his philosophy of non-violence and civil disobedience is thought to have inspired freedom fighters around the world, including Martin Luther King, the Dalai Lama, Nelson Mandela, Steve Biko and Aung San Suu Kyi. But according to Gandhi himself, his teachings and peaceful protests were nothing new: as he often stated, 'Truth and non-violence are as old as the hills.'

POLICE LINE DO NOT CROSS

Giovanni Falcone

The assassination of Judge Giovanni Falcone was a dark day in the history of the Italian nation. Falcone was known as a tireless crusader against the Mafia, a secret society whose influence had come to dominate the economy of Sicily, the largely agricultural island in the southern part of Italy. Falcone was killed in revenge for having imprisoned several major Mafia figures, and is remembered as the man courageous enough to take on the most violent, ruthless and corrupt elements in Italian society – and who lost his life as a result.

PERSUADING THE MAFIA
Born on 18 May 1939 in Palermo, Sicily, Giovanni Falcone grew up in a part of the city that was heavily bombed by Allied forces in 1943. His father, Arturo Falcone, was director of a chemical laboratory. Giovanni studied law at university and also attended the naval academy at Livorno, before becoming a practising lawyer. In 1964, he passed his examinations to become a judge, and after serving as a district magistrate, began to specialize in penal law.

During the 1970s, Falcone started to make a name for himself with his work on cases involving organized crime. He made many inroads in this area, including liaising with the police in the United States to track down Mafia members there. He also managed to persuade several important Mafia figures, including Tomasso Buscetta, a leading

Giovanni Falcone was an Italian judge who specialized in investigating Mafia crime

member of one of the top Mafia families, to work with the police and the legal authorities. Buscetta had seen many of his loved ones killed by rival families, and was among the first of the Mafia members to realize that the constant bloodshed they engaged in was entirely destructive to everyone concerned.

WIPING OUT CORRUPTION
By the mid 1980s, Falcone was focusing on prosecuting Mafia members for a variety of crimes, including murder. Together with other magistrates, he pioneered the famous Maxi Trials, which charged and convicted hundreds of Mafia members, in an attempt to wipe out the

corruption endemic in Sicilian society, thus making everyday life safer and more prosperous for the ordinary citizen there.

For many years, the existence of a Mafia network controlling almost every aspect of the economy and bureaucracy in Sicily had been quietly ignored. There was, however, evidence to show that this secret society had been controlling many activities since the 19th century, and that its influence had now penetrated into the police, legal and civil authorities. The reasons for the silence surrounding this state of affairs were twofold: first, many officials were receiving pay-offs from the Mafia

POLICE LINE DO NOT CROSS

POLICE LINE DO NOT CROSS

The debris after the car bomb that killed Judge
Falcone and his wife

and stood to gain if it continued its
stranglehold on the economic life of the
area; second, ordinary Sicilians were
terrified of the Mafia, whose culture of
machismo and violence was notorious,
and whose many bloody reprisals often
took place in public. For example, when
communist politician Pio La Torre
suggested that Italian law should be
changed to make being a member of the
Mafia a criminal offence, he was shot
in cold blood. The law was eventually
passed, but not surprisingly, there were
few other people brave enough to come
forward and incriminate Mafiosi.

'YEARS OF LEAD'

By the 1980s, the warring families of
the Mafia were engaged in tremendous
conflict for control of the black economy,
giving rise to hundreds of violent killings.
Not only Mafiosi, but politicians, police
and legal figures were drawn into the
conflict, and were murdered as well:
Cesare Terranova, Rocco Chinnici,
Emanuele Basile, Guiseppe Montana and
Salvatore Lima, to name but a few.
The victims of the 'years of lead', as the
decade became known, were by now so
many that the public became outraged at
this failure of the authorities to prevent
complete lawlessness in the region. The
politicians, many in the pay of the Mafia,
seemed unable or unwilling to solve the
problem. Something had to be done.

Enter Judge Giovanni Falcone.
Together with close friend and fellow
magistrate Paolo Borsellino, Falcone led
the movement to confront the situation

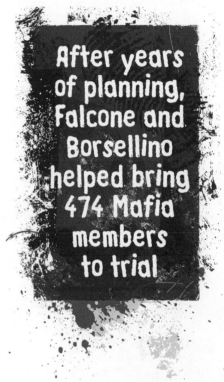

After years
of planning,
Falcone and
Borsellino
helped bring
474 Mafia
members
to trial

head on. They came up with a plan to
charge hundreds of Mafia members at
one time, hoping that by delivering such
a fatal blow, the organization would be
weaker and retaliations fewer. Of course,
both Falcone and Borsellino knew
that they were risking their lives, but
nevertheless, they continued in their
work. After years of planning, they
helped to bring a total of 474 Mafia
members to trial.

On 10 February 1986,
the Maxi Trial, as it
was called, began

POLICE LINE DO NOT CROSS

in a blaze of publicity. The charges ranged from murder, drug trafficking and extortion to being a member of the Mafia. Out of the total number of defendants, some of whom were tried in their absence, 360 were convicted, with a total of over 2,000 years in prison sentences. Some of these were important Mafia figures, such as Michele Greco, Salvatore Riina and Bernardo Provenzano. There were also over a hundred acquittals, demonstrating that the exercise was not merely a 'show trial': of these, eighteen were later killed by the Mafia. One of them, Antonino Ciulla, was actually gunned down on his way to attend a celebration for his release.

CORRUPT JUDGES
Sadly, much of Falcone's work was undone by corrupt judges, through the appeals system. One particular judge, Corrado Carnevale, who was later found to have been taking bribes from the Mafia, became known as 'The Sentence Killer' because he let so many of the convicted men go, often on specious grounds of ill health. For example, there was one Mafia boss who claimed to be suffering from a brain tumour; he was allowed to live in a private hospital, with his cronies around him attending to his every need, despite the fact that his 'tumour' had no symptoms at all.

At the beginning of the 1990s, Falcone and Borsellino succeeded in recouping some of the gains made at the Maxi Trial. They managed to turn down some of the appeals, and returned several Mafiosi to prison, much to their fury. In particular, they angered Mafia boss Salvatore Riina, who had been tried in

his absence, and was hoping, after his appeal, to return to his home and live in luxury for the rest of his life: instead, his appeal was turned down, and he found himself still facing a prison sentence.

DEADLY REPRISALS
On 23 May 1992, Falcone was travelling by car between the airport and the city of Palermo with his wife, Francesca Morvillo, who was also a magistrate. As the car sped along the motorway, it was blown up by a bomb placed on the side of the road. The bomb also killed three policemen. In the same year, Falcone's long-standing colleague and partner in the anti-Mafia offensive, Paolo Borsellino, was also murdered in a bomb attack.

It was not long before Salvatore Riina was arrested for the crimes, which were clearly reprisal killings in response to Falcone and Borsellino's determination to make his conviction stick. Riina was duly charged with the murder of both men, and is currently serving a life sentence for his part in the crimes. Another Mafioso, Giovanni Brusca, was convicted of detonating the explosives that caused their deaths.

Today, the airport at Palermo has been renamed Falcone-Borsellino in honour of the two men who tried to stamp out corruption in their city and who – to some degree, at least – succeeded in doing so. According to many reports, the Mafia still holds sway in Sicily, but Falcone and Borsellino will be remembered as the men who tried to prove that the rule of law is stronger than that of brute force, and that the safety and security of ordinary citizens is of paramount importance.

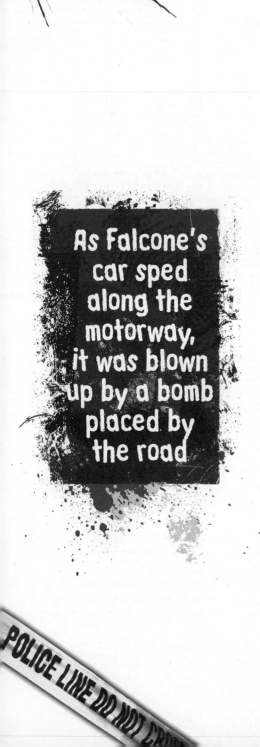

As Falcone's car sped along the motorway, it was blown up by a bomb placed by the road

POLICE LINE DO NOT CROSS

Abraham Lincoln

The assassination of Abraham Lincoln on 14 April 1865 was, arguably, the first modern political assassination.

This was not an especially mysterious crime. Abraham Lincoln had led the Union side throughout the extraordinarily bitter and bloody conflict known as the American Civil War (or the War Between the States to a southerner). At the time of his death the Union forces had finally prevailed. Not only that, but during the course of the war Lincoln had proclaimed emancipation, freeing the slaves in those southern states that the northern Union forces occupied.

As a result, there were many who wanted Lincoln dead: supporters of the southern Confederacy in general and pro-slavers in particular. One such man was the actor John Wilkes Booth, born on 10 May 1838. Booth had achieved some success on the stage, including several parts in Shakespeare plays. As a confirmed racist and southern sympathizer, he loathed Abraham Lincoln.

Abraham Lincoln led the Union side throughout the American Civil War and was a staunch defender of the emancipation of the slaves

ABDUCTION PLAN

In the late summer of 1864 it was becoming clear that the Union forces were winning the war. Booth's original plan (whether devised by himself alone or in collaboration with more senior Confederate figures) was to kidnap Lincoln, take him to Richmond, the Confederate capital, and hold him in return for Confederate prisoners of war. By January 1865, Booth had organized a group of helpers that included Samuel Arnold, Michael O'Laughlen, John Surratt, Lewis Powell, George Atzerodt, and David Herold. He used a boarding house belonging to Mary Surratt to meet with his co-conspirators.

The kidnap was planned for 17 March 1865, when Lincoln was due to attend a play at a hospital near Washington. However, the president changed his schedule at the last moment. Before the plot could be rearranged, General Robert E. Lee surrendered to General Ulysses S. Grant at Appomattox on 9 April 1865, effectively bringing the Civil War to an end. Two days later, Booth was present as Lincoln made a speech in Washington suggesting that voting rights be granted to certain blacks. Booth then decided it was time for yet more desperate action.

POLICE LINE DO NOT CROSS

On 14 April 1865, John Wilkes Booth shot Abraham Lincoln in the head at near point-blank range with a single-shot Derringer

POLICE LINE DO NOT CROSS

With his comrades, Booth came up with an ambitious plot to assassinate not just Lincoln but also the vice-president and the secretary of state. Booth wanted to be the one to actually shoot Lincoln. The aim was to kill the president and to cause chaos, so that the Confederates would have one last chance to strike back.

AT THE THEATRE

On the morning of Friday, 14 April, Booth visited Ford's Theater and was delighted to discover that the perfect opportunity was about to be presented to him. The president was planning to attend the theatre that very evening to watch a play called *Our American Cousin*. Booth held one final meeting with his co-conspirators. He would shoot Lincoln at the theatre; Atzerodt was to shoot Vice-President Andrew Johnson; and Powell was given the job of shooting Secretary of State William Seward. Herold would accompany Powell. All three attacks were planned for 10.15 pm that night.

The president arrived at the theatre at about 8.30 pm. An hour later Booth arrived, carrying a single-shot Derringer and a hunting knife. Booth gave his horse to a boy who held it for him in the rear alley, while he went to the saloon next door for a little Dutch courage. At 10.07 pm he came back into the theatre, and gradually made his way toward the state box where the Lincolns were sitting. Lincoln's personal bodyguard, meanwhile, had left his post. At about 10.15 pm, Booth opened the door to the state box and shot Lincoln in the back of the head at near point-blank range. As chaos broke out, one of Lincoln's companions, Henry Rathbone, tried to restrain Booth. Booth stabbed Rathbone in the arm and jumped about 3.3 m (11 ft) to the stage below, breaking his leg as he landed. He dragged himself to his feet, shouted 'Sic Semper Tyrannis' (Latin for 'As Always to Tyrants', and the Virginia state motto) and hobbled off the stage before anyone could stop him. Booth went out of the back door, climbed on his horse, and escaped via the Navy Yard Bridge.

His cohorts were less successful. Atzerodt never even tried to kill Johnson, and Powell stabbed Seward but failed to kill him. At midnight Booth reached Mary Surratt's tavern in Surrattsville where he met David Herold, before heading off to a sympathetic doctor who set and splinted Booth's broken leg.

Back in Washington, Lincoln never regained consciousness and finally died at 7.22 am the next morning. Booth and Herold remained at large for another eleven days before the authorities caught up with them and found them hiding in a barn near Port Royal, Virginia, on 26 April. Herold surrendered but Booth refused, so the forces set the barn on fire. Booth was eventually shot dead by Sergeant Boston Corbett.

Within days, Booth's co-conspirators were arrested by the government. They were tried by a military tribunal and found guilty. Powell, Atzerodt, Herold and Mrs Surratt were all hanged on 7 July 1865.

CONSPIRACY THEORIES

That was the effective end of the story. The assassin and his henchmen had been found and hanged. However, speculation has raged ever since that there may have been a wider conspiracy behind the assassination. Some suggest that the vice-president himself might have been behind it; others point the finger at the secretary of war. Others still have suggested such unlikely culprits as international bankers or the Vatican. Rather more plausible, though, is the idea that Booth's operation may have been directed by more senior Confederate leaders, in particular Judah Benjamin, the Confederate secretary of state. Today, many modern historians support this view.

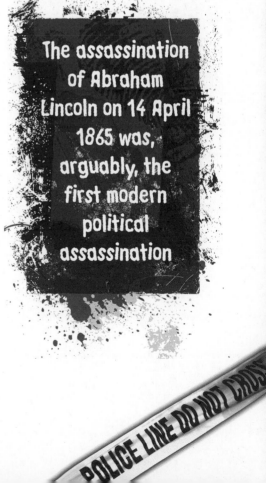

The assassination of Abraham Lincoln on 14 April 1865 was, arguably, the first modern political assassination

POLICE LINE DO NOT CROSS

Gianni Versace

The murder of Gianni Versace horrified the world when it took place on 15 July 1997. At the time, Versace was at the height of his success as one of the foremost fashion designers in the world, having designed highly glamorous, flamboyant clothes for rock stars such as Elton John. With his trademark T-shirts and unstructured suits, first designed for the cult TV series *Miami Vice*, Versace had also pioneered a more relaxed look for men that had become synonymous with 1980s style.

His killer was Andrew Cunanan, a gay man who inhabited the fringes of Versace's social world, and whose apparent frustrations with his lack of success erupted in a killing spree that was as violent as it was senseless. After killing a string of men, both friends and strangers, Cunanan travelled to Miami and lay in wait for Versace, shooting him on the front steps of his palatial home, Casa Casuarina, at South Beach. Afterwards, the killer fled and went into hiding. He was found eight days later on a houseboat, having committed suicide.

A RELAXED LOOK

Gianni Versace was born on 2 December 1946 in Calabria, Italy. His father sold electrical goods and his mother owned a dressmaking store. As a boy, Gianni learned the tailoring trade, both sewing and designing clothes. In 1972, he began receiving commissions to design for clothing companies and later opened his own store. During the 1980s, his own collections became hugely popular, and he became known as the designer who dispensed with the old-fashioned tie, yet still managed to make men look stylish and well-groomed. He also began to dress some of the most famous names of the day, in the world of film, pop and even royalty – Princess Diana was one of his close friends. By the 1990s, along with Ralph Lauren and Giorgio Armani, he had become one of only a handful of world-famous designers with a huge clothing empire to his name.

GLAMOROUS LIFESTYLE

By the time he reached fifty, Versace had about as much success as any man could want, and was talking about leading a more relaxed life with more time for entertaining. He had bought a large property on Ocean Drive, overlooking the sea at Miami Beach, and transformed it into an Italianate palace for himself and his friends. At the time, Miami Beach was the hub of a fashionable gay social life, and there was an array of ever-changing restaurants and clubs to see and be seen in. However, there was also a darker side to this sophisticated world of money, glamour and power; AIDS was terrifying the gay community, and there was a constant undertow of drug abuse and violent sex lurking below the glittering surface of the gay lifestyle.

Enter Andrew Cunanan, a good-looking, personable young man who became part of this lifestyle but who – unlike Gianni Versace – never had the talent or application to do more than drift on its treacherous currents. Cunanan was born on 31 August 1969. His father, Modesto, was Filipino, a fact that Andrew later often disguised,

There was a darker side lurking below the glittering surface of the gay lifestyle in Miami

POLICE LINE DO NOT CROSS

Gianni Versace at the height of his glittering career as a fashion designer in 1994

pretending that he came from a Latino background instead. His mother, Mary Ann, was a strict Catholic, and she was not happy with her husband and his authoritarian ways. Modesto's job in the hospital corps of the navy often took him away from home, and when he returned he often became paranoid that his wife had been having affairs, even accusing her of giving birth to a child that was not fathered by himself.

The couple had four children, the youngest of whom was Andrew. When Andrew was born, his mother suffered a bout of depression, and he was mainly cared for by his father. Andrew grew up to be extremely bright with a high IQ but often played the fool, finding it difficult to settle down to work at school. The tensions of his home life were evident in his behaviour, but people found him entertaining and fun, and on the whole were happy to accept his obvious homosexuality from a young age.

SELLING SEX

From the age of about fifteen, Andrew began to frequent gay bars and clubs, often changing his name and appearance and making up stories about his life. Before long, he was selling his body as a male prostitute to rich older men and spending the money on flashy new designer clothes. His parents had no idea what was going on, but they were having troubles of their own. Modesto had changed his employment and become a stockbroker, but had lost money and the couple split up. Modesto returned to the Philippines. Andrew quarrelled with his mother and followed his father there, but was horrified to find him living in squalor, and soon returned – after prostituting himself once again to earn the fare home.

NEW LIFE

Once back in America, Andrew carved out a new life for himself in San Francisco, often posing as a young naval officer. There, he began to lead the high life, and once actually met and chatted briefly to Gianni Versace at a party. At the same time, his life was beginning to spin out of control. He was acting in gay porn videos, some which were very violent, and his self-destructive mood was beginning to sour. He was drinking excessively, and became angry and unpredictable with friends; he was also paranoid that he might have contracted AIDS, but was afraid to seek medical help; and he was also broke, having been abandoned by his rich lovers.

For reasons that are still unclear, Cunanan's anger suddenly spilled over into violence, and he accused two ex-boyfriends, Jeff Trail and David Madson, of having an affair with each other. The men were both well-to-do, which also fuelled Cunanan's jealousy. Cunanan's behaviour became abusive and he telephoned Trail, threatening to kill him. He then went to visit Madson in Minneapolis, who tried to reassure him by inviting Trail over to his house, but a bitter argument broke out. Cunanan found a hammer in the kitchen and clubbed Trail over the head with it repeatedly, smashing his skull and killing him. Madson panicked, and helped Cunanan roll the body up in a rug;

A couple look on in shock at the blood-stained steps of Versace's Miami Beach villa on Ocean Drive

POLICE LINE DO NOT CROSS

Frustrated with his own life, and no longer able to control his anger, Andrew Cunanan (left) went on a killing spree which included gunning down Gianni Versace

that caused much criticism of the local police force when it came to light after Versace's killing. During this time, he followed Versace's movements, and noted that the designer often went to a café on his own in the mornings. On the morning of 15 July 1997, he followed Versace home and shot him twice in the head as he was opening the gate of his house.

The fact that Versace was so famous prompted the FBI to immediately launch a huge search for the killer, who was found only eight days later, hiding out on a private houseboat. A caretaker discovered Cunanan there and alerted the police, who quickly surrounded the houseboat. A dramatic standoff took place, with Cunanan refusing to come out and give himself up. When the police finally moved in, they found Cunanan dead on the floor. He had shot himself with his murdered friend Jeff Trail's pistol.

POST-MORTEM

A post-mortem revealed that Cunanan was not suffering from AIDS, despite the rumours that this was what had sent him over the edge and caused his demonic behaviour. It still remains unclear exactly what exactly motivated Cunanan, beyond a generalized sense of jealousy and anger at the world. Because of this, there have been conspiracy theories since Versace's death, seeking to explain what happened, including the theory that his assassination was masterminded by the Mafia. However, it seems that to date no one has a clear answer as to why Versace met his death that day, and the murder will continue to puzzle us for many more years to come.

and a couple of days later, the pair took off together in Madson's jeep. Later, Cunanan inexplicably pulled a gun on Madson and shot him dead as well.

The next two victims were complete strangers to Cunanan. The first was an elderly man named Lee Miglin who just happened to be standing outside his house when Cunanan approached for directions. He took Miglin into the garage and bound, tortured and killed him before spending the night in the house and taking off in Miglin's car the next day. The second was 45-year-old William Reese, the caretaker of a cemetery, whom he held up and shot.

SHOT TWICE IN THE HEAD

Amazingly, Cunanan managed to escape the police, who were by now on his trail, and hole up in Miami Beach. There, he checked into a hotel, dined in restaurants and wandered the streets for two months without anybody noticing him – a fact

POLICE LINE DO NOT CROSS

Tsar Alexander II

One of the most shocking assassinations in history was that of Alexander II, who was Tsar of Russia from 1855 until his death in 1881. Alexander II was in some ways one of the more liberal monarchs of Russia, and it was under his regime that the emancipation of the serfs took place. However, his reforms did not go far enough, and poverty was still a huge problem throughout Russia, so that a revolutionary fervour gripped the country.

BLOODBATH

There were several attempts on Tsar Alexander's life, and by the time he died, his security forces were on high alert. However, despite their caution, the tsar was eventually killed in a bomb attack that not only blew him apart, but also killed his assassin, and twenty others, as well as injuring many more. According to onlookers, the scene of the crime was a bloodbath, the snow turning red as the wounded bled to death, with fragments of human flesh hanging from the trees and lamp posts in the street.

Ironically, the assassination of the tsar only led to worse problems in Russia, as his successor Tsar Alexander III was profoundly reactionary, and became so unpopular that by the end of his reign he was virtually a prisoner in his own palace. By the time his son Nicholas II came to the throne, repression had reached such a level that there was a massive revolution, led by the Bolsheviks, and Nicholas was brutally assassinated,

along with his whole family. Thus, Alexander's assassination was the beginning of the end for the tsars of Russia, whose despotic rule came to an end with the Revolution of 1917.

BRUTAL REPRESSION

Alexander II Nikolaevitch was born on 17 April 1818, the eldest son of Tsar Nicholas I of Russia. As a boy, he was kind-hearted and even-tempered, to the disappointment of his father, who wished that he would display virtues more suited to a military leader. The young Alexander showed little interest in military affairs or politics, and seemed disinclined to change the status quo, which was one of extreme inequalities between rich and poor, together with brutal repression and censorship of any criticism about the government of the day.

In 1841, Alexander married Princess Marie of Hesse, with whom he had six children. His wife later died, and he married his mistress, Princess Catherine Dolgoruki, who was mother to four more children. When his father died, Alexander became tsar, and spent his initial years in power overseeing the Crimean War. When this was over, he devoted himself to reforms that were desperately needed to put the country back on an equal footing with other European powers. Without relinquishing his autocratic powers, he began to pass laws to help modernize industry and commerce, and planned the creation of an infrastructure of railways across the

Alexander II, Tsar of Russia, normally travelled with two trains, one to test the safety of the tracks, the other to carry him. Yet he was not always in the second train

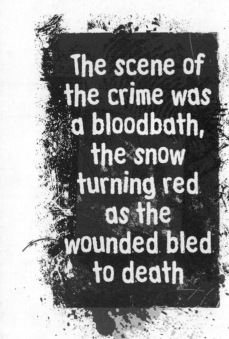

The scene of the crime was a bloodbath, the snow turning red as the wounded bled to death

POLICE LINE DO NOT CROSS

country. He also realized, unlike his predecessors, that Russia could not advance any further under the system of serfdom, by which peasants were tied to the land with very few rights of their own. Accordingly, he passed laws to emancipate the serfs, and make them independent; however, he also imposed heavy taxation on them, so they were not a great deal better off in the long run.

In addition, the government brutally suppressed the January Uprising of 1863, killing and deporting thousands of Poles. Criticism of the regime grew stronger, until Alexander felt forced to adopt repressive new measures, including the banning of minority languages in some parts of the country. Not surprisingly, this led to a great deal of unrest and bitterness, and it was not long before Alexander and his government realized that their days were numbered.

MISFIRED SHOTS

There were, in fact, several assassination attempts on the tsar. In 1866, Dmitry Karakozov, a student and revolutionary, arrived in St Petersburg with the intention of assassinating Alexander. On 4 April, he went to the gates of the Summer Garden, drew his gun, and was about to shoot the tsar when a bystander, Osip Komissarov, prevented him by jostling his elbow. Some argue that Komissarov, a peasant who had come to work in St Petersburg as a hatter's apprentice, intervened because he loved the tsar, while others allege it was an accident, or perhaps that it never happened at all. Whatever the truth, Karakozov tried to make a run for it, but

was arrested. He was later hanged in public in St Petersburg. Komissarov, on the other hand, was rewarded with a title and money, but went on to embarrass the government with his uncouth behaviour, and was sent to live out of town. The tsar commissioned a new gate for the city, to commemorate his lucky escape.

The next attempt on his life came on the morning of 20 April 1879, when a student, Alexander Soloviev, walked towards the tsar holding a gun. The tsar quickly retreated, but Soloviev fired at him. There were five shots, but miraculously all of them missed the target. Soloviev was arrested and hanged the following month.

OUTWITTED

Also in 1879, a group of radicals called 'Will of the People' attempted to blow up a train in which the tsar was travelling. The attempt failed when explosives did not detonate as planned, blowing up a train – but the wrong train. The tsar normally travelled with two trains, one to test the safety of the tracks, and one to carry him; but in this case, the first train had been carrying the tsar. The plotters were outwitted for now.

In 1880, there was another amazing attack. This time, assassins blew up the dining room of the tsar's Winter Palace. This was a spectacular attempt, but it too failed – because the tsar and his family had been late arriving for dinner.

After these terrifying attempts, the tsar's advisers were determined to

There were several attempts on the life of the tsar: on one occasion a student threw a bomb at his passing carriage

POLICE LINE DO NOT CROSS

keep him out of harm's way, and arranged for him to cut down on his public appearances. He was also advised to discontinue travelling by railway, and to travel by boat instead as often as possible. However, Alexander was determined to continue his activities as monarch, and refused to be hemmed in by his security men. He announced that he did not fear death, and pointed out that he had already survived several assassination attempts, and had lived longer than most of his ancestors.

CHANGING THE ROUTE
But his confidence was misplaced, as it turned out. On 1 March 1881, Alexander went to review his troops. A group of radicals were waiting for him, including Andrei Zhelyabov, a brilliant leader who had been born a serf and had educated himself so that he had eventually gained a scholarship from the University of Odessa. With Zhelyabov was his lover, Sophia Perovskaya, also a political activist. The pair had rented a shop in one of the streets the tsar and his family were due to ride through, and had pretended to be cheese sellers at the shop in the days running up to the event. In fact, what they had been doing was tunnelling under the street and planting explosives in a spot where they would blow up the tsar's carriage as it passed by. They also positioned four men in the street, all armed with bombs to throw at the tsar if the explosion failed.

The police were on Zhelyabov's tail, however, and just before the event took place, they arrested him. Perovskaya was left to manage the attack,

but the plan failed when the tsar took an unscheduled route. Instead of passing down the street where the explosives were planted, the carriage went another way, which meant that the bomb attackers had to leap into action. The job was left to a 19-year-old student, Rysakov, who emerged out of the crowd, dressed as a common peasant. He threw the bomb right at the tsar's carriage, damaging the door of the vehicle and rocking it from side to side. The tsar was unhurt, but a boy who was standing in the street was not so lucky and was killed. Two of the tsar's Cossack escorts, and several horses, were also killed, and some soldiers were also hurt. Rysakov was arrested, taken into police custody, and later executed.

LEGS BLOWN OFF
The tsar stopped his carriage and got out to see what was going on. He walked around, offering assistance to those who were wounded. He then turned towards another carriage, determined to travel on and continue the day's scheduled events. However, just as he was doing so, another assassin, Ignaty Grinevitsky, quickly ran towards the tsar, throwing a nitroglycerine bomb right at him. This time, there was no escape: the bomb blew up Alexander's legs, and took out one of his eyes. It was clear that the tsar was about to die, and Grinevitsky too was fatally wounded. Not only this, but around them, twenty onlookers also lay dead, and many more in the crowd had been injured by the bomb.

By now, the dying Alexander knew that his time was up, and managed to order his aides to get him to the palace

as quickly as possible so that he could say farewell to his loved ones. An hour later, he died, attended by his closest family members.

TYRANNICAL RULE
The aftermath of the assassination was a dismal one. Instead of heralding change and revolution, liberal and left-wing opposition to the regime collapsed. The six main conspirators involved in the plot were tried and found guilty. All six of them were executed.

Radicals all over the country went into hiding, disbanding their organizations. Partly as a result of the bloody end to Alexander II's regime, his successor, Alexander III, clamped down on any form of political activism, and proved an extremely repressive monarch, deeply opposed to any kind of reform, and determined to turn the clock back as much as possible in Russia. For over a decade, any kind of opposition to the government was banned, and Russia's social system returned to the miserable backwardness that had characterized it before the reign of Alexander II.

When Alexander III died prematurely in 1894, the hapless Tsar Nicholas II took over. He became the last of the tsars to rule Russia. He and his entire family were eventually shot by ruthless revolutionaries in the Russian Revolution, bringing to an end the tyrannical rule of the tsars of Russia, and ushering in a new, equally turbulent, era of socialism. Thus Alexander II's brutal assassination proved the first of a long line of violent actions whereby the members of the Romanov dynasty lost their place as rulers of the Russian empire.

Leon Trotsky

The assassination of Leon Davidovitch Trotsky was one of the most dramatic murders in history. The revolutionary was savagely attacked at his house in Coyoacán, Mexico, by a Soviet agent, Ramón Mercader. Mercader hid an ice pick in his coat, then pulled it out while Trotsky was reading his script and dealt him a massive blow on the head, mortally wounding him. Bleeding profusely, Trotsky struggled with his attacker, but eventually collapsed and died. Although Trotsky had been one of the major figures of the Russian Revolution, he was never honoured as such in his home country; however, his theory of communism, and his implacable opposition to Stalinism, continue to this day to be significant contributions to political thought. His life had been full of drama, adventure, activity and passion; and as he lived, so he died.

THE PASSIONATE REVOLUTIONARY

Trotsky was born Leon Bronstein on 7 November 1879 in the tiny village of Yanovka in the Ukraine. (It has also been noted that, according to the ancient Julian calendar, his birth date actually fell on 26 October, the same day that the Russian Revolution of 1917 broke out.) His father was a farmer who was unable to read or write, but the family were quite wealthy so the young Trotsky was sent to Odessa to be educated. As a young man, he studied mathematics at university, but spent most of his time writing Marxist pamphlets under the name 'Lvov', until he was arrested and jailed. So began his

Bolshevik leader Leon Trotsky, one of the major figures of the Russian Revolution and a fierce critic of Stalin, was killed in exile by a Soviet agent with an ice pick

first spell in prison. During this time he studied philosophy and married a comrade, Aleksandra Sokolvskaya. He was then sent to Siberia, where he remained in exile for four years before escaping to join fellow Russian revolutionaries such as Lenin, Plekhanov and Martov in London. It was at this time that he acquired the name 'Trotsky', which was the name on his stolen passport.

At the time of the outbreak of the

POLICE LINE DO NOT CROSS

Russian Revolution in 1917, Trotsky was living as an exile in New York. He managed to make his way back to his homeland, and became part of the new government of Lenin and his Bolshevik party. Trotsky formed and led the new government's military force, the Red Army, which went on to brutally suppress the Kronstadt Rebellion, an uprising of working people in 1921. This was a crucial event in the history of the USSR, and ushered in a new phase of repressive state bureaucracy that was to continue throughout most of the 20th century.

EXILED ONCE MORE

When Lenin became ill and died in 1924, a bitter power struggle, both ideological and personal, took place between Trotsky and Joseph Stalin. Stalin triumphed; Trotsky was expelled from the party, and once more found himself in exile. He travelled around Europe and then went to live in Mexico, where he continued to write about the progress of the revolution, and to agitate against Stalin's increasingly vicious regime. Not surprisingly, Trotsky's activities made him extremely unpopular with Stalin and the communist government in the USSR. It was not long before he began to receive visits from the NKVD, the Russian Secret Service, at his home in Coyoacán, Mexico City. In May 1940, assassins conducted a raid on the house, aided by the Mexican painter David Siqueiros, who supported the Stalinist regime. Even though the attackers fired several rounds of bullets at the house, miraculously all the occupants escaped

8 November 1921: Red Square is packed with thousands of hushed soldiers and citizens listening to Leon Trotsky's passionate words

unharmed. A few months later, however, on 20 August, a second attack took place; this time, it was successful.

THE FATAL ICE PICK

Having failed to kill Trotsky in a hail of bullets, the agents of the Russian secret service now decided on a different plan of action: to hire an assassin who would do the job with an ice pick. They had just the man to carry out the attack: Jaime Ramón Mercader. Mercader's mother, Caridad, had once worked as a Soviet agent and Mercader junior had continued the family's line of business, training in Moscow as a saboteur and assassin. Posing as a Canadian, Frank Jacson, Mercader had travelled to Mexico City and had become friendly with members of Trotsky's family and entourage, feigning an interest in politics. Unbeknownst to the Trotskys, 'Jacson' had been involved in the first raid on the family house, but this fact did not emerge until later.

On the fateful day of 20 August, 'Jacson' visited the house, pretending to have revised an article that Trotsky had previously corrected for him. He carried a coat with him, under which he had hidden a steel ice pick, the handle shortened so that it would be easier to conceal. (The 'ice pick' method was well tried and tested by the NKVD, and had been used on several occasions before; it was held to be a quick, easy murder method.) Up the street, his mother Caridad and another agent were waiting in a car for him to make his getaway.

Trotsky had not been very impressed with his new friend's political writings so far,

POLICE LINE DO NOT CROSS

and had told members of his family that he considered 'Jacson' a little 'light-minded', but out of politeness he agreed to look over the revised article again.

The men went to Trotsky's study, and the revolutionary sat down to re-read Jacson's article. As Trotsky bent his head over the paper, 'Jacson' saw his golden opportunity, picked up the ice pick, and dashed it into Trotsky's skull.

TREATED AS A HERO

Unfortunately, the blow was badly aimed, and although blood gushed from Trotsky's head, he remained alive and extremely vocal for quite some time. According to Mercader, he let out a blood-curdling yell, which was to haunt the murderer for the rest of his life, and then began to fight with his attacker. Hearing the commotion in the study, Trotsky's bodyguards rushed in from another room. They were always on hand, since by this time Trotsky lived each day in fear of his life. Rational to the last, Trotsky told the guards not to kill Mercader, saying, 'He has a story to tell.'

A doctor was immediately called, and police surrounded the house. Mercader's mother and the other agent, sensing that the plan had failed, escaped. By the time Trotsky's grandson, Seva Volkov, returned home from school, he found a scene of murder and mayhem, with his grandfather lying on the floor covered in blood.

Trotsky was quickly rushed to hospital and operated on but he died the next day, 21 August 1940, as a result of severe damage to the brain, aged sixty years.

He had put up an extraordinary struggle, remaining conscious for several hours even though the wound to

Sheer treachery: Trotsky was struck on the back of the skull with an ice pick while helpfully reading an article that his assassin had written

his head was deep. Mercader received a twenty-year jail sentence for murder but did not reveal his true identity. In 1960,

he was released, went to Cuba and then to the USSR, where he was treated as a national hero. He died in 1978.

POLICE LINE DO NOT CROSS

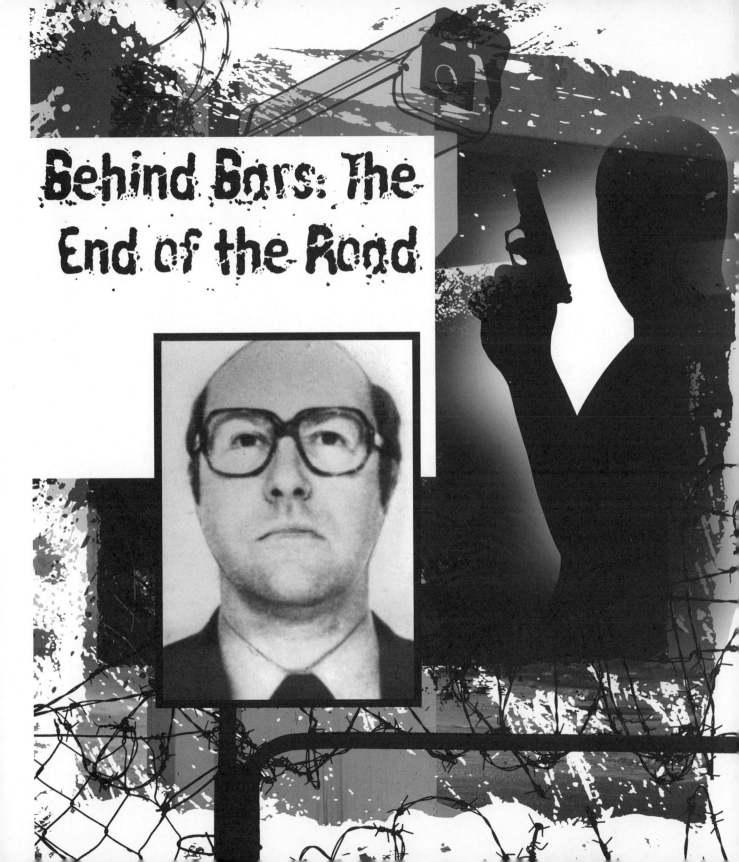

Behind Bars: The End of the Road

Jacques Mesrine

Jacques Mesrine was an infamous French bank robber and kidnapper who became known for his daring prison escapes. During the 1960s and 1970s he became popular in France as a romantic 'Robin Hood' figure, who would rob the rich and, allegedly, give to the poor. He was also admired by the public for his ability to outwit the French police force, who were unable for many years to capture him, and eventually named him 'Public Enemy Number One'. The police finally caught up with him on 2 November 1979, and shot him dead.

Mesrine was born into a middle-class family in Clichy, France, in 1936. As a child, he got into trouble at school for his violent behaviour, and was expelled twice. As a young man, he served in Algeria, and then returned to France, where he embarked on a career of crime. A good-looking man, he charmed those around him – sometimes even those he was robbing. However, his courteous exterior belied his true nature, which was that of a ruthless criminal who would stop at nothing to get what he wanted.

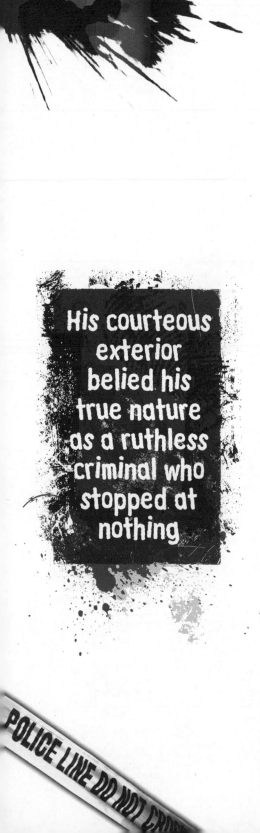

His courteous exterior belied his true nature as a ruthless criminal who stopped at nothing

A LOVE OF PUBLICITY

Mesrine liked to live well, enjoying good food and wine at the best restaurants in France. He was extremely attractive to women, and had a succession of beautiful girlfriends, who sometimes accompanied him on his bank-robbing sprees. He liked to dress well and often conducted raids wearing the latest fashions. All this,

of course, together with his love of publicity and his talent for sensational escapades, made him a tremendously popular figure in the national press.

Mesrine's first arrest took place in 1962, when he attempted to rob a bank with three accomplices. He served a sentence in prison and was released the following year. After a short stint working for a design company, he resumed his criminal activities in Spain, and was arrested but set free after only six months. He then opened a restaurant in the Canary Islands, but left to pursue a life of crime once more, first robbing a hotel in Chamonix, France, and then attempting a kidnap in Canada.

Together with his girlfriend, Jeanne Schneider, Mesrine had planned to kidnap a Canadian grocery and textile millionaire named Georges Deslauriers. Deslauriers had employed Mesrine and Schneider as domestic servants and then sacked them. The kidnap failed, and Mesrine and Schneider were sentenced to ten years in prison for the attempt. However, they managed to escape in style, capturing a prison warder, stealing his keys, locking the warder in a cell and fleeing to live in the local woods.

SENSATIONAL ESCAPES

Mesrine was soon recaptured, and this time sent to the high-security Saint Vincent de Paul prison outside Montreal. Before long, he had led five inmates in a daring escape that involved using a pair of pliers, which had been stolen from a workshop, to cut through several fences. After managing this extraordinary feat, the group then flagged down cars on the highway, and got clean away.

POLICE LINE DO NOT CROSS

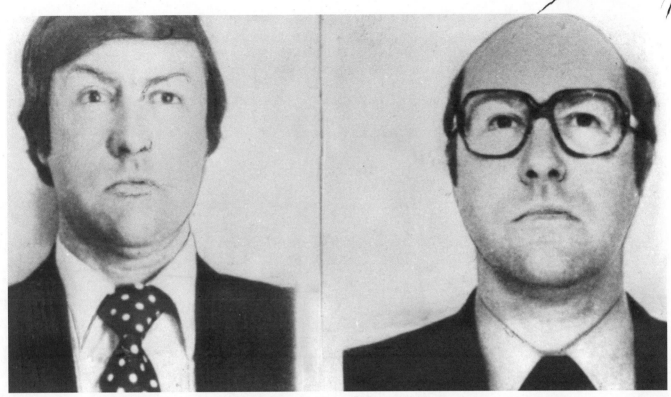

The changing faces of Jaques Mesrine. The criminal seemed to delight in coming up with different disguises with which to outwit the police

Mesrine's next move was audacious in the extreme: he decided to return to the prison and help the remaining inmates of the prison to escape. He robbed a number of banks to raise the money he needed, and then went back, armed with shotguns and wire cutters. However, the complicated plan failed and Mesrine had to make a quick getaway. He was on the run again.

COURTROOM DRAMA

With his accomplice Jean-Paul Mercier, Mesrine fled to Venezuela. However, before long he was back in France, robbing banks again. In 1973, he was caught and tried. During his trial in court,

he caused a sensation by managing to take a judge hostage. An accomplice had hidden a gun for him in one of the toilets of the court, which he stuffed into his belt and pulled out as his charges were being read. Holding on to the judge and using him as a human shield, Mesrine ran under a hail of bullets from police, jumped into a getaway car and sped away. He was only arrested several months later and duly imprisoned once more.

Mesrine's next sensational exploit was to escape from his maximum security jail at La Santé de Paris. Using a secret stash of guns, Mesrine and two other prisoners held up guards, stole their uniforms and

locked them in the cells. They then commandeered some ladders and climbed over the prison walls, using ropes and grappling irons. They became the first prisoners ever to escape from La Santé. The incident infuriated the French authorities, who were humiliated by Mesrine's disappearance from their top-security prison. Mesrine now became the most wanted man in the country.

THE FINAL SHOWDOWN

Free once more, Mesrine continued his criminal career, becoming ever more daring –

and ruthless. He used many disguises to evade police during his exploits, including wigs, which he sometimes wore one on top of the other for quick changes. He kidnapped rich individuals, robbed banks and jewellery shops, and smuggled arms. He boasted that he had killed over thirty victims in the process of committing his crimes, although this figure has never actually been verified.

ROBIN HOOD?

Despite this, sections of the French press continued to view him as a romantic figure, painting him as a kind of Robin Hood, a thorn in the side of authority. Mesrine, too, evidently saw himself as a folk hero, and often attempted in interviews to convince journalists that his crimes were motivated by radical political ideas rather than by self-interest. The fact that he had boasted about cold-bloodedly murdering scores of victims, and that he obviously spent more money than he ever gave away, did not stop the tabloid press from seeing him as something of a hero – perhaps because his escapades made the authorities look so foolish and inept.

As Mesrine's criminal activities continued, the French government became more and more embarrassed by him, and ordered police departments to intensify their efforts to apprehend him. On 2 November 1979, police found out where he was living and ambushed his car, surrounding it as he waited at traffic lights in the street. They shot nineteen rounds of bullets through his windscreen, killing him instantly.

The legend ends: Mesrine was gunned down at close range while waiting at traffic lights

He used a variety of disguises to evade police during his exploits, including wigs

POLICE LINE DO NOT CROSS

Eric Rudolph

When the Olympics came to Atlanta, Georgia, a bubbling carnival atmosphere pulled in the crowds and 44-year-old Alice Hawthorne was not about to miss out on the chance to party.

'If somebody went to all the trouble to bring the Olympics to Atlanta, the least I can do is go,' the woman from Albany, Georgia, told friends. So it was with high spirits that she and her 14-year-old daughter Fallon set off on 26 July 1996 to savour the buzz of an international event.

FUNDAMENTALIST

Tragically, a visit that day to the same place by domestic terrorist Eric Rudolph ensured that this would be the last trip Alice ever made. Rudolph was not there to celebrate sporting excellence or relish a vibrant ambience. Rather, to 'confound, anger and embarrass' the government on the abortion issue, he came armed with a vicious pipe bomb and planted it where an R & B band was playing. One moment Alice was dancing delightedly with her daughter in the early hours of 27 July, the next she lay fatally wounded from bomb shrapnel. It was the biggest pipe bomb the FBI had ever seen. Another man, camera crew member Melih Uzunyol from Turkey, died of a heart attack as he rushed to the scene of the bombing.

Investigators mistakenly believed a security man was to blame. He was ultimately cleared of involvement but it was seven years and three bomb attacks later before Rudolph was finally arrested while he was scavenging for food by a store in the early morning hours.

ANTI-ABORTIONISTS

Rudolph was responsible for planting two bombs at a women's health clinic in Atlanta on 16 January 1997, injuring four people. Another bomb, which wounded four women at a nightclub with a predominantly lesbian clientele the following month, was also his work. A second bomb planted at the same venue fortunately failed to detonate.

On 29 January 1998 an off-duty policeman died and a nurse was severely injured in an explosion outside an abortion clinic in Birmingham, Alabama. The outrage was followed up with a chilling note that read: 'The bombing in Birmingham was carried out by the Army of God. Let those who work in the murder mill's [sic] around the nation be warned once more – you will be targeted without quarter – you are not immune from retaliation. Your commissar's [sic] in Washington can't protect you.'

The Army of God is a terrorist Pro-Life offshoot of a hardcore fundamentalist group known as Christian Identity, which espouses white supremacist and anti-Semitic beliefs. Like the rest of the group, Rudolph, a Catholic, believed that their aims were legal and theologically justified. One of their main activities is their fervent opposition to abortion.

PRIME SUSPECT

In Birmingham, Rudolph's truck was identified close to the scene of the carnage and he became a prime suspect. Once that was known Rudolph vanished. It soon became clear that he was a keen survivalist and was living rough, with the help of supporters, in Nantahala National Forest in northwest North Carolina.

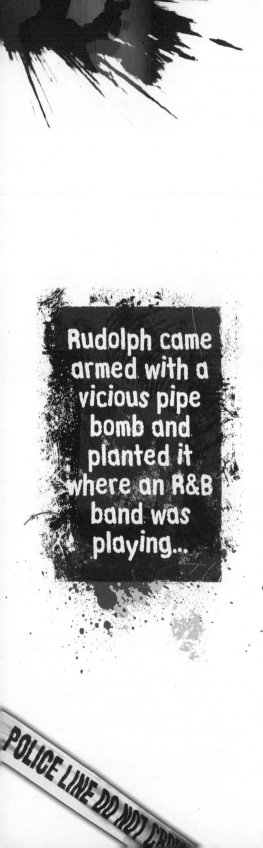

Rudolph came armed with a vicious pipe bomb and planted it where an R&B band was playing...

POLICE LINE DO NOT CROSS

His family shared the same extreme anti-establishment views. Indeed, after being pressured by police investigators, Rudolph's younger brother Daniel protested by cutting off his hand with a radial saw while a domestic video camera rolled. The severed limb was later successfully re-attached.

Rudolph was someone with an agenda, a message to spread among society. Apart from a statement read out at sentencing,

this was never broadcast. The man who once headed America's 'most wanted' list pleaded guilty to the bomb attacks in order to avoid the death penalty.

THREE LIFE SENTENCES

Rudolph received three consecutive life terms without parole before he had an opportunity to preach his message of hate extensively in the courtroom. And when the bomber became prisoner number

On 16 January 1997 two bombs were detonated at a women's health clinic in Sandy Springs near Atlanta, Georgia. The bombs were later linked to Eric Rudolph

No. 18282-058 at the ADX in Florence, Colorado, he was effectively buried alive. For a man who loved living outdoors, the contrast of incarceration after years spent as a fugitive in the wild must have been hard – not as hard, though, as losing one's life.

POLICE LINE DO NOT CROSS

Devil's Island

Devil's Island was just about the most notorious of all prisons, perhaps the international benchmark in appalling prisons. The name is misleading. Devil's Island was only one of three islands that, together with a sizeable slice of mainland French Guiana, comprised the penal colony opened in 1852 by Napoleon III. It operated for nearly a century, during which time thousands of hardcore and novice criminals were sent there from mainland France. The aim was clear: to rid mother France of trouble-makers and dissenters. The ploy was brutally effective.

ONE-WAY TICKET

Forty per cent of new arrivals to the colony died within the first year. Of the 80,000 or so who were transported there during the colony's 94-year existence, few made it back to France. Vulnerable to the effects of tropical diseases and exhaustion, prisoners existed in a state of perpetual terror, not knowing if the fierce guards or unfamiliar environment would deal them a deadly blow.

Shackled prisoners worked twelve hours a day in the sun and oppressive heat and faced perils as diverse as poisonous snakes and malaria-carrying mosquitoes. They survived on starvation rations.

Many men worked and died waist-deep in water in the timber camps, where they were forced to meet an arduous daily quota or suffer dire punishment. The most deadly camp was at Kourou, where convicts were made to build a road – Route Zero – though

The infamous Devil's Island, set up as a penal colony under Napoleon III

many suffered from the twin plagues of disease and hunger. So few survived that the road never stretched beyond 25 km (15 miles). Solitary confinement, another commonly employed punishment, was in a roofless, airless, subterranean cell on the island of St Joseph, known among inmates as the 'devourer of men'. Armed guards, peering in as they paced its grounds, saw crouching, cowed prisoners staring back.

For those guilty of minor infringements the shadow of the guillotine still loomed large. The unforgiving blade was then

France's chosen method of delivering capital punishment and was in regular use. Victim's heads were preserved in alcohol and sent back to France as proof that justice had been done.

UNCOMFORTABLE MINDS

Devil's Island was often earmarked for political prisoners. It became famous for one of its inhabitants, Alfred Dreyfus, a Jewish French army officer wrongly accused of spying in a case that dragged on for years and became known as the 'Dreyfus Affair'. Dreyfus and his supporters

POLICE LINE DO NOT CROSS

Guiana: by sea, by crossing into Dutch Guiana (Suriname) or by hacking a path through virgin jungle into neighbouring Brazil. Those who chose the sea had to contend with strong currents and shark-infested waters.

Anyone heading for Dutch Guiana probably went via dugout canoe and risked ending up as food for the ravenous piranha fish that patrolled the River Maroni. Convicts choosing to travel by land were likely to have their bones picked clean by giant marauding ants. Even if they survived the mortal threats posed by natural predators, convicts had to avoid the merciless bounty hunters who roamed the region, eager to cash in on the reward offered for escapees. And prisoners were always sent back if they were captured by Dutch guards, who were weary of convict excesses.

To enter Brazil meant almost certain death from encounters with any number of fierce or poisonous jungle creatures lurking beneath the rainforest canopy. Of course any choice of escape was accompanied by a real threat of disease.

ATROCIOUS CONDITIONS
In addition to Dreyfus, two other men brought to public attention the atrocious conditions that inmates had to suffer. Perhaps the most famous was the Frenchman Henri Charrière (1906–73), better known as 'Papillon' – the Butterfly (see pages 264–6).

The other was Rene Belbenoit (1899–1959), who was sent to Devil's Island in 1920 after stealing pearls from the Countess of Entre-meuse, in Paris. As prisoner number 46635 he tried to escape four times, on one occasion helping to

eventually unveiled corruption and anti-Semitism among the top brass as well as unmasking the true traitor, a Major Esterhazy. Dreyfus was eventually exonerated in 1906.

Those fortunate enough to survive their sentences, which usually amounted to a minimum of eight years, were then obliged to spend a similar length of time in French Guiana as authorities in France tried to financially improve the colony.

ESCAPING THE DEVIL
There were only three ways of fleeing the purgatory of forced labour in French

The aim was clear: to rid mother France of trouble-makers and dissenters

POLICE LINE DO NOT CROSS

butcher a fellow escapee who turned murderer. For these breakouts he earned 50 months in solitary confinement.

At this time he provided material for author Blair Niles, who would write two books exposing the horrors at Devil's Island based on a manuscript written by Belbenoit. Only when he had completed his sentence in 1934 and was working in French Guiana as a 'compulsory volunteer' did he make good his escape using a dugout canoe.

As Belbenoit paddled to freedom he reflected that only fifteen men, including himself, of the 700 sent across the Atlantic with him seventeen years before had survived.

He worked his way up the South American coast, aided by the British in Trinidad, and survived a close shave with French authorities keen to return him once more to Devil's Island.

Belbenoit financed his adventure through South America through the sale of exotic butterflies that he captured in the jungle with a long-handled net. Despite the deprivations of his fugitive life, he continually wrote in his journal.

He published a book, *Dry Guillotine*, in 1938 after reaching the United States, which ultimately became his home. He spent the rest of his life attacking the inequities of the French justice system.

END OF THE COLONY

The last of the colony's inmates were repatriated to France in 1952 as Devil's Island at last fell victim to its outrageously high running costs and a concerted campaign by the French

Perhaps the most famous inmate of Devil's Island was Alfred Dreyfus, a French army officer who had been wrongly convicted of espionage and was later exonerated

Salvation Army to halt the brutal punishments. Like many other places

marked by the depths of human misery it has become a tourist attraction.

Eight former inmates of Devil's Island who succeeded in escaping in August 1940 as the prison regime fell into chaos following the surrender of France to Germany during the Second World War

POLICE LINE DO NOT CROSS

Papillon

Henri Charrière was a small-time Parisian crook who achieved lasting fame when he wrote his life story, entitled *Papillon*. The book told of the many thrilling adventures that befell this highly intelligent, resourceful criminal as he planned his various escapes from different prisons in South America, where he was sent after being convicted of murder in 1931. Charrière's escapes were very carefully planned, but he also learned to take opportunities when they arose, using the skills he had learned as a thief on the streets of his native city. The title of the autobiography, French for 'butterfly', was Charrière's nickname, which derived from a tattoo of a butterfly that he had on his chest.

Charrière grew up in Paris and, as a young man, began a criminal career as a thief and safe-breaker. He managed for the most part to evade the law until, in 1931, he was accused of murdering a pimp known as Roland le Petit. He maintained that he had been framed for the murder, but no one believed him. When the case came to trial, he was found guilty and sentenced to a term of life imprisonment with hard labour. He was ordered to serve out his sentence at a penal colony in French Guiana, which was infamous at the time for its brutality and tough living conditions.

PRISON CAMP ORDEAL

In the book, Charrière described in detail the horrific conditions for prisoners in the penal colony of French Guiana at that period. He also made it clear that, although he was no angel, and had for many years made his living as a thief, he was innocent of the crime of murder that he had been convicted of. His abiding sense of outrage and the claim that he had become the victim of a miscarriage of justice carries the reader's sympathies; it also helps to explain the iron determination that Charrière showed throughout his long career as an escape artist, making an effort to break out of his confinement at every opportunity, whatever the cost.

Once at the penal colony, Papillon made the first of his many bids for freedom. He escaped from hospital on the mainland in the company of two other prisoners, and made his way to Riohacha, Colombia. He sailed along the coast, via Trinidad and Curaçao, for hundreds of miles in an open boat. After this gruelling ordeal, he finally reached Colombia, only to be caught there and imprisoned again.

ESCAPE AND CAPTURE

Undaunted, Charrière escaped and went on the run again, this time to Guajira, where he lived in a native village and took two wives as his consorts. This episode in his eventful life was a relatively quiet one, in which he lived in peace and harmony with his wives, Lali and Zoraima. Their relaxed attitude towards sex pleased him greatly, differing entirely as it did from the mores of the French women he had known. Both of his wives eventually became pregnant by him. However, although he could probably have carried on living in the village for the rest of his life, working and raising his children in obscurity, his lust for adventure caused him to move on. When he did so, he was once again captured and imprisoned, this time at Santa Marta.

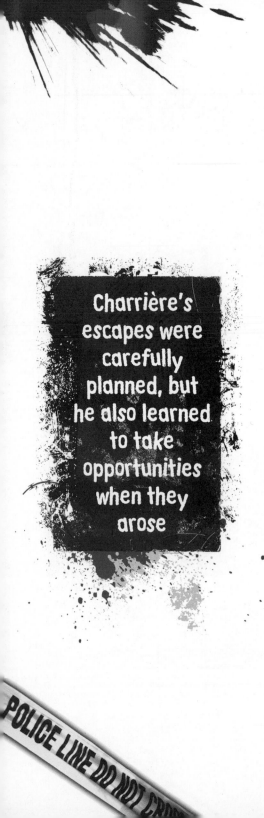

Charrière's escapes were carefully planned, but he also learned to take opportunities when they arose to escape. However, on this occasion his attempt was foiled by an informer, whom he murdered in revenge.

Once again, Charrière was punished; and once again, he continued to make his escape attempts from wherever he was imprisoned. It seemed that nothing would deter him. His next ruse was to pretend to be mad, so that he was sent to the mental hospital on the island of St Joseph. He attempted to escape from the hospital, but was caught and sent to the most infamous of all places – Devil's Island.

FREEDOM AT LAST

As its name suggests, Devil's Island was a hellish place, rife with disease, where prisoners lived under a brutal regime in fear of their lives. Legend had it that no prisoner had ever managed to escape from the island. Not surprisingly, soon after arriving, Charrière made his bid for freedom, throwing himself into the shark-infested sea surrounding the island with only a makeshift raft of coconut sacking to keep him afloat in the water. Against all odds, he succeeded in reaching the mainland, and once there travelled on to Georgetown, the capital of British Guyana. In company with five other fugitives, he managed to get to Venezuela, but once there, was taken prisoner at El Dorado.

Henri Charrière was finally given his much-desired freedom in 1945. He settled in Venezuela, and opened a restaurant in Caracas where he entertained diners with stories of his many adventures on the run from the law. He died in 1973, at the age of sixty-six.

The lined face of an experienced escape artist – Charrière's adventures made for a lively story

Charrière was then transferred to Barranquilla, where he made various audacious attempts to escape, but these all failed. In 1934, he was sent back to French Guiana, where he was punished for his escape attempts by being put into solitary confinement on the island of St Joseph. After two years of a miserably lonely existence, he was sent to another island, Royale, where he again attempted

POLICE LINE DO NOT CROSS

Today, some critics question Charrière's innocence, wondering whether he was in actual fact the unfortunate victim of a miscarriage of justice that he made himself out to be. Others claim that he exaggerated his story, and that parts of it cannot be true. Another criticism levelled at him is that his casual attitude to his two native wives (whom he impregnated and then left), not to mention his disregard for his own family back home in France, showed him to be a heartless philanderer. However, despite these criticisms, his autobiography continues to be read by hundreds of new readers every year, and is still enjoyed as an inspiring testament to the human spirit of endurance, determination, and the search for justice.

His autobiography continues to be read by hundreds of new readers every year

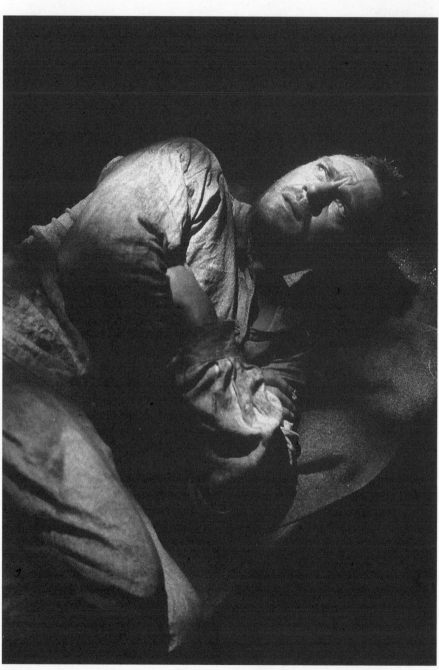

Charrière's book Papillon was made into a film of the same name, which starred Steve McQueen

Brazil

With a population of some eleven million, São Paulo is by far the biggest city in the southern hemisphere. It stands proud with its skyscrapers, its bustling business community and its vibrant culture that captivates residents and visitors alike.

Yet for four days in May 2006 the place was paralysed after street warfare that left 170 people dead and ninety-three more wounded. More than sixty buses were burned. Government buildings were firebombed, roads were impassable and residents stayed at home. All seventy state penitentiaries were hit by riots.

The carnage and destruction was breathtaking. But perhaps the most eye-opening aspect of the bloody episode was that it began on the orders of a prison gang boss, given from inside his cell by mobile phone. It was his response to a government plan to kill off prison gang power. Ironically, perhaps, in a city with the motto 'I am not led, I lead', 'Marcola' Comacho was making a direct challenge as to who really ruled the city.

SECRET PLANS

The government's idea was simple and strategic: significant players from the prison gang First Capital Command, better known by its Portuguese initials PCC (Primeiro Comando da Capital), would be removed from São Paulo to jails in remote areas in order to take them out of the communications loop.

The plan was unveiled at a secret meeting and surprise was to be a key element of its success. However, the architects of the ploy didn't reckon on

the long tentacles of the prison gang. Its hierarchy knew about the plans almost instantly when a government employee divulged the meeting's secrets to a PCC lawyer. In the mayhem that followed prison guards were killed at their homes and off-duty police officers were gunned down as they relaxed in bars.

The *Folha de São Paulo* newspaper reported receiving a video – supposedly produced by the PCC – featuring a masked man flanked by machine guns and sticks of dynamite. In the video, he reportedly made demands in the name of the 'party', saying: 'Don't mess with our families and we won't mess with yours.' Threats of violence also circulated via the internet.

The gang's ominously precise organization chilled the hearts of the city's residents, who found themselves faced with the reality of daily battles between trigger-happy policemen and vicious gunmen, although some remained convinced that the gang was merely the scapegoat of an incompetent government.

'They link this to the PCC because the government doesn't want to take responsibility for controlling delinquency,' said Bezerra da Silva, standing next to a wooden stool that he keeps padlocked to a streetlight. 'They blame the PCC, saying it's a huge problem they can't control, and they wash their hands of everything.'

A HISTORY OF VIOLENCE

Terrible though events in São Paulo were that month, the episode was just one in a series linked to the PCC that shocked the world. In December there were twelve orchestrated attacks in just four hours on buses and police targets, which left

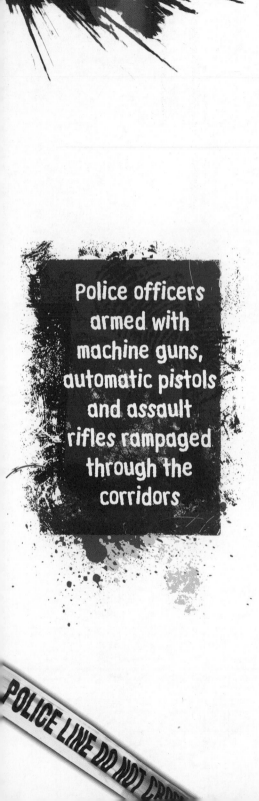

Police officers armed with machine guns, automatic pistols and assault rifles rampaged through the corridors

POLICE LINE DO NOT CROSS

The courtyard of the Carandiru prison in São Paulo, Brazil, since demolished

nineteen dead and twenty injured. Again the go-ahead was given from inside jail.

In June 2005, a PCC riot at Presidente Venceslau Penitentiary, 600 km (373 miles) west of São Paulo, ended in the death of five prisoners, whose decapitated heads were then paraded on long poles atop the prison roof. It is thought that the victims were former members of the PCC who were being kept in isolation for their own protection when the riot broke out. Rioters told local reporters that they erupted into violence because they had suffered 'humiliations and repression'.

Judge Machado Dias was assassinated by the PCC in 2003 after dispatching high-profile members to a maximum-security prison.

In February 2001 more than 8,000 prison guards and

POLICE LINE DO NOT CROSS

visitors, including 1,700 children, were taken hostage when trouble flared at eighteen prisons in and around São Paulo. Eight people – both prisoners and prison staff – died before peace was restored.

Violence in Brazilian jails has shocked even experienced observers. 'What is peculiar to Brazil is the exceptional level and type of violence,' Andy Barclay, project director of the International Centre for Prison Studies, said. 'There are, of course, killings in other systems around the world but I've never come across elsewhere the torture and decapitation like you find in Brazil.'

SOUND BEGINNINGS

However, the PCC initially had sound reasons for its formation. It was founded in Taubate Prison in 1993 from the ranks of the prison soccer team as a response to the massacre of prisoners at Latin America's biggest penitentiary, the notorious and hellish Carandiru Prison in the suburbs of São Paulo in 1992. When the killing stopped, 111 inmates lay dead.

The shocking incident had unremarkable beginnings. A fight between two inmates – nicknamed 'Barba' and 'Coelho' – had been broken up by several prison staff who subsequently locked down the cellblock.

That might have been the end of the trouble were it not for the chronic prison overcrowding. Carandiru, built to hold some 3,000 prisoners, was packed with a population of at least 7,000. Prisoners were compelled to sleep in shifts because there were too few beds. They were vulnerable to diseases such as scabies and tuberculosis, which only contributed to the jail's tinderbox atmosphere.

When the rioting started, the prisoners had taken control of the area within a few hours. Observers insist, however, that no hostages had been taken and there had been no attempt to escape.

The authorities lined up São Paulo's military police to regain control of the prison. Inmates apparently tossed their weapons out of the prison windows and hung lengths of material down the outside walls to denote a truce.

Yet police officers armed with machine guns, automatic pistols and assault rifles rampaged through the floors and the corridors, mowing down any prisoners as they dived for cover.

An official report discovered that 515 shots were fired, killing 103 inmates. Eight died of other wounds, possibly those administered by fellow inmates. No policemen were killed. Forensic reports proved that the shots were fired into rather than out of the cells, casting doubt on police claims that they acted in self-defence. The majority of bullet wounds were to the heads and chests of the dead, suggesting a 'shoot to kill' policy.

It all unfolded on the eve of municipal elections, during which law and order had been a key issue. An investigation into the episode took years to complete, by which time the PCC was in full swing. At last, it seemed that justice would be done.

'REPRISAL' KILLINGS

In 2001 Colonel Ubiratan Guimarães, who had commanded the police during the trouble, was sentenced to 632 years in jail for sending in the riot police to quell the disturbance. However, the astonishing sentence was overturned on a technicality the following year.

When the body of 63-year-old Guimarães was found in 2006, having bled to death after being shot in the stomach, it was thought a vengeful PCC might have been responsible. Carandiru chief prison warden, José Ismael Pedrosa, who was also implicated in prisoner deaths, was likewise killed in suspicious circumstances in 2005 amid rumours of PCC involvement.

The government acknowledged the mistakes that had been made at Carandiru and the prison was demolished in 2002. However, it was already too late to stem the influence of the gang which was by now widespread due to the squalid conditions in other overcrowded jails.

'BLOODING A FINGER'

Today the PCC has an estimated 125,000 members, making it the largest gang in the western world. To be inducted into the PCC requires 'blooding a finger', that is, swearing to observe a sixteen-point constitution that includes kidnapping officials. The ceremony involves cutting a finger to produce blood. That is why prison guards have been taken hostage by the hundreds since its inception. Without any sense of satire, its slogan is 'Liberty, Justice and Peace'.

It has won significant victories against the authorities, including the provision of better food, increased visiting rights and, allegedly, extra television sets in prisons during the football World Cup.

With prisoners deprived of the bare necessities, the gang has strengthened its core support by providing essential items that include toothbrushes, soap and food. It also has a network of 'brothers' and 'sisters', prisoners who support the gang but who are not themselves members. But if it began with fraternal and gallant intentions, it has now moved into the murky realms of organized crime. Efforts to improve prison conditions have subsequently been sidelined.

APPALLING CONDITIONS

Five years after the PCC began, the conditions in Brazilian prisons were still sufficiently poor to attract the vocal condemnation of the human rights group Amnesty International. In a 1998 report it gives some insight into why the gang has hit such a rich vein of support. 'Weekly riots and almost daily serious assaults indicate that in many prisons the authorities have lost control. Corruption is rife. Staff entrusted with the care and rehabilitation of prisoners do not have the resources to carry out their jobs.

'Doctors who fail to turn up for work are not disciplined, and there are simply too few legal aid lawyers to guarantee prisoners an adequate defence. Prison guards do not receive professional training in important skills such as restraint methods, and themselves risk violence and illness. Despite the enormous responsibilities of their work, they have no official guidelines to direct them and are not effectively monitored. If they beat, torture or kill a prisoner, there are no effective complaint mechanisms in place to hold them accountable for their actions. Very few investigations result in a criminal prosecution.'

CELL PHONES

In the 21st century the prison gang has continually improved its profile. One of the key tools of its organization is the mobile phone, smuggled into every prison and cloned so that tracing it is impossible. It is vital for co-ordinating attacks on both sides of prison walls. Since 2002, when Marcola, or 'Playboy', Camacho took control of the PCC, the expertise of the Colombian gangs has been sought, as well as guns from counterparts in Paraguay. Camacho is serving a 44-year sentence for bank robbery. According to the Brazilian news source Epoca, he is a dapper intellectual. During a recent search of his cell several political manifestoes were found, alongside Sun Tzu's *The Art of War*, Machiavelli's *The Prince* and biographies of Che Guevara. Following media coverage of the May 2006 fighting he was featured on the front cover of several magazines in Brazil, enhancing his iconic status among inmates.

The PCC members who are in charge of communications are known as pilots, while those in charge of prison discipline are referred to as 'Bin Ladens'. As a result of its expanding influence, instances of violence between inmates have plummeted as no one dares to scrap without official sanctioning by the PCC.

The PCC has struck an agreement with its counterpart in Rio de Janeiro, the Red Command. Such blanket coverage means there is little opportunity for rival gangs to gain a foothold. Hostage-taking continues to be one of its favourite tools.

One unnamed prison officer told a newspaper that he was in no doubt about who called the shots in Brazilian prisons. 'Everyone in the prison is a hostage of the PCC. They make all the decisions, not the prison administrators.'

His words were echoed by BBC reporter Tom Gibb, who says the PCC and its associated gangs possess enormous power within Brazil's prison system. 'A lot of the prisoners are very frightened of it,' he said. 'A lot of the prisoners who are not involved may themselves in many ways be hostages.'

LINES OF SUPPLY

Heidi Cerneka, who works for the Catholic prison ministry in São Paulo, concurred with this troubling theory. 'The State, according to many prison employees that we know and even some directors, no longer controls the prisons. The PCC does. Prison directors have been known to make implicit or explicit agreements with the leaders of the PCC. Directors agree that they'll let them do whatever they want on the inside, as long as no riots occur in that particular prison.

'Unfortunately, the best place to buy drugs in the state of São Paulo is inside the prisons. One can purchase alcohol, drugs, arms and cell phones in the prisons if one has enough money or connections. According to inmates, most of these products enter the prison in the hands of corrupt and greedy guards.

'According to the prison system, most of it enters through family members on visiting day. However, family members are literally strip-searched before entering. Recently, a machine gun was confiscated at the end of a rebellion. It is hard to imagine a family member managing to sneak in a machine gun without the assistance of some guard somewhere.'

With the Brazilian prison population trebling between 1992 and 2004, the government supplied numerous new recruits to the prison gangs on a regular basis.

United States

Prison gangs are common to all countries and continents. It was during the 1990s that this new threat to prison stability in the United States was identified, as behind-bars disturbances leapt by 400 per cent. For the first time the muscle wielded by prison gangs was understood by prison authorities. From their cells US gang leaders could control extortion, drug dealing and prostitution and even order murder to take place. Gangs and gang membership have been mushrooming in recent years and prison authorities have been fighting a rearguard action to contain the gangs' power.

THE GANGS OF AMERICA

One survey put prison gang membership in the United States at more than 300,000. In Illinois it is estimated that 60 per cent of the prison population is affiliated to a gang.

Renowned for their slick organization, the gangs orchestrate the supply of drugs in prisons. In the United States, gangs generally divide along racial lines and their existence, at least in the beginning, had an almost meritorious rationale – they claimed to stand for the defence of vulnerable minorities behind bars.

The biggest and most threatening of the gangs – known to the authorities as Security Threat Groups or STGs – have been identified as follows.

ARYAN BROTHERHOOD

A white supremacist gang, the Aryan Brotherhood, also known as the Brand, has been in existence since the 1960s, evolving out of a white, Irish-influenced gang known as the Blue Birds. It devised an oath of allegiance to bind its members together, which still holds good today:

'I will stand by my brother.
My brother will come before all others.
My life is forfeit should I fail my brother.
I will honour my brother in peace
as in war.'

Although it still indulges in Nazi insignia, it is better known by the symbols of the shamrock, the initials AB and three sixes; and it is these that feature in tattoos denoting gang membership. Wannabes who display such tattoos before being accepted into the Brotherhood are likely to have them burned off – they might even be killed. Like other white supremacist groups, it cherishes the number 18, which denotes the first and eighth letters of the alphabet, the initials of Adolf Hitler.

The Brotherhood functions best in an atmosphere of fear and loathing. A peerless reputation for ruthlessness is rooted in numerous killings – it is said that in 1969 Charles Manson, the convicted serial killer and race-hate preacher, was not sufficiently violent to join its ranks. A blip in AB power was reported to the director of the FBI in 1982 following an interview with an informer.

'The AB was organized in the California state prison system but within the last several years they have become an influence within the federal penal system and their activities tend to be uncontrolled. Things are not currently going well within the AB as many members have become users of drugs, act in a petty manner and do not live by their lifelong sworn code of conduct.'

Nonetheless it has survived and thrived. Like other prison gangs, its primary

> For the first time the muscle wielded by prison gangs was understood by prison authorities

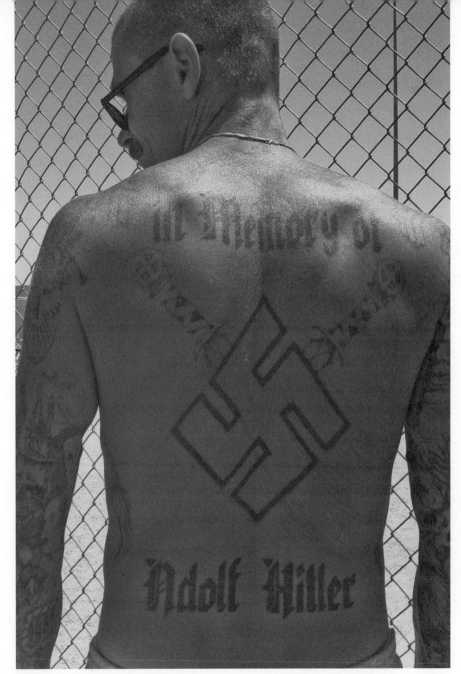

A member of the Aryan Brotherhood displays his gang tattoo in a California state prison

murder, assaulting and threatening those who violate the enterprise's rules or pose a threat to the enterprise … Inmates and others who do not follow the orders of the Aryan Brotherhood risk being murdered, as is anyone who uses violence against an Aryan Brotherhood member. Inmates who co-operate with law enforcement authorities are also subject to being murdered.'

David Grann, a gang investigator, told *The New Yorker* magazine: 'The gang selects only the most violent and capable individuals to become "made" members – individuals who are, as one former gang member put it, "master manipulators". But I also think that the leaders have been able to operate for decades because so many of their crimes are done in the cloistered world of prison, where the public doesn't see them and where many of their victims are hardened cons.'

He believes prisons and gangs like the AB bring out the worst in people. 'I do think that there are instances where individuals come in as bank robbers or drug dealers and, after being socialized in the violent, apartheid world of prisons and the gangs there, are transformed into conscienceless killers.'

BLACK GUERRILLA FAMILY
At first the agenda of the Black Guerrilla Family (BGF) was political. It was formed in 1966 inside San Quentin Prison, California, by George Jackson, a former member of the Black Panthers, with the express aims of eradicating racism, maintaining dignity for inmates in prison and overthrowing the US government.

business these days is trading drugs, extortion, racketeering and prostitution. Members released from prison are expected to do their utmost to support those still incarcerated. In 2002 an indictment against forty alleged AB members and associates revealed the long and violent arm of the gang.

'The Aryan Brotherhood enforces its rules and promotes discipline among its members and associates by murdering, attempting to murder, conspiring to

Mourners give the Black Panther salute at the funeral of founder and gang member George Jackson on 21 August 1971. Jackson had been killed attempting to escape from the notorious San Quentin Prison in California

Among its members were men from the Black Family, the Black Vanguard, the Black Liberation Army, the Symbionese Liberation Army and the Weathermen Underground, all demonstrably capable of extreme violence.

TEENAGE JAILBIRD
Chicago-born Jackson was still a teenager when he was thrown in jail following a $70 gas station hold-up. He would never be a free man again. In 1970, along with two others, he was charged with murdering a guard at California's Soledad Prison. The slaying was carried out in retaliation for the killing of three black activists by a prison guard, who was later acquitted of murder charges. Afterwards Jackson became known as one of the Soledad Brothers. While in solitary confinement for twenty-three hours a day, he devoted himself to reading and writing. His two works, *Blood in My Eye* and *Soledad Brother*, which expounded his Marxist ideology, were widely acclaimed.

Also in 1970, Jackson's 17-year-old brother Jonathan burst into a Marin County courtroom aiming to free a trio of San Quentin prisoners. At the same time he took Judge Harold Haley hostage, demanding the liberation of his brother in exchange for Haley's life.

However, police opened fire on the getaway car, killing Jackson and two of the prisoners. It's likely a gun carried inside the vehicle killed Haley. The prisoner who survived the shoot-out was given a life sentence for his involvement.

George Jackson did not live much beyond his brother. He was gunned down in the prisoner yard at San Quentin in 1971, where he had been transferred prior to his trial. Prison authorities insisted that Jackson had been armed and was instrumental in a prison riot that day that claimed the lives of three guards and two prisoners – charges denied by his fellow prisoners. Opinion remains sharply divided about Jackson.

LAWLESSNESS

Stanley Williams, a founder of the Crips gang, dedicated his 1998 book *Life in Prison*, in part, to George Jackson. Unfortunately, it did him no favours. In his response to Williams' appeal for clemency, Californian Governor Arnold Schwarzenegger claimed that the writer's dedication to Jackson was 'a significant indicator that Williams is not reformed and that he still sees violence and lawlessness as a legitimate means to address societal problems'.

With George Jackson dead the highbrow aims of the group dissipated. The BGF became immersed in drug trafficking, prostitution and racketeering like other prison gangs.

Recently it has formed alliances with street gangs including the Crips, the Bloods and the up-and-coming Gangster

Disciples to maintain its stranglehold on narcotics transactions in certain areas. It has adopted a new profile or identity known as New Man/New Woman or New Afrika Revolutionary Nation. However, the old tattoo of a dragon that encircles a prison tower with a guard at its mercy, plus crossed weapons and the letters BGF, still stands.

MEXICAN MAFIA

The roots of the Mexican Mafia lay in the 1950s when a group of thirteen Mexican inmates at the Deuel Vocational Institute, a correctional facility in California, formed a gang to protect each another from their hostile inmates. When prison authorities tried to break up the gang by sending members to other prisons, they only succeeded in boosting its membership as each gang member turned recruiter. When members were released from prison and returned to the streets the gang went from strength to strength.

Another arm of the Mexican Mafia is the Sureños, Spanish for 'southerners', which strictly speaking applies only to those from southern California. It is also known as 'La Eme', and its members used to be distinguishable by wearing red bandanas or T-shirts.

As if to underline its success, La Eme even sold protection to imprisoned godfathers of the Italian Mafia. One of the gang's architects, Joe 'Peg Leg' Morgan, was a white man who adopted Hispanic culture, and in the past there have been blacks and Caucasians in its ranks. However, at the moment the gang's hierarchy has given the green light for ethnic cleansing in its strongholds on the streets.

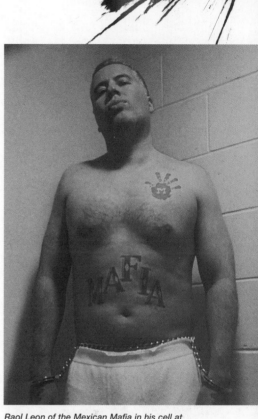

Raol Leon of the Mexican Mafia in his cell at California's Pelican Bay prison

DANGEROUS SHOES

After a prison bust-up at San Quentin in 1968 over the theft of a pair of shoes the Mexican Mafia and La Nuestra Familia (NF) – the prominent and adversarial Latino gang – became sworn enemies. The owner of the shoes was Hector Padilla, a member of La Nuestra Familia who shared a cell with Robert 'Robot' Salas of the Mexican Mafia. Carlos 'Pieface' Ortega, one of Salas' comrades, apparently stole the shoes and Padilla was killed in the fight that ensued.

One of the gang's early leaders, Rudy 'Cheyenne'

POLICE LINE DO NOT CROSS

Cadena, encouraged recently released members to take part in such laudable community work as drug rehabilitation programmes. By doing so they gained access to millions of dollars in government grant money, the proceeds of which they passed on to the Mexican Mafia. This was to lead to a wave of corruption scandals in California that exposed the deep involvement of the Mexican Mafia in every aspect of public life.

UNITED IN FIGHT

A visionary who believed that criminal gangs could unite to challenge the US government, Cadena organized a truce with the Black Guerrilla Family in 1970, and in the following year he urged Latino gangs to unite.

It was with this ambition in mind that he arranged to meet the leaders of La Nuestra Familia (NF), the northerners of California, in a second-floor prison cell at Palm Hall, in the Chino Institute for men on 17 December 1972. The NF response was uncompromising. Two members of the NF repeatedly stabbed Cadena. His stricken body was tossed over the guard rail and another NF member weighed in. Cadena died from over fifty stab wounds.

Cadena was among thirty-six inmates to be murdered that year in California – but only one of six whose assailants were not thought to be from the Mexican Mafia.

The practice of milking various federal programmes continued. In 1976 paroled gang member Michael Delia launched Project Get Going, ostensibly to assist drug users, with $228,000 of government money. He accessed the cash through the talents of his wife, Ellen, who was adept at filing grant applications.

Within a year Ellen was shot dead in Sacramento, apparently on her way to tell the authorities about gang involvement in the project. Her husband ordered the hit. Eighteen days earlier the same gunmen assassinated Gilbert Roybal after he announced he was leaving the gang.

The extraordinary ability of the gang's top brass to look after business from within a prison cell has continued. In 1990 Joe Arriaga was murdered, presumably as punishment for owing $30,000 in taxes to the Mexican Mafia, which takes 10 per cent of every drug transaction carried out in the areas it controls.

Activities were further expanded in 1984 when a Texas branch of the Mexican Mafia was started. Organized by 'Herbie' Huerta after he brokered an agreement with the existing California Mafia, it is known as Mexikanemi or La Emi.

CONSTITUTION

According to analyst Robert Fong (1990), the Texas Mafia's Constitution outlines twelve principal rules:

- Membership is for life.
- Every member must be prepared to sacrifice his life or take another's life at any time when required.
- Every member shall strive to overcome his weakness to achieve discipline within the Mexikanemi brotherhood.
- Never let the Mexikanemi down.
- The sponsoring member is totally responsible for the behaviour of the new recruit. If the new recruit turns out to be a traitor, it is the sponsoring member's responsibility to eliminate the recruit.
- When disrespected by a stranger or a group, all members of the Mexikanemi

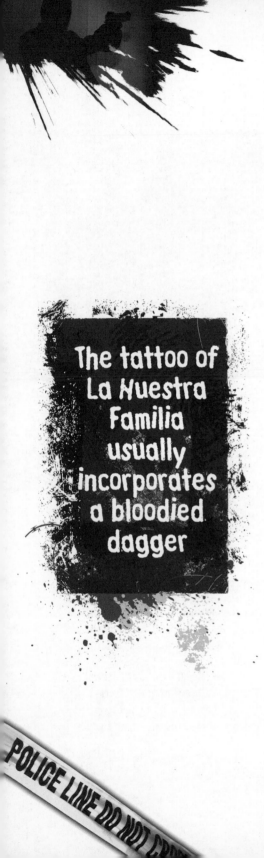

The tattoo of La Nuestra Familia usually incorporates a bloodied dagger

will unite to destroy the person or the other group completely.

- Always maintain a high level of integrity.
- Never release the Mexikanemi business to others.
- Every member has the right to express opinions, ideas, contradictions and constructive criticisms.
- Every member has the right to organize, educate, arm, and defend the Mexikanemi.
- Every member has the right to wear the tattoo of the Mexikanemi symbol.
- The Mexikanemi is a criminal organization and therefore will participate in all aspects of criminal interest for monetary benefits.

LA NUESTRA FAMILIA

A potent prison force, La Nuestra Familia was created as a response to the Mexican Mafia by rural Hispanics in Northern California known as Norteños. They took exception to the muscle-flexing of the urban gang members in the south of the state – the border between north and south lies at Fresno and Bakersfield – and banded together to better retaliate. Its tattoo usually incorporates a bloodied dagger and its favoured colour is blue.

The NF is paramilitary in organization with a supreme commander, generals, captains and lieutenants in charge of its soldiers. Recruits are schooled in weapons-making, sports, Mexican-American history and boot camp-like chants, which are used at night to intimidate other inmates as they try to sleep. This is done to prepare aspirants for twenty-one questions they must successfully answer before they can be admitted into the NF.

A member of the Latin Kings gang in the Bronx declares his allegiance by wearing a crown as he carries his baby

Affiliation to the NF is for life. Its long and detailed manifesto includes the maxim: 'A *familiano* will remain a *familiano* member until death or otherwise discharged from the organization. He will always be subject to put the interests of the organization first and always above everything else, in prison or out.'

It was, in part, the automatic death sentence invoked against NF members perceived to be traitors, cowards or deserters – costing hundreds of lives – that prompted a massive law enforcement operation against it beginning in 1998. Operation Black Widow, which cost five million dollars, was also an attempt to mop up the massive amount of drug activity in gang strongholds. Detectives benefited from high-level informants and

one man helped to secure taped and video evidence. Despite accusations that law enforcement officers stood by while gang assassinations were carried out, thirteen defendants – including six from the secure unit at Pelican Bay Prison – were eventually found guilty of scores of crimes. However, the police were not convinced that the gang had been shut down, even temporarily.

'[This is] at best, the cutting off of the head of a poisonous snake – knowing that as we speak it is already growing a new head,' Santa Rosa Police Chief Mikael A. Dunbaugh said at a press conference.

One man caught up in Operation Black Widow has risked his life to speak out against the NF killing culture. Armando Frias Jr

POLICE LINE DO NOT CROSS

was born into a family affiliated with the NF. At seventeen he saw his best friend shot in a robbery. Later, a mentor, Chente Sanchez, received an order to kill a drug dealer who had not been paying his dues to La Nuestra Familia. The man was Sanchez's friend. Sanchez took a noble but foolhardy decision and refused the order, knowing full well that the NF code would be enforced.

Within three weeks he was found on Pacheco Pass with a bullet in his head. Frias learned of the death in a newspaper clipping he read while he was locked up.

Initially, Frias was convinced that Chente Sanchez had sacrificed himself for a worthy cause. For a time Frias was a member of the lesser-rated street gang, Nuestra Raza, but he soon got deeply involved in the NF. He began selling drugs on the street and willingly became enmeshed in gang life, obedient to the orders smuggled out of Pelican Bay.

'When you make that step and you start functioning with them, there ain't no stepping back,' said Frias. 'I thought what I was doing was right.'

IGNORED WARNINGS

That's why in 2001, when he was out of jail, he shot Raymond Sanchez, an NF dropout who had been selling drugs in NF territory. Sanchez had repeatedly snubbed warnings to get out of the area and had refused to share his proceeds with the gang. When Frias found himself in the same bar as Sanchez he knew what he had to do. Indeed, had Frias been spotted in the same room as Sanchez without taking action he would have been branded a coward and subject to a death

sentence himself. The job was done without emotion. 'The truth is, I really didn't feel nothing. The life I chose let me know those things are going to happen.' Predictably, Frias was sentenced to life. But during the long hours available to him for contemplation he began to question the gang's commitment to its own mission. 'I started seeing abuses of authority, people wanting something done for their own personal gain, not for Norteños in general,' he said.

BREAKING THE RULES

He started seeing gang members using drugs, which is strictly against the gang's constitution. Members who had been tagged 'no good' by the leadership, in theory a permanent label and a death sentence, were able to buy their redemption by sending money to Pelican Bay.

'I tried to feel what (Sanchez's) family was feeling,' he said. 'I put myself in their position. I can imagine what they're going through. If the same thing happened to my dad, he's my best friend, I'd go crazy. The same thing with my son.

'If I could go back and change it, I would. I wasted my life. I took a life and I've affected my son's life. And for what?

'I saw (the gang) as a movement, a cause, like Pancho Villa or Emilio Zapata or Cesar Chavez. I thought it was pure. But really it's all corrupted by greed and drugs and money.'

It finally came to light that the street general who ordered the hit carried out by Frias, Daniel Hernandez, was in fact working for the FBI.

Now Frias only sees his young son through a pane of glass at the Monterey County Jail and can talk to him only over the phone on the wall nearby. When he gets home, the boy picks up the phone and tries to talk to his dad again.

Frias fervently hopes his son will sidestep gang culture. In the meantime he knows his disparaging comments about the gang will be noticed and could well bring retribution, but he says he's not afraid.

He never expects to be paroled and intends to write a book to discourage young Latinos from the gang lifestyle. 'Being proud of one's heritage does not require a life of crime,' he says.

TEXAS SYNDICATE

Since its inception in California's Folsom Prison, the Texas Syndicate has set out to prove itself the most violent of prison gangs. Its members are drawn from Cuban, Colombian and Mexican immigrants. Identifying tattoos are various and often the key initials TS are cleverly disguised in the artwork.

THE BEST OF THE REST

New gangs and splinter groups are swift to form. They are eager to surpass in violence and ruthlessness those already in existence, like the Latin Kings, who were launched in the 1940s and are linked to East Coast prisons and to Chicago. Among the fastest growing of these new groups is Public Enemy Number One (PEN1), which has a white supremacist agenda and is active mainly in California. Not strictly a prison gang – it boasts members and activities inside and out of jail – PEN1 activists have proved valuable in carrying out Aryan Brotherhood orders beyond prison boundaries.

Known as 'needle Nazis' because of their very heavy drug use, they can count an estimated 400-plus members. Unlike other gangs, there is no binding code or recognized hierarchy although certain individuals have gained a reputation for being the kingpin.

PEN1'S NO. 1

Donald Reed 'Popeye' Mazza was Public Enemy Number 1's 'shot caller'. A heavy heroin user, he has a violent criminal history. One incident on his prison record amply illustrates his commitment to the gang. In April 1999, according to state prosecutors, only ten hours after being released from prison, Mazza stabbed PEN1 associate William Austin, while Dominic 'Droopy' Rizzo, the No. 2 leader in PEN1 (and godfather to Austin's child), held Austin down. Austin was a member of the Los Angeles Death Squad, another white supremacist gang, and an active participant in PEN1 and the Nazi Low Riders (NLR) activities. Austin was said to have been attacked in this 'prison-ordered hit' because some of his fellow gang members believed he had turned informer. According to prosecutors, an Aryan Brotherhood member is believed to have overseen the attack.

In 2003 'Popeye' Mazza was convicted of attempted murder and is currently serving fifteen years at Pelican Bay. In the summer of 2005 he reportedly earned his Aryan Brotherhood 'dancing shoes', meaning that he was inducted into the AB. Mazza's elevation into AB ranks is likely to boost PEN1's position and power in California's prison system.

NETA

Neta is a long-standing gang believed to have chapters inside and out of prisons in thirty-six cities across nine states. In Florida, authorities have identified 240 different gangs operating in its prisons.

There has been some success in blunting the potency of the gangs. In 2002 a court heard about the activities of the Barrio Azteca (BA) in West Texas. Formed in 1986, allegedly to protect and unite all Hispanic inmates from the El Paso area, it remained under the radar despite a long-running spat with the Mexikanemi gang, which officially ended when a peace treaty was agreed in 1998.

This was, an attorney remarked, 'an extremely violent gang operating in the El Paso/Ciudad Juarez area as well as in federal correctional facilities, the state prison system and local jails. Their enterprise included extortion, assault, murder, attempted murder, money laundering and narcotics trafficking.' A civil injunction against thirty-five members and their associates slowed the gang's activities.

DRUG MONEY

Allegiances struck up between gangs mean that members of one often mingle with members of another. The Aryan Brotherhood will co-operate with the Mexican Mafia, the Dirty White Boys and Nazi Low Riders. Long-standing rivalries dictate that gang members occasionally target competitor gangs, seeking to beat or murder the membership. This can happen during 'cell pops', when a prison's mechanical cell doors open accidentally. Occupants are ever-ready to rush out and attack nearby rivals. But while gangs claim that long-standing feuds are the cause of the violence, drugs turf wars are more often at the heart of the problem.

Violence between gangs on the inside is also infecting city and urban streets on the outside. In California the rise in crime carried out on the say-so of prison gang bosses in previously peaceful communities has become an issue.

'The spike in black and Latino hate crime violence is due in part to the undeclared war between blacks and Latinos that has raged in some of California's jails and prisons,' explained Earl Ofari Hutchinson, a political analyst and social issues commentator. 'That battle has spawned an even bigger fight in poor neighbourhoods between gangs over crime and drug turfs. The violence has resulted in dozens of injuries and a few deaths. There are rumours that black and Latino prison gangs have ordered hits on other blacks and Latinos on the streets as part of their turf battles.'

KEEPING IN TOUCH

Just how the gang leaders establish such sophisticated communications networks is a matter that is currently being studied by prison authorities.

Clearly, gang barons can issue orders by telephone although calls are supposed to be monitored. With access to a phone they can make calls to members in other prisons via the 'three ways' system' – bosses simultaneously call a member on the outside, who holds the two phones to one another. Just as troubling is a 1999 report by the Justice Department that found that just 3.5 per cent of all calls in federal prisons came under scrutiny. Usually, known gang leaders are kept incommunicado while in prison to eliminate the option of telephone conversations. Still they find ways of flicking the reins of power. They can send orders to the outside through other convicts' letters home, using code to avoid detection by prison censors.

CODES AND LANGUAGES

Sometimes the codes are so obscure that FBI cryptologists must be called in to crack them. A few prisoners have even mastered the double alphabet pioneered by Sir Francis Bacon. Organizers of La Nuestra Familia are well versed in the Huamanguillo dialect of the ancient Aztec language of Nahuatl and choose to communicate in this obscure language.

Also they can send coded messages and documents, such as hit lists, inside reams of legal papers that are off limits to guards' searches, thereby using their lawyers as unwitting couriers.

Some gang bosses have written letters using their own urine, realizing that the words vanish when dry only to reappear when the paper is heated. Small letters have also been secreted on the inside of envelopes where joins overlap. Notes bearing tiny writing, known as 'kites' or 'wilas', can be smuggled out of prisons in body orifices. At Pelican Bay maximum security prison a fourteen-page list which contained the names of 1,500 Hispanic gang members was recovered from the rectum of a prisoner.

To communicate between themselves prisoners can 'fly kites'. These are minute written notes attached to a strand of elastic pulled from the waist band of prison jumpsuits and then expertly flung into another cell. In some cases leaders can simply talk face-to-face in the exercise yard. Men who have been paroled are commonly used as mules to carry messages to the outside world.

Not all gangs live by the same rules, of course, but there are some common conventions. It is usual to 'blood in – blood out' of gang membership. This means that aspirants must kill at the behest of gang leaders to win acceptance into its ranks – and that they will be killed if they choose to leave. Having killed, the new member will be expected to swear an oath of loyalty that is binding, as many gang members have discovered to their cost.

LIFE AND DEATH OF A GANG MEMBER

Robert Viramontes, known as 'Brown Bob', spent most of his life inside California's state prisons, rising to become one of the highest-ranking members of La Nuestra Familia. After serving the NF for twenty years, Viramontes opted for 'semi-retirement', guaranteed, according to the NF constitution, to any member who survives two decades. In effect, it is the only safe way to get out alive.

While still loyal to the NF, Viramontes began having second thoughts about the vicious lifestyle membership entailed.

Although he never spoke out against the gang or informed to police he did caution newly arrived gangsters through a programme called 'Mothers Against Gangs'. Significantly, he asked tattoo artists to cover the massive 'Nuestra Familia' emblem on his back. To earn a living once out of the gang lifestyle he worked as an office cleaner. He lived at a one-storey home with his wife, Esperanza, and his two sons, aged seventeen and six, and took up gardening.

Indeed, he was tending his rose bushes the day his assassins called. In the early evening of 19 April 1999 a Ford Explorer carrying three young men pulled up to the kerb in front of Viramontes' home. It had been stolen from a local driveway.

The driver, Albert 'Beto' Avila, waited at the wheel while two men in T-shirts and shorts leapt from the passenger-side doors. The first was David 'Dreamer' Escamilla, a member of the NF who was out on parole after doing time for attempted murder. He was accompanied by Santos 'Bad Boy' Burnias, a longtime NF member who had also done a stint for attempted murder. A fourth person, Antonio 'Chuco' Guillen, the San Jose NF underboss, supervised everything from a car parked down the street.

Seeing his assailants, Viramontes turned towards the open garage and tried to run into his home. As he crawled towards the door, he was hit seven times in the chest, back, legs and arms. One bullet grazed his left cheek. Dreamer got so close to his target that blood splattered back on to his hands.

DEATH SENTENCE

The murder of Robert Viramontes was, like most hits on higher-ups, ordered from inside Pelican Bay State Prison, La Nuestra Familia's headquarters. He knew his murder was on the cards and was even warned by a long-time comrade that the death sentence had been issued. In gang parlance, he could 'smell the blood' or sense the threat. If Viramontes believed his long, loyal service would help him sidestep the killing he was sadly mistaken.

Viramontes had been 'blooded in' to the NF in 1978 when he and some other

La Nuestra Familia members were convicted of manslaughter for hanging an inmate they thought was a snitch.

When Viramontes was first paroled from San Quentin in 1992, he returned home to the South Bay and took a tentative step toward loosening ties with the NF. He approached Mothers Against Gangs about being a speaker, getting so nervous before his first presentation that he asked his family to wait outside. After each subsequent speech, he took notes on his own performance, clearly committed to an anti-gang agenda.

At the same time, the Santa Clara County district attorney's office was engaging in a thorough and costly war against La Nuestra Familia, a clean sweep that would eventually involve Viramontes.

PERJURY
Eventually he was subpoenaed to testify before a grand jury, but was one of the few witnesses who refused to talk about his role in the gang. The answers he gave contradicted other sworn testimony so Viramontes was convicted of perjury and sent back to San Quentin in 1994.

Inside, Viramontes came across Chuco, who was serving time for drug possession. Chuco noticed Viramontes' back, and saw a recently tattooed Aztec figure disguising his NF emblem of a large sombrero with a knife and three drops of blood. According to NF member Anthony 'Chavo' Jacobs, Viramontes' cover-up tattoo work caused Chuco to feel 'ashamed'. And when he learned Viramontes had spoken on behalf of Mothers Against Gangs, Chuco said: 'He's poisoning young minds.'

Unaware that doubt was being cast on his commitment, Viramontes made what

Deported back to Honduras, these 18th Street gang members retain their allegiance

proved to be two fatal mistakes. First, he announced he wanted to revise the gang's policy about attacks on other gangs, suggesting that NF members now 'stand their ground and act aggressively only if the enemy acts aggressively'. He then called for a truce with the NF's greatest enemy, the Mexican Mafia.

By now suspicion was rife about where exactly Viramontes stood, and a whispering campaign circulated through the prison. The death penalty, ordered by men with whom he had once rubbed shoulders, was apparently given before Viramontes had left prison. Twenty years of service and a respected constitution ultimately counted for nothing. There was, in reality, no such thing as 'semi-retirement'.

CODES OF CONDUCT
It is not unusual for tightly run gangs to boast a ruling council or commission. There may be a single, all-powerful commander but there will also be generals, captains and lieutenants to oversee the grisly activities of the foot soldiers. It is at this level of pseudo-sophistication that corrupt prison guards are likely to be lured into co-operation.

Gang hierarchies encourage their underlings to study subjects as diverse as philosophy, military strategy and corporate management. This helps engender trust, discipline and respect.

Tattoos have long been used to denote gang membership, but

POLICE LINE DO NOT CROSS

as prisons attempt to weed out gang power these are now being disguised.

Part of gang wealth comes from levies paid by its members or their families. Those on the outside pay substantially more than those in jail. Of course, if they falter on payments they are usually given the chance to act on behalf of the gang in a robbery or a hit to wipe out the debt. Most comply, knowing that their families could be at risk if they don't.

POPULAR MUSIC

Gang culture is also detectable in popular music. From the favelas of São Paulo to the back streets of Los Angeles, entire neighbourhoods are ringing with the sound of CDs extolling the goodness and the power of prison gangs.

This music helps to enhance the image of the gang and means that crimes ordered by gang leaders from inside their cells are not the only problem facing lawmen in big cities. Generations of disaffected young people are unduly impressed by the conduct of prison gangs and commit brutal crimes so that they can be sent to jail, to be in the company of those they admire most. And it is the young men among them, inducted as they serve their sentences, who will willingly step into the shoes of gang leaders snared by vigilant authorities.

Sociologist David Ward believes prison gang supremos achieve their status by being perceived as 'the strongest of the strong': 'In some quarters these would be the people who would be in combat; they would be your medal of honour winners because they would never give in, they would never give up. Their strength under circumstances in which all the rest of

Even when not directly linked to a gang, prison tattoos can be lurid and violent like the ones proudly displayed here in Midway prison, Texas

us would have folded long ago is something that really is extraordinary. I don't say this in a way of admiration as much as in a way of wondering how people can survive this kind of regime forever.'

GETTING OUT

By committing known gang members to the Security Housing Unit (SHU) in Supermax prisons the authorities hoped to smother their power. The policy appears to have failed. One man who joined a white gang learned his criminal trade after being sent to the SHU.

'I always looked at the SHU as like a piece of steel that you could sharpen yourself with. You're not going to get that kind of opportunity to look at who you are and what you need to change about yourself to be stronger like you will in the SHU,' he explained.

'All I was waiting for was someone who was in trouble so I could stab them. That's all I looked forward to.

'I think that it's hard for normal people to understand but the way I used to look at prison when I was younger was like it was a kind of college. I had to go there to further myself. If I wanted a career in what I was doing then I needed to go to prison and make a name for myself in there in order to do so.

'By all standards my whole philosophy was wrong. But I thought that by creating my own system of morality, that by living within the codes of the prison, doing what's right in there, being respected in there, that I had created my own society.'

In addition to those who aspire to join prison gangs there are those who join after being preyed upon by existing members who have little to lose. Given the monotony of life in a SHU, it's easy to succumb to the apparent advantages of gang membership.

In some ways, gang members found guilty of ordering crimes in the outside world are beyond punishment. Typically, they are already serving life terms in the harshest prison regime the United States can offer. There's little that can make a real difference to their torpid daily routine and the gang masters know this. Extra years added to the end of a sentence seem meaningless to those who know they are likely to die in jail.

DEBRIEFING

Choosing a different route to undermine gang supremacy, some prisons now offer disenchanted or desperate men the chance to leave both a gang and the SHU through a process called debriefing. Some states offer the reformed gang member a route out of the Supermax and into anonymity and ordinary prison once gang membership has been renounced.

However, at Pelican Bay the exit from the SHU could have an unacceptably high price. It involves snitching on other gang members, for which the penalty may be death. In a debrief lasting several hours the inmate is expected to spill all he knows about gang life in and out of jail, including the names of the major players.

At Pelican Bay there is a unit for former gang members, kept segregated from the other prisoners – for they are acknowledged as marked men by prison authorities and prison gangs alike. Here, they can enjoy being outside without handcuffs for the first time since entering the SHU. Classes in computer skills, victim awareness and anger management are at last available. It's a pivotal part of rejoining society outside. But some prisoner welfare groups are opposed to the debriefing ideal, believing prisoners should not be encouraged to put themselves and their families at risk as informers.

And, as one informer put it: 'I've burned my bridges. There are no more bridges. When you take that step you're done. Period. There's no going back. And you'd better hope that nobody catches you because if they do then you're going to become another statistic.'

The debriefing process is certainly not providing an answer to the problem of prison gangs. Most prisoners are deterred by the stigma attached to being an informer. And for every reformed character there are untold numbers of new recruits waiting in the wings.

At the moment no ideal solution to the perils of prison gangs is unknown. El Salvador pursues a policy of jailing any known associate of a prison gang. This merely has the effect of concentrating members in easy reach of the gang masters.

South Africa

In South Africa the authorities can do little in the face of powerful 'number gangs'. The lure of the gangs is so great that members prefer to be inside prison, where they get free medical care, a bed, food and the respect that gang membership confers. These benefits are not always available in the slums outside jail.

There are three number gangs – the 26s, the 27s and the 28s. Generally speaking, the 26s are linked to robberies and cash accumulation and the 27s are associated with blood-letting while the top-of-the-pile 28s are known for sexual domination. The subtext with regard to the 28s is that young men sent to prison to await trial are likely to be raped during their first night behind bars and as a result may well contract HIV/Aids. The only liberation from gang life is death.

NUMBERS ADDING UP

South Africa's biggest prison is Pollsmoor, about 40 km (25 miles) from Cape Town. Nelson Mandela was held there for a time during the apartheid era. Built for 4,000 inmates, it usually holds at least double that number and up to sixty men might share a cell designed for only eighteen. There is only one toilet and obviously not enough beds to go around.

Although estimates vary there is thought to be just one warden for every hundred prisoners. This means that access to supervised recreational and educational facilities is limited.

It also explains why prisoners enjoy various unofficial privileges, including drugs and porn. There simply aren't enough staff to crack down. Wardens also tread warily around gang members as recruits frequently earn their stripes by wounding or killing prison personnel. Staff who have upset gang hierarchies are targeted. Sometimes wardens learn that an attack against them has been ordered yet they must continue working, not knowing when they may be attacked.

On arrival prisoners are fingerprinted and subjected to a strip-search during which they must squat to prove they are not carrying drugs anally. At this stage existing gang members, with their razor and ink tattoos, are swiftly identifiable. High-ranking members have stars tattooed like epaulettes on their shoulders. The British actor Ross Kemp is an expert on the

Inmates at Pollsmoor Prison in Cape Town, South Africa, the largest in the country, pictured here leaving the polling station during the 2004 elections

number gangs at Pollsmoor. Although better known as a soap opera star, in 2006 he became a roving reporter for a documentary about gangs for Sky TV, which included a trip to Pollsmoor.

A HUMAN ZOO

'It is like entering a human zoo,' he said. 'The smells, sights and sounds are overwhelming and I don't mind admitting, I'm frightened.'

Nonetheless, once inside he roamed the security wings and entered cells containing South Africa's most deadly prisoners. For a while he came up against the strict code of silence that governs the numbers gangs. Infringements usually bring about a dire punishment. But

eventually he earned their trust and learned about the perils of being confined at Pollsmoor, especially its dark and violent undercurrents.

SEXUAL INITIATION

Ultimately he interviewed John Mongrel, the highest-ranking 28 in the prison at that time, to learn more about the sexual initiation that takes place. Mongrel was given a nine-year sentence for murder at the age of fourteen. But offences committed in jail mean he has not yet been released. He himself entered the 28s by stabbing another prisoner through the heart soon after arriving in prison.

Now he orders other would-be gang members to commit murder or maiming and will go along to watch it take place.

And for those who don't go down the road of violence there is always the alternative path of sexual submission. Mongrel forces new inmates to have sex – they submit through fear and the unspoken threat of violence – although he denies being homosexual.

'I'm a man. He is a woman or wifey. He must wash my clothes. I give him food and I give him a bed,' Mongrel told Kemp.

Sex has been part of 28 culture virtually since its formation in 1906 when black prisoners first banded together, claiming that the prime motivation was to protect themselves from whites.

RAPE AND POWER

An estimated 65 per cent of inmates in South African jails currently participate in sexual activity of one kind or another – and none consider themselves homosexual. Indeed, consensual same-sex relationships are frowned on in prison gang culture.

In prison, sex is about power rather than sexual fulfilment and may involve 80 per cent of those awaiting trial. Rape is, said one inmate, 'an every night, every day occurrence'. Those who cannot afford gang protection, are unable to pay debts or return favours or are disinclined to violence use sex as a currency.

Sexual activity behind bars inevitably has an effect on the outside. Victims of male rape in jail often try to regain their manhood by raping women or even children when they return to their communities. Protection against sexually transmitted diseases isn't used in either instance and so HIV/AIDS is rampant.

Five years previously BBC reporter Allan Little went behind the scenes at Pollsmoor Prison and soon discovered that the same violent, sexually charged scenario operated inside. He met Mogamat Benjamin, an inmate for thirty-four years and veteran of many violent excesses. Not only has he beheaded corpses, he has, he claims, cut out the victims' hearts and eaten them in a ritualistic bid to claim their life force.

'I am powerful,' Mogamat bragged to Little. 'I am partly God. No man has a higher rank in Pollsmoor than me. In the camp of the 28s a person's life is in my hands. The final decision is mine. There are people who I said should be killed and they were killed.'

Although every numbers gang is distinct – the 27s were formed as a direct response to the sexual preoccupation of the 28s – each is linked to the others by the twin threads of violence and strict ritual. It is, it seems, possible to move between the groups but only after carrying out some prescribed and horribly violent act. Those who are in the 27s act as intermediaries between the 26s and the 28s, who are generally prohibited from contacting each other. There remains a mix of respect and suspicion between the three.

THE VIEW FROM INSIDE

One man, Magadien Wentzel, was the subject of an enlightening biography that revealed the view from the inside. He outlined the aspects of violence most admired by gang members.

'The brave part is not the stabbing. It is what happens to you after that. Because they are going to beat the s**t out of you. And if you cry out, just once, the stabbing means nothing: you have failed. After they have f***ed you up, they are going

to put you in a dark cell, with not enough food, for a long time. And if you go mad in there, if you come out crying like a baby, the stabbing means nothing.'

Gang members at Pollsmoor are so institutionalized that many would prefer to commit a fresh crime behind bars or confess to something they didn't do rather than face life with all its uncertainties on the outside.

Until the mid-1980s, the numbers gangs existed only in prisons and the streets were left in the hands of different, equally violent, gangs. However, keen to cash in on the drugs trade that took off at the time, each numbers gang has aligned itself with equivalents on the outside to reap the rewards of drug involvement, including cash and drugs supply.

Northern Ireland

Over twenty-five years the activities of two rival political factions in Ireland degenerated into gangsterism. One prison became an especially potent symbol of the era. It held men from both sides of the divide and placed the guards whose task it was to supervise them at huge risk.

The place was Northern Ireland. The rival factions were the Irish Republican Army (IRA) and the Ulster Volunteer Force (UVF), along with their numerous offshoots with various identities. The prison in question was the distinctively shaped Maze – originally known as Long Kesh, a disued Royal Air Force base near Lisburn.

After 1971, when the government of Northern Ireland tried to clear the province of terrorist activity by arresting suspected IRA sympathizers and detaining them without charge, the Maze became home to a long line of terrorists.

This, it turns out, was not the smartest move the authorities could have made as the Maze soon gained a reputation for being a 'University of Terror'.

One former Republican prisoner recalled: 'We went in bad terrorists and came out good terrorists. We learned how to strip and handle weapons, how to make booby-trap bombs, how to stand up to interrogation and, basically, how to be a professional terrorist.'

For a while prisoners were granted special status by the government, reflecting the political nature of their crimes. They were allowed free association and extra visitors and were excused from penal work. However, when this status was scrapped in 1976, Republican prisoners began an orchestrated campaign designed to cause maximum embarrassment to the British government, which governed Northern Ireland direct from London.

DIRTY PROTEST

At first, prisoners refused to wear prison uniforms and went naked, wrapping themselves in rough, prison-issue blankets. When this had no effect they refused to use toilet facilities, smearing the cell walls with faeces in a 'dirty protest'. The brand-new H-blocks at the Maze were thus transformed into cell hells.

By 1980 Republicans began to adopt a different approach to garner national and international

POLICE LINE DO NOT CROSS

support. A number of inmates went on hunger strike, hoping that the threat of prisoner deaths in custody would squeeze concessions out of the British government. To the great delight of Republicans, one of the hunger strikers, Bobby Sands, aged twenty-seven, was even elected to the British parliament, thus further highlighting their campaign.

But by the time Bobby Sands died of starvation, sixty-six days after he began his hunger strike, there was still no offer for negotiations on the table from the British government. A further nine prisoners died before a tacit move by the authorities at last brought an end to the hunger strikes. Critics argued that special status was ultimately restored in all but name.

LOST IN THE MAZE

Nonetheless, there remained palpable tensions inside the prison walls. There were numerous escape attempts, the most successful being on 23 September 1983 when thirty-eight Republican prisoners hijacked a prison meals lorry and smashed through security gates. One prison officer, James Ferris, died of a heart attack when he was threatened by an inmate.

One of the least successful attempts occurred the following year when Loyalist Benjamin Redfern stowed away aboard a waste disposal lorry. He died when the driver switched on the rubbish-crushing mechanism without realizing there was an additional passenger on board.

The Maze was again in the spotlight following the 1997 murder of 37-year-old Billy Wright, a prominent and controversial Loyalist who had survived six death sentences that were issued by the

Rioters in Belfast in 1981 show their support for IRA hunger strikers in prison

Republicans and who predicted that he would meet his end at their hands. He was also a target for Loyalists dismayed by his uncompromising approach. When Wright was jailed on perjury charges, members of the Irish National Liberation Army decided to wreak revenge on behalf of the Catholics he had previously targeted. As he waited inside a prison van before a visit three men clambered over a roof from a neighbouring yard and, using pistols smuggled into the prison, shot Wright in the heart and the lungs. Afterwards the

killers calmly turned over the weapons to a Catholic priest and gave themselves up.

Peace initiatives gained momentum as the 21st century approached and by 2000 the last 'terrorist' prisoners were released from the Maze as part of the Good Friday Agreement, which had been fashioned to bring peace to the province. One of the last men to gain his freedom was Michael Stone, a Loyalist whose crimes included shooting three mourners at a funeral.

Demolition of the Maze prison, a focus for hatred, was begun in October 2006.

Joseph Riordan

Joseph Riordan, nicknamed 'Whitey', was one of the few prisoners to escape from the legendary Sing Sing, New York's maximum security prison. Riordan came up with a master plan to make the perfect escape, and succeeded in breaking out of the jail. His daring breakout, along with two other prisoners, took place on 13 April 1941, and went down in history as the most serious breach of security ever to occur at the prison.

Riordan and his two accomplices, John 'Patch' Waters and Charles McGale, were all prisoners who had been convicted of armed robbery and sent to Sing Sing

A grim place, the interior of Sing Sing no doubt spurred on Whitey Riordan's endeavours to escape

POLICE LINE DO NOT CROSS

to serve out their sentences. They met when they were being held in the prison hospital, and between them hatched an audacious escape plan. They contacted outside accomplices, who smuggled in guns while they were in the hospital. Armed with the guns, they chose a quiet moment to launch their attempt, when few guards were on duty.

THE BID FOR FREEDOM

At 2.30 am the prisoners pulled out their guns and began their bid for freedom. A prison guard, John Hartye, was then making his rounds of the wards; when he tried to stop them, they shot him in the back. This incident caused another inmate, McGowan Miller, who was ill in hospital, to suffer a serious heart attack. He died instantly from the shock.

Leaving this trail of devastation behind them, the three prisoners then made their way down into the prison basement. There they found another guard, pulled their guns on him, and forced him at gunpoint to lead them out of the prison. The group made their way through a tunnel they knew about that led out into the street outside the prison. They had previously arranged, with outside accomplices, for a getaway car to meet them there and it was waiting for them.

UNLUCKY TIMING

As the escapees ran towards the waiting car, two police officers, William Nelson and James Fagan, just happened to be walking up the street. When they saw the prisoners, they became suspicious, and stopped them. Riordan lost his head and drew out his gun. He began to

shoot wildly, at which point Waters and McGale also pulled out their revolvers and joined in. The policemen responded by opening fire as well, and soon a street gunfight was raging, with bullets from both sides ricocheting all around. During the battle, one of the prisoners, Waters, was shot dead with two bullets in the head; one of the policemen, Fagan, was also wounded by a shot to the head. The police officer was rushed to hospital, but it was too late to save him: he was pronounced dead on arrival.

BROUGHT TO JUSTICE

Riordan and McGale fled the scene, and went down to the riverside. There, they found a fisherman, Charles Rohr, to carry them across the Hudson River in his boat. Once on the other side, they disappeared into the woods and hid, but not for long. They were eventually found by the police, using a pack of bloodhounds to sniff them out. The pair of escapees were arrested, as were their accomplices who had supplied the prisoners with guns.

When the case came to trial, Riordan mounted his own defence, claiming that police officers had beaten him until he made a confession.

He recounted how he and McGale had been kicked, punched and knocked to the ground hundreds of times while in custody. He also alleged that they had been strung up and tortured. However, the judge and jury were not sympathetic, and both men duly received the death sentence. Their accomplices were given life sentences.

In a final irony, Riordan was executed on 11 June 1942 – his birthday.

The most serious breach of security ever to occur at the prison

Jack Sheppard.

Jack Sheppard was an 18th-century thief who achieved notoriety because of his amazing ability to escape the long arm of the law. Arrested and imprisoned several times, he managed to escape from some of the harshest prisons in England, using a combination of meticulous planning, sharp-witted resourcefulness and street savvy. After his death, he went down in history as one of the great characters of British crime history. He was immortalized in poems, books, plays and films.

John Sheppard was born in Spitalfields, London, in 1702. He was the son of a carpenter, but while he was still a boy his father died, and the family became poverty-stricken. His mother found him an apprenticeship in his late father's trade. While he was working, he began to mix with London low-life, frequenting a London pub called the Black Lion in Drury Lane. Here he consorted with prostitutes and, at their suggestion, began to supplement his meagre earnings by stealing goods from the houses where he was working. He then, under the bad influence of a woman named Maggot, progressed to breaking and entering.

A LIFE OF DEBAUCHERY

Before long, Jack fell out with his erstwhile employers, who disliked the company he was keeping and suspected him of stealing. He was by now leading a wild, debauched life in the company of

Sheppard's former home was as unprepossessing in the 20th century as it had been in his day

villains, so he gave up his apprenticeship entirely and began thieving full time. He achieved notoriety when, on a visit to a woman named Edgworth Bess – one of his prostitute friends in prison – he had a violent altercation with a guard, knocked him down, and carried the lady out of the prison. This exploit made him popular with the prostitutes of London, and also endeared him to the British public generally.

Jack then went into partnership with his brother Thomas, and together the brothers and Edgworth Bess committed a series of robberies in London. This continued until one of his drinking cronies – hoping to gain a reward – told the police of his whereabouts. Sheppard was arrested and sent to St Giles' Prison.

PRISON ESCAPES

At St Giles', Sheppard made his first escape by sawing through the wooden ceiling of his cell. Once outside, he met up with Edgworth Bess again and committed several more offences, until he was rearrested and this time, sent to the infamous Newgate Prison, at the time said to be one of the most secure prisons in Britain. However, Sheppard managed to escape from Newgate not just once, but three times during that year. On the first occasion, he cut a hole in his cell wall and used his bedsheets to climb down to the street.

On the second attempt, he cut a metal spike out of a window. He was then locked up in a strong room called the 'castle', from where he made his third escape.

Jack Sheppard during one of his escape attempts from the feared Newgate Prison, with the help of some knotted bedsheets and Edgworth Bess

POLICE LINE DO NOT CROSS

In the castle, Sheppard was put in handcuffs and leg irons which were chained to the floor. His jailors were doing their best to ensure he had no means of escape. He was allowed visitors – and he had many, his fame having spread far and wide – but they were very carefully monitored so that they could not pass him items such as knives, chisels, and so on. However, Sheppard managed to find a small nail in the room, and somehow unlocked the padlock that connected the chain to the staple on the floor. He was able to take off his handcuffs and fetters, and then found a large iron bar in the chimney, which he took with him. To leave the prison he then had to pick the locks of several bolted doors, wrench off bars and break down walls with the iron bar he had got from the chimney. He used some bedclothes to swing up to the roof of a house nearby the prison, and made his escape over the rooftops of the city.

SENTENCED TO BE HANGED

After two weeks, Sheppard was arrested again. He was once again sent to Newgate, and this time was sentenced to be hanged on the gallows. Still undeterred, he planned another escape. One of his visitors had given him a penknife, which he was apparently going to use to cut the ropes binding his body as he was led to the gallows. His plan had been to jump into the crowd, which he knew would be friendly and help him to escape. However, before he set off for his final journey, a prison warder found the penknife.

As Sheppard went through the streets of London, he received a hero's welcome. He was then hanged at Tyburn, at the

JACK SHEPHERD,
Drawn from the Life.
A. The Hole he made in y Chimney when he got loose.

Jack Sheppard's exploits caught the imagination of the popular press and pictures tended to portray him in quite a dashing light

tender age of only twenty-three years. Afterwards his body was cut down and taken by friends to a pub in Long Acre. In the evening, the body was buried at the church of St Martin's-in-the-Fields.

Jack Sheppard's life and exploits were remembered long after his death. In the early 18th century, he became the model for the character of Macheath in John Gay's *The Beggar's Opera*. In the 19th century he was immortalized in a variety of plays and a novel, while in the 20th century he reappeared in Bertolt Brecht and Kurt Weill's *Threepenny Opera*.

Prison Riots

Attica

In 1971 a volatile political atmosphere
infected an overcrowded New York
prison, with deadly consequences.
Anti-war sentiment was at fever pitch
as America's involvement in Vietnam
dragged on. The public mood had soured
further the previous year when the
National Guard had opened fire on
unarmed student protesters.

America's Civil Rights Act was only
seven years old and symptoms of racism
were still keenly felt. Although more than
half the inmates inside Attica Prison were
black, all the prison officers were white
and some were openly racist. When the
black population of Attica heard about the
death that year of icon George Jackson
at the hands of a white prison officer
tensions soared. However, there was no
evidence that a riot was imminent.

TWO BUCKETS

Aside from the political stirrings, the
general conditions inside the prison were
poor. Men were given two buckets in
their cells, one for food, the other to use
as a toilet. But after they had been emptied
there was no way of telling which was
which. The inmate population stood at an
estimated 2,200 – about 1,000 more than
the prison was intended to house.

A considerable number of the white
prisoners were subjected to the same
deplorable squalor, among them the anti-
capitalist protester, Sam Melville. The
man who bombed New York's financial
district was nonetheless settling in well
in prison. In a letter to a friend written

Rioting prisoners at Attica State Prison, New York, raise their fists in a show of solidarity, October 1971

before the riot he concluded: 'I think the
combination of age and the greater coming
together is responsible for the speed of
the passing time. It's six months now and
I can tell you truthfully few periods in my
life have passed so quickly. I am in excellent
physical and emotional health. There are

doubtless subtle surprises ahead but I feel
secure and ready.'

Before the infamous Attica Prison
riot was to end, however, Sam
Melville would be lying dead
from gunshot wounds
to the head.

POLICE LINE DO NOT CROSS

REQUESTS DENIED

It began on 9 September 1971, after a prisoner was locked in his cell while fellow inmates went to breakfast. When the rumour circulated that he was going to be tortured, five inmates freed him. Shortly after that, violence erupted and prison officer William Quinn, aged twenty-eight, was allegedly tossed out of a window, dying two days later from his injuries. Three inmates were also killed by the rioters. Prisoners armed with pipes, chains and baseball bats took forty-two hostages in all and occupied one wing of the prison.

'If we can't live as men we sure as hell can die as men,' said one of the rioters. Still, they catered thoughtfully for their hostages, became well-organized and entered into negotiations.

For their part, the authorities were willing to concede negotiating points to the prisoners. However, they refused to grant an amnesty to those involved. The somewhat optimistic request by the prisoners to be taken to a 'non-imperialistic' country was also denied.

After four days New York governor, Nelson Rockefeller, decided to break the palpable tension at the prison by sending in armed troops. On a damp Monday morning helicopters fired teargas into the yard which was controlled by the prisoners. Then law enforcement officers fired 2,000 rounds in six minutes, killing twenty-nine prisoners and ten hostages. Claims made to the media that prisoners had slit the throats of the hostages proved to be totally false.

It has often been called the bloodiest one-day encounter between Americans since the Civil War. Ironically, while libertarians believed vile conditions were the cause of the unrest, local people thought the permissive regime at the prison was to blame. When prison officers reclaimed the jail, the subsequent punishment of inmates involved in the riot was merciless.

The harsh post-riot treatment was the basis of a lawsuit filed by inmates and victims' families and in 2004 the lawyers agreed a $12 million settlement.

Santa Fe

While events at Attica were marked by solidarity among prisoners, the riot that took place nine years later in Santa Fe is remembered more for its appalling savagery. And this time it was not a case of armed guards lashing out at inmates. In the New Mexico penitentiary prisoners turned on one another with merciless and unimaginable barbarity.

DRUNK ON HOOCH

The trouble began in the early hours of 2 February 1980 when two guards came across a couple of inmates drunk on home-made hooch. Perhaps fuelled by the alcohol, the men overpowered the guards, ran from the scene and dashed into a nearby control centre. The guard in charge fled, leaving a set of keys. With these the prisoners could release the other inmates at will.

Informers who had been fostered by the prison authorities were kept in separate quarters for their own protection. Now, outraged inmates sought out the so-called snitches to exact revenge. If they could not find the right keys to open the

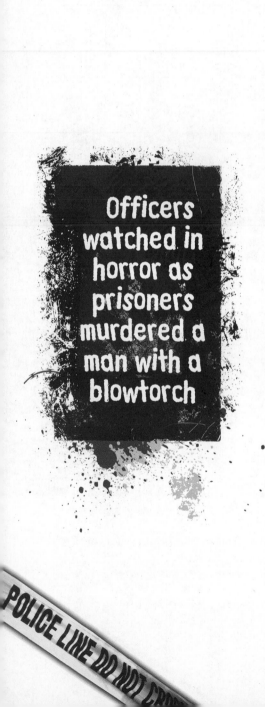

Officers watched in horror as prisoners murdered a man with a blowtorch

POLICE LINE DO NOT CROSS

A National Guardsman keeps a wary watch on the prisoners in the aftermath of a riot at the New Mexico State Prison during which many were savagely killed. The inmates wrapped themselves in blankets to stave off the cold

doors, the rampaging men simply used a blowtorch to burn a route to their terrified quarry.

'THERE'S BLOOD ALL OVER THIS GODDAM CORRIDOR'

One man was found hanged with the word 'rat' carved into his chest. Another was discovered with an iron bar run through his skull from ear to ear. Law enforcement officers gathering at the perimeter watched in horror as prisoners murdered a man with a blowtorch. Thirty-three inmates were killed, dismembered and burnt; one was decapitated.

As the torture and killing unfolded, the authorities decided against intervention in the hope of saving the lives of the ten guards being held hostages inside. Remarkably, although beaten, stabbed and sodomized, none were murdered. Two guards and a medical technician, who were hidden by inmates during the violence, remained undiscovered.

However, it was starkly obvious that violence on a major scale had been unleashed inside. An ominous and chilling message came through on a two-way radio from inside. 'Attention, attention, all units. You stop killing each other. There's blood all over this goddam corridor.'

POLICE LINE DO NOT CROSS

In addition, the rioters attacked the very fabric of the prison, built in 1956. They battered holes through 15 cm (6 in) thick reinforced concrete, burned down steel doors and smashed furniture to matchsticks. They also emptied the shelves of the pharmacy of drugs. Some broke into workshops to sniff glue.

Eventually, though, the perpetrators came down from their variously induced highs and began to give themselves up to the patiently waiting state troopers standing by the 4.5 m (15 ft) fences. They joined other prisoners gathering there, putting themselves out of harm's way.

GHOST FIGURES FROM A NETHER WORLD

Secretary of Corrections Adolph Saenz described the scene like this: 'To the north of the city of Santa Fe, the sun crested the snow-covered Sangre de Cristo Mountains. Below the highlands, on the desert plateau, dark smoke from the burning penal institution spiralled upward in the windless sky. National Guard troops and State Police surrounded the penitentiary.

'They stood immobile, twenty to thirty yards apart, outside the barbed wire fence encircling the prison, watching for signs of escape. During the night, approximately two hundred inmates had managed to flee the violence inside the prison walls, seeking refuge in the prison yard.

'Injured inmates, some with mutilations, wandered aimlessly in the smoke-filled courtyard. Outside the perimeter fence, prison officials watched and waited...'

There seemed little cohesion among the rioters, about a dozen of whom were thought to have been responsible for the killings. Eventually a list of eleven basic demands was issued, one being the attendance of journalists at the scene. In return some hostages were released.

One of the first journalists to arrive was Steve Northup of *Time* magazine. 'There was smoke everywhere. You could see people giving themselves up – ghostlike figures coming out, waving white sheets. It was a nether world.'

After thirty-six hours the troopers moved in and regained control of the prison without firing a shot. Ninety prisoners needed hospital treatment, many for the effects of drug overdoses. Overcrowding, unsanitary conditions and lax security probably contributed to the catastrophe. Race does not appear to have played a part.

It may well have been that having so many vicious men locked in one place led to the rage that engulfed the jail. In any event, prisoners were dispersed among several jails in case bad chemistry between inmates had played its part.

Although the penitentiary was partially refurbished, it was finally closed in 1997.

Strangeways

In Great Britain, the worst prison riot was not coloured with blood; it earned notoriety because of its longevity, lasting no fewer than twenty-five days.

Nobody died in the unrest at Strangeways Prison, in Manchester, although 200 inmates and staff were injured. The damage inflicted during the

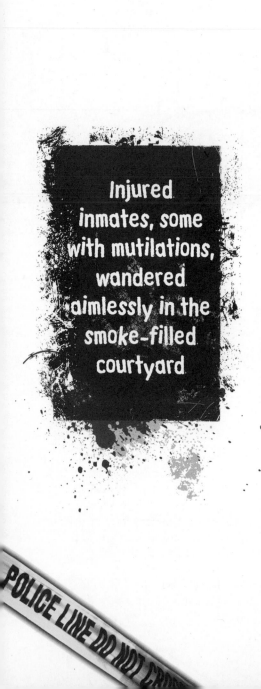

Injured inmates, some with mutilations, wandered aimlessly in the smoke-filled courtyard

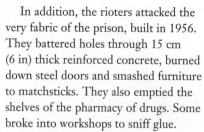

The 1990 riot at Strangeways Prison in Manchester was the most violent, long-lasting and expensive in British history

riot on the Victorian building cost about £100 million to repair.

Trouble started on 1 April 1990 – April Fools Day – following a sermon in the prison chapel. There was a healthy congregation that morning of about 300 inmates – implying that the action was planned. A prisoner, later identified as Paul Taylor, stood up and said: 'This man has just talked about the blessing of the heart and how a hardened heart can be delivered. No it cannot, not with resentment, anger and bitterness and hatred being instilled in people.'

Prison officers beat a hasty retreat – but not before a prisoner had grabbed hold of a set of keys, which meant other inmates could be released with ease.

MASKED INMATES

Masked prisoners soon made their way to the chapel roof where they hurled slate tiles at the police and prison officers gathering below. 'Stop the brutality. We are not taking it any more,' one bellowed through a loudspeaker. 'We are up here because we have had enough of being treated like s**t. We're not animals. We are human beings.'

Rioters set fire to the gym, chapel and some cells. Early reports that rioters had forced their way into E-wing, where sex offenders were held in isolation, and killed twelve later proved to be wrong.

One prisoner was 17-year-old Jason Ogden, who later recalled the terror he had felt at the time:

'It was horrific. I just wanted a way out. One bloke handed me a meat cleaver and I just took it because I didn't want to look like I wasn't doing anything. I just threw it down when I got round the corner.

'I saw people slashed, and the place was six inches deep in water because the toilet block was smashed up. One lad was on protection on the landing above us, but he wasn't a sex offender, he just wouldn't take the sentence for his co-accused. Lads were making their way up there carrying sticks and shouting. I never saw him again.'

> I saw people slashed, and the place was six inches deep in water because the toilet block was smashed up

POLICE LINE DO NOT CROSS

SLOPPING OUT

While prison officials attempted to evacuate as many prisoners as possible, the ringleaders climbed up onto the roof every evening to entertain local people and the assembled media. It was not until 25 April that the last five surrendered peacefully.

Afterwards the harsh conditions within the prison, built in 1869 and barely modernized, became known. Up to three prisoners were sharing single cells and they had to 'slop out' each day (empty a bucket of urine and faeces) because they had no access to a toilet. As a result of the riot, slopping out was ended and authorities pledged to improve conditions in Britain's many Victorian jails.

Fremantle

On 4 January 1988 a prison in Fremantle, Western Australia, was partially destroyed in a riot that began when two prisoners delivering tea threw 50 litres (11 gallons) of boiling water from the urns at their guards. In the mayhem that followed, seventy prisoners from the wing housing the prison's most violent inmates rushed the gates, forcing them open. They then lit a fire, fuelling it with furniture ripped from cells that were opened with stolen keys.

The fire turned into an inferno and the prison roof collapsed. Firemen arriving on the scene discovered

The imposing walls of Fremantle Prison, Western Australia, now a popular tourist attraction

that the prison gates, built by convict labour more than a hundred years before, were too narrow for the fire engines to get through. It took nineteen hours before the fire was brought under control, by which time damage valued at Aus $1.8 million had been caused.

In fact, it was not the riot but a later escape attempt that got out of hand which became the big story. The brains behind the bid was Brenden Abbott, a notorious bank robber who had collected the petrol used to spark the original blaze from the prison lawnmowers. Evidently, he was not enjoying incarceration at Fremantle. As he later recalled: 'Fremantle was a right shithole. I remember one night waking up because of a cockroach having a feed from my mouth.'

Unable to make good his escape in the chaos that day he waited a year before breaking out of Fremantle. On the run for nearly six years, Abbott was eventually recaptured in 1995 yet succeeded in escaping from the Sir David Longland Prison in Queensland two years later.

POSTCARD BANDIT

A career bank robber, Abbott continued to pursue his trade, to the frustration of the police. To the public he was the Postcard Bandit, taunting police by sending them postcards of his travels. In fact, these stories were invented.

Abbott was finally captured again in 1998 and kept in solitary confinement for five years, the longest detention of this type ever given to any Australian inmate, and a reflection, perhaps, of his capacity to embarrass

POLICE LINE DO NOT CR

the authorities. His release date is 2020,
and he will still have further charges to
face in two other Australian states.

Alcatraz

As long as there are prisons there will be
jail breaks; some prisoners like Abbott
seem to have the need to flee written into
their DNA. For these inmates there are
prisons like Alcatraz. Perched on an island
in the swirling currents of San Francisco
Bay, Alcatraz became a federal jail in
1934, during the heyday of organized
crime in America's big cities. It was the
destination for 300 of the system's most
hardened inmates, each occupying a
single cell sited by a perimeter wall to
reduce the opportunity for escape.

Alcatraz was not only a suitable
holding pen for notorious offenders, it
was a chilling symbol of an impenetrable
penitentiary, visible from the city. It had
its fair share of infamous inmates including
Al Capone and Robert 'Birdman' Stroud,
a murderer who earned his ornithological
reputation at a previous prison and was
not permitted to keep birds on the island.

ESCAPE FROM ALCATRAZ
But the prison is probably best remembered
for escape attempts, none of which are
believed to have been successful. There
were fourteen different attempted
breakouts involving thirty-six inmates,
two of whom tried to escape twice.

The island prison of Alcatraz stands in
San Francisco Bay, close to the famous
Golden Gate Bridge

POLICE LINE DO NOT CROSS

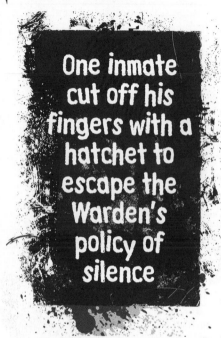

One inmate cut off his fingers with a hatchet to escape the Warden's policy of silence

Seven were shot dead in the process, twenty-three were recaptured and three drowned. Five men from two different escape bids are unaccounted for but are thought to have disappeared in the dark waters of the bay.

MILITARY UNIFORM

In 1945 an inmate who worked on the prison docks loading clothes made by inmates stole, over the course of several months, individual items until he had assembled an entire military uniform. One day he hid the clothes by the dock, put them on while the guards were distracted and leapt aboard a departing boat. Unfortunately for him, his absence was noticed immediately. The prison radioed the ship to return, thus ending the convict's brief spell of liberty.

Another man, in 1962, fared little better. He had loosened and removed a bar across a storage room window and covered himself with lard to slither through the small gap. He survived the bay's dangerous currents and beached himself near the Golden Gate Bridge. But he was so tired from his exploits that he fell asleep and was recaptured before leaving the shore.

An attempt at a mass jailbreak in 1946 resulted in a shoot-out between prisoners and officers. Alcatraz warden James A. Johnston was so alarmed that he called in the Marines, Coast Guard and Navy to help contain the situation. The prison officers soon won back the cell block where some of their colleagues had been taken hostage, though not before two of these were killed. Three of the inmates were killed and two were sent to the gas chamber at San Quentin for their role in the mutiny. Another was sentenced to ninety-nine years.

Perhaps the best-remembered escape also took place in 1962, when four men broke out by surreptitiously drilling holes into a utility corridor behind their cells. To prevent their absence from being immediately detected, they left hand-made heads in their beds. Earlier they had hidden a hastily constructed raft at the water's edge with which to cross the treacherous straits to freedom.

In the end, one man was left behind because the hole he had dug was not large enough to squeeze through. The fate of Frank Morris and the brothers John and Clarence Anglin is, however, unknown. There was at least one report from a ship in the area of seeing a body in the water soon after the break-out, though no conclusive evidence ever emerged about whether the men drowned or lived thereafter incognito, having pulled off an extraordinary feat.

THE HOLE

The daily schedule was harsh, beginning at 6.30 am and involving hard labour. All privileges, including visits, had to be earned. The existence there was highly regimented, with twelve headcounts a day, and transgressors often found themselves in 'The Hole', a row of solitary cells with sink, toilet and a single low-wattage bulb. Perpetual offenders were sent to the dreaded 'strip cell', a dark, steel-encased tomb-like place without lights or a sink. The toilet was a hole in the ground. There, prisoners were forced to remain naked day and night. They were handed a mattress for the concrete bed only at night. Luckily for them, confinement in the strip cell usually lasted only a few days.

However, the worst aspect of a term at Alcatraz was the policy of silence instituted by Warden Johnston. Its effects were so disturbing that one prisoner, convicted gangster Rufe Persful, cut off his fingers with a hatchet while in a workshop to get away from the aching isolation it created. Yet even when the silence rule was relaxed, life in Alcatraz was tough.

By the 1950s life behind bars on the island had eased and Alcatraz came to resemble almost every other American prison – except for the cost of running it. The prison finally closed in 1964 when the last prisoner, Alf Banks, was shipped out. It now attracts a million tourists a year.

Burt Lancaster starred in the movie The Birdman of Alcatraz, which was based on true events in the notorious prison

POLICE LINE DO NOT CROSS

INDEX